AN INTRODUCTION TO RISK ANALYSIS

SECOND EDITION

SECOND EDITION

AN INTRODUCTION TO
RISK ANALYSIS

ROBERT E. MEGILL

PennWell Books
PennWell Publishing Company
Tulsa, Oklahoma

Other Books by Robert E. Megill

An Introduction to Exploration Economics
Second Edition   1979

May I Touch Your Life?   1979

How to Be a More Productive Employee   1980

Life in the Corporate Orbit   1981

Copyright © 1977, 1984 by
PennWell Publishing Company
1421 South Sheridan Road/P.O. Box 1260
Tulsa, Oklahoma 74101

Library of Congress Cataloging in Publication Data

Megill, R. E.
  An introduction to risk analysis.

  Includes bibliographical references and index.
  1. Risk—Mathematical models.   2. Petroleum
industry and trade—Mathematical models.   3. Gas
industry—Mathematical models.   I. Title.   II. Title:
Risk analysis.
HB615.M43 1984   519.5′4   84-4315
ISBN 0-87814-257-6

Printed in the United States of America

1 2 3 4 5   88 87 86 85 84

Contents

Acknowledgments

Special thanks are due to Messrs. R.I. Swanson, C.R. Clark, and J.E. Smitherman. Each read early drafts of the manuscript and gave important criticism. Their efforts contributed to a better finished product.

To G. Rogge Marsh, who has reviewed carefully all of my published works to date, go my deepest thanks and appreciation. He not only provided important criticism but contributed ideas that were incorporated in the final draft. Each of the prior books owes much to his insights and candid questions. This book also benefited from his questioning, and I am sincerely grateful.

To Margaret Richards, my thanks for her valuable help in proofing the final manuscript for mathematical errors.

To my wife, Margaret, my thanks for putting up with me during the three years of research and writing and for typing each draft. It could not have been done without her.

Preface

My first published book, a success in a narrow field, was a simplification of established economic concepts; my second, a statement of opinion about a personal work ethic and personal productivity.

This book presents a little of each. Part is simplification of established concepts and part is opinion. Presentations of opinion carry their own burdens, especially when they refer to an area, such as risk analysis, where many opinions are possible. Any writing on risk analysis can never be other than part opinion and can also never be the "end-all" to a problem with innumerable solutions.

It is hoped, however, that both the mathematical simplifications and opinions on risk analysis will provide a beginning—an introduction to a very complex subject.

Risk analysis is becoming a bonafide segment of all modern decision-making, economic evaluation, and forecasting. If this treatise can help to broaden the base of understanding and increase the number of persons with a beginning comprehension of the fundamentals of risk analysis, it will have served its purpose. In this book you will find many useful references at the end of each chapter. These have been carefully selected for their ease of reading. The more complex writings in the area of risk analysis have been omitted. However, as you read further on risk analysis you will find other references that will increase your knowledge. It is my fond hope that what you read in this book will spur you on to further reading.

The words that follow were not recorded for the expert. They are a personal effort to make simple a few of the basic fundamentals in the analysis of risk. Every chapter has been constructed with the underlying purpose of providing a truly introductory explanation to an important method or concept in risk analysis. Only you can judge whether this goal was achieved.

How to use this book

An Introduction to Risk Analysis is conceived as a companion volume and sequel to my earlier book, *An Introduction to Exploration Economics*. It is in essence a major expansion of Chapters 8 and 9 of *An Introduction to Exploration Economics*, which dealt but briefly with an analysis of risk. The book will borrow a few illustrations from *Exploration Economics*. It will not, however, cover the economic analysis of prospects or plays, which the earlier book reviewed.

In keeping with its predecessor, this book assumes that the reader must start from the very beginning on all concepts. It is divided into two parts. Part I deals with simple mathematical concepts that will be helpful in understanding Part II. If you already have a strong statistical background you may wish to skip directly to Part II, which deals with the important concepts and methods in risk analysis. If not, you may wish to review specific chapters prior to beginning the second part. Portions of the book can be read in an isolated manner, i.e., many of the chapters stand on their own. An example is the chapter on competitive bidding. Since it is primarily a review of published literature, it can be read without considering most of the other chapters. Even here, however, it is of value to understand the importance of lognormality in oil and gas field-size relationships.

Throughout the book the positive as well as the negative aspects are reviewed for each concept. Anyone wanting to utilize the basic concepts of risk analysis will still find some problems in acceptance. The fear that a few geologists have of the quantification of uncertainty is akin to the early fears about the use of the computer in mapping. This fear stems largely from misinformation and lack of knowledge of both the benefits and limitations of risk analysis. The difficulty in comprehending a new concept always stands in the way of its acceptance. Not everyone appreciates the value of an analysis of risk. You need to understand the psychological problems associated with the hangups potential users of your work may have.

In my opinion much of the fear about using the techniques of risk analysis is the fault of the teacher and not the student. Many are willing to learn, but in all too many cases the teacher has failed to show in easily understandable terms the beneficial self-interest of risk analysis.

The following paragraphs briefly describe each chapter. From the description you may determine for Part I just what reading is necessary for you or of special interest or whether you can go immediately to Part II.

In Chapter 1 the groundwork is laid to show the value of a histogram in sorting masses of data. A cumulative frequency distribution is introduced.

Chapter 2 dwells on the binomial and normal distributions. A penny-tossing example is used to show important characteristics of a binomial distribution. If you already understand binomial distributions (two outcome distributions), skip to the next chapter.

In Chapter 3 the characteristics of a distribution are defined and illustrated. You need to understand thoroughly the mean and standard deviation. They are the two key characteristics most frequently used for any distribution.

Lognormal distributions are the subject of Chapter 4. This chapter is important background for later discussions on field-size distributions and competitive bidding. In Chapter 4 you will learn why calculations involving multiplication yield lognormal distributions.

Chapter 5 deals with histograms and frequency distributions and their shapes when converted to cumulative frequency distributions. This chapter is of particular value for those who have trouble mentally going from the shape of a distribution to its cumulative frequency.

Chapters 6 and 7 prepare the reader for a discussion of Gambler's Ruin. They provide background data on permutations, combinations, and binomial probability.

Chapter 8 is the beginning of Part II. It discusses Gambler's Ruin; it explains what is meant by a *normal run of bad luck.*

Chapter 9 discusses the need for analyses of opinion; it presents the pros and cons of subjective probability.

Because triangular distributions (three points) are so popular, Chapters 10 and 11 illustrate certain facts about this tool.

In Chapter 12 an example of the use of opinion analysis is given. Chapter 13 illustrates how types of uncertainty can be quantified for later use in a computer model.

Basin assessment is reviewed in Chapter 14. The important role of attainable potential and field-size distributions is reviewed.

Competitive bidding is reviewed in Chapter 15. The significant papers covering this important aspect of exploration are listed and briefly discussed.

The second edition contains three *new* chapters: 16, 17, and 18.

Chapter 16 is the most significant addition to this treatise on risk. It is a complete discussion of risking prospects and includes a methodology by which all prospects can be risked in a consistent manner. The method allows full reign to the explorer's geology; but given the geology, each prospect is handled in a consistent manner thereafter.

Chapter 17 is an additional discussion on prospect risking. It discusses the allocation of dry risk to tracts and certain aspects involving prospects with multiple reservoirs.

In Chapter 18, a complete discussion and history of the overbids in sealed-bid sales are included. This addition to the book is in recognition of the vast sums of money invested in bidding in sales in the Outer Continental Shelf.

Chapter 19 is a wrap-up of the fundamentals of risk analysis and has additions not included in the first edition.

Appendix A contains an expanded mathematical explanation of why the three values of maximum, minimum, and most-likely for a triangular distribution completely describe the probabilities shown by its cumulative-frequency distribution.

Appendix B is a major revision of the original appendix in the first edition. It reviews several methods of determining the mean of a cumulative-frequency distribution. The major emphasis is on the method known as Swanson's rule, and the rule's strengths and weaknesses are discussed.

Appendix C contains several tables of individual and cumulative binomial probabilities.

In your future reading and work in the analysis of risk, perhaps a few ideas from this effort will help your understanding of risk and will enable you to explain its fundamentals to others. The significant additions to the second edition are intended to provide you with major contributions to both the understanding and the explaining of this difficult subject.

PART I

MATHEMATICAL CONCEPTS

*A*n *Introduction to Risk Analysis* is truly an entry-level book on the subject of risk. All readers are assumed to have little or no prior knowledge about the subject. Thus, Part I begins with the simple, fundamental mathematical concepts needed to understand the principles reviewed in Part II.

The extensive discussions about distributions prepare the reader for the important role that distributions play in the field of probability. Every formula and graph are part of the base upon which we will build understanding.

We use probabilistic methods to apply to single events. You need, therefore, to have in your background knowledge a clear understanding of the basis for all concepts on which the applications of probability are based. Having mastered the basic statistical concepts, you will have a fundamental appreciation for the approaches to and limitations of the analysis of risk.

Again, if you have a strong statistical background, you may wish to advance to Part II immediately. The choice depends upon the status of your understanding of distributions and combinations. If these are well within your grasp, go to Part II.

CHAPTER 1

Managing lots of data

I n business and professional fields men and women are confronted daily with masses of data. Often these masses of data are more than the human mind can grasp or comprehend. No profession escapes this dilemma. Faced with this problem, what do we do? How does one manage lots of data?

In the first part of this book, we are going to explore mathematical concepts that help to manage data and build understandings of what the data mean. We begin the search with two fundamental but simple principles:

1. We manage masses of data by simplifying and searching for meaning.
2. We do this by
   • sorting
   • classifying
   • analyzing

THE ACT OF SORTING

We sort data for meaning by searching for and finding a common base, characteristic, or concept. We may sort by definition or objective. For instance, how many bits of the data fit a given characteristic we wish to measure? We can sort by time sequences, age, dimension, color, or many other characteristics.

We often have preconceived ideas about data and its separation. Thus, separations (or even the data selected) may not always be independent of the thoughts or theories for which they were collected. The *a priori* influence in data selection presents a greater danger on unfamiliar ground; yet ignoring the personal bias or prejudice can trip you up even in an area of experience.

The establishment of information systems has increased the explorationists' ability to obtain sorted data quickly. A well data system usually stores data on a hierarchical system. Such a system permits rapid sorting and retrieval of precisely defined segments of data.

A WELL DATA SYSTEM

In the United States the American Petroleum Institute (API) has established a unique number for each well drilled. To this number in a well data system is "attached" all of the pertinent data about a well. A well data system usually sorts wells first by their spot on the globe. A hierarchical system might be as follows:

Level of Separation	Description of Separation
1	State
2	County
3	Township and range
4	Section
5	Location within the section

These data would be the first to be attached or added to the data bank of a particular well. Other data are added depending upon frequency of usage and storage capacity of the system. Geologic data, such as formations tested, formations penetrated, and logs run, can all be recorded for a particular well. Any geologist working with a data bank gets the benefit of much sorting by those who stored the data in the system originally.

OTHER SYSTEMS

The geological profession is not the only one to value data sorting. A doctor can establish a data system for his patients and attach records to the name of each patient. The federal government and many commercial institutions attach data to social security numbers. A few cities store data about property. Rather than a complex property description, the data can be attached to the geographic location (latitude-longitude) defined as the center of the property. Utility companies set up data banks on their electric lines with the telephone pole as the equivalent of an oil or gas well to which data are attached.

What would you record about a telephone pole? You might be surprised at the available facts that are useful to a utility company:

- geographic location
- distance and direction to preceding and following pole
- number of cross bars (arms)
- wires per cross bar
- voltage carried by wires
- wire size or type
- age of pole
- type of pole (aluminum, creosoted, etc.)
- number of transformers per pole

Can you think of other facts?

The point of our digression is this—when you have lots of facts, you can begin to get meaning by carefully sorting them.

CLASSIFYING

Perhaps sorting and classifying have the same meaning to you. As used herein, classification is an interim step between sorting and analyzing. A rough sort of data can still leave much classifying to be done. Sorting the wildcat wells may leave much additional sifting if you are looking for only those wildcats with gas shows in a specific formation. Even when you have separated these wells, you may wish to make further refinements in your selection, such as gas shows in sands thicker than 15 ft or gas shows confirmed by sidewall cores.

Classification can be thought of as grouping things already sorted. Again, we group for meaning and simplification. Once data have been sorted to give the ability to retrieve selected portions, we can perform other calculations to classify the data.

Grouping data by percentage is an example of classification. If you have sorted out all of the wells that were wildcats and that were offshore, you might want to classify them by some other characteristic such as depth. If you use a common class interval (such as every 2,500 ft), you arrive at the basis for a frequency histogram.

In Table 1.1 a set of data is provided that will be used for several figures. The data concern a sorting and classification of wells, drilled offshore, in a specific year in a given area.

TABLE 1.1 Offshore wells, area A

1	2	3	4	5
			Percent	
			Cumulative*	
Total Depth (Class Interval)	No. of Wells	Of Total	Shallower Than	Deeper Than
0–2,500	20	5	5	100
2,501–5,000	40	11	16	95
5,001–7,500	60	16	32	84
7,501–10,000	100	27	59	68
10,001–12,500	80	22	81	41
12,501–15,000	40	11	92	19
15,001–17,500	20	5	97	8
17,501–20,000	5	3	100	3
Total	365	100		

*Cumulative percentages refer to the high side of the class interval in column 4 and the low side in column 5.

ANALYZING WHAT IS CLASSIFIED—A DISTRIBUTION

The data in Table 1.1 show how 365 wells can be grouped into depth intervals of 2,500 ft. These data can be plotted two ways, as shown in Figs. 1.1 and 1.2.

In Fig. 1.1 the wells are plotted by the number occurring in each class or depth interval. The most common depth interval is from 7,501 to 10,000 ft with 100 of the 365 wells bottomed in this interval.

In Fig. 1.2 the vertical scale is not the number of wells but their frequency, expressed as a percent of the total wells. Fig. 1.2 is a plot of the data shown in column 3 of Table 1.1. Note the change in appearance from Fig. 1.1. The shape of the graph in Fig. 1.2 is flat relative to the first figure. The flatness is a function of the vertical scale. It could have the same shape as Fig. 1.1 by expanding the vertical scale. Fig. 1.2 tells us that even though 100 wells were drilled to depths between 7,501 and 10,000, these 100 wells represent only 27% of the total wells drilled.

CUMULATIVE FREQUENCY DISTRIBUTIONS

The percentage graph is very useful in comparing one distribution to another. It also allows us to compile a second graph that has wide-

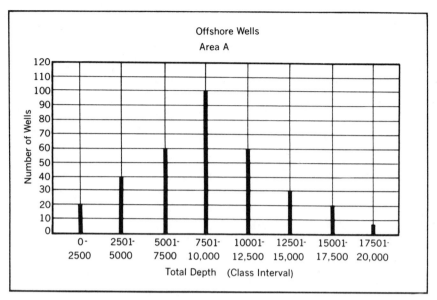

FIG. 1.1   Wells plotted according to number of wells vs total depth

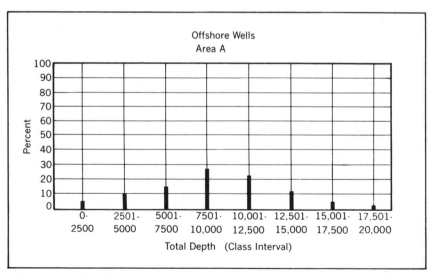

FIG. 1.2   Wells plotted according to frequency vs total depth

spread use in risk analysis. This use is illustrated by Figs. 1.3 and 1.4, which were constructed from the data in column 4 in Table 1.1. Column 4 represents the cumulative frequency of the wells drilled. In Fig. 1.3 it is plotted as "stairsteps" rising to 100%. In Fig. 1.4, the cumulative percentage points appear as individual points connected by a smooth line.

Both figures, however, tell the same story as the fourth column in Table 1.1. They say, for example, that 81% of all of the 365 wells were in the 10,001–12,500-ft depth interval or shallower; or to put it another way, only 19% of the wells were deeper than 12,500 ft. You now see the usefulness of the cumulative percentage distribution over the numbers alone. It tells instantly how many wells were deeper or shallower than a certain percentage. We will find this graph extremely useful in the chapters ahead.

Sometimes the data on cumulative frequencies are plotted slightly differently, shifting the emphasis to deeper or greater than. To graph the data this way we use the percentages from column 5 in Table 1.1. They are plotted on Fig. 1.5. This figure shows the same basic data as the two previous figures, but the cumulative percentages begin from the deeper end—to illustrate the "equal to or deeper than" concept. You can read the third point from the bottom as 19% of the wells are in the interval 12,501 to 15,000 ft *or deeper.*

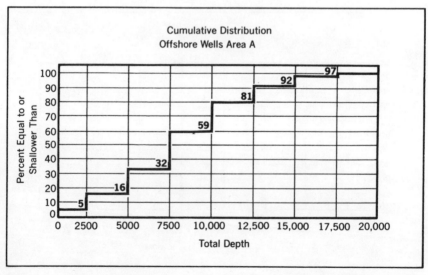

FIG. 1.3   A cumulative frequency distribution of offshore wells in area A

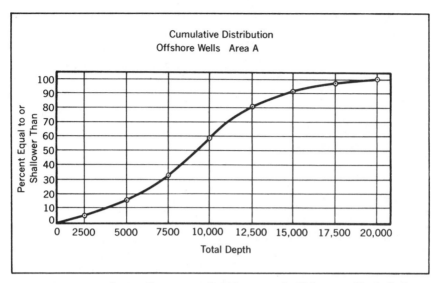

FIG. 1.4   A cumulative frequency distribution of offshore wells drilled in Area A in one year—less-than plot

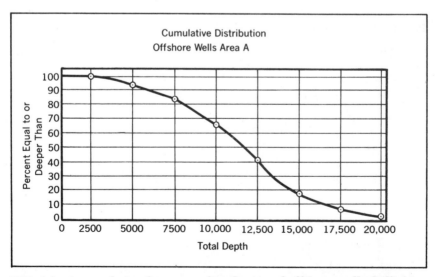

FIG. 1.5   A cumulative frequency distribution of offshore wells drilled in Area A in one year—greater-than plot

From these figures we can see the first use of a simple mathematical concept to help us understand a mass of data. In the illustration the mass of data was 365 wells drilled offshore. We examined certain characteristics of these wells as related to depth. Depth was the common classifying point. Grouping the data enabled us to grasp depth relationships quickly. Just imagine trying to gain the same insight from a list of 365 wells and their depths. Your mind would boggle trying to make sense from such a mass of data.

Managing lots of data begins with some form of simplification.

REVIEW

As the human mind grapples with masses of data it searches for meaning. The initial step in this search for meaning is sorting or grouping data by common characteristics. Such groups can be further classified by more specific characteristics. A common mathematical classification is the frequency distribution. In this classification a graph displays either by percentages or actual values the number of times a factor occurs within carefully defined boundaries called class intervals. Cumulative frequency distributions are an important extension of a frequency distribution.

The beginning of understanding of masses of data starts with the proper sorting and classifying.

Recommended Reading

Bernstein, Leonard A. *Statistics for the Executive.* New York: Hawthorn Books Inc., 1970.

CHAPTER 2

More about distributions

A brief description of a frequency distribution was in the preceding chapter. A frequency distribution tells something about a mass of data. It is a step beyond sorting. A frequency distribution is a special arrangement or classification of data. It reduces a mass of data to a few manageable relationships. The 365 wells, for example, were reduced to eight numerical or percentage values.

Within the broad range of possible distributions there are some very specialized distributions. One of these is the Binomial Distribution. *Bi*, meaning two, and *nomial*, referring to number, give the clue to a special two-number distribution.

One can think also of the two ingredients in this distribution as two events or two outcomes. For example, you could consider dry or successful for a wildcat well, or you could consider heads or tails in the toss of a coin.

We can learn a lot about distributions, particularly continuous distributions, by creating our own distribution. We can simulate a *continuous distribution* (a smooth curved distribution indicating almost infinite possible outcomes or events) by designing a distribution in which only 11 possibilities can occur. Because only 11 possibilities can occur, our distribution is called a *discrete distribution*. Another discrete distribution would be one in which the variable would be days in a week, months in a year, etc.

A BINOMIAL DISTRIBUTION

We shall create our distribution with pennies. A single penny tossed can produce only two outcomes—heads or tails. Furthermore with a fair coin, each event is equally likely, i.e., there is a 0.5 probability of heads (50% chance) and a 0.5 probability of tails. Only one

11

event can occur (symbolized as 1.0), so **the probability (P) of a head (H) plus the probability of tails (T) equals one.** In equation form this would be

$$P(H) + P(T) = 0.5 + 0.5 = 1.0$$

Suppose we have ten coins. Let's toss these into the air ten times to see what happens. One toss of the ten coins equals one event. What happened in an actual experiment is shown in Fig. 2.1, Graph A. Graph A shows a frequency on the vertical scale (ordinate) and the total possible number of events on the horizontal scale (abscissa). Events are shown as the numbers of heads that occurred in each toss of ten coins. The number of tails would obviously be 10 minus the number of heads. Note that 11 and only 11 possible outcomes can occur. A toss resulting in no heads is the eleventh possible outcome. These are called discrete probabilities.

Now let's see what happened in 10 tosses of 10 coins. Amazingly enough, in only 10 tosses *only four* of the 11 possible outcomes occurred. The four events were as follows:

2 heads	twice
4 heads	twice
6 heads	five times
8 heads	once
Total	10 tosses

Please note. The most-likely event—5 heads—did not even occur in 10 tosses of 10 coins.

What happens if you toss the 10 coins 50 times? This result is shown as Graph B in Fig. 2.1. Now *seven* of the possible events occurred. However, we still had, in 50 tosses, four possible events that did not occur. None of the 50 events produced:

> 1 head
> 8 heads
> 9 heads
> 10 heads

The distribution is a little smoother but is still erratic. Note also that the separate session of 50 tosses of 10 coins produced no case of 8 heads, whereas the 10 tosses before produced one such outcome.

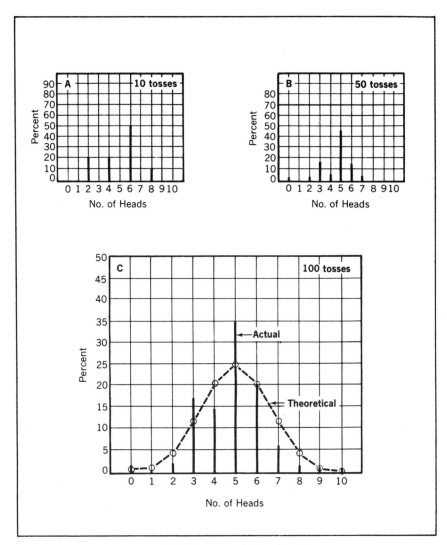

FIG. 2.1 Many tosses needed for smooth distribution

Graph C, Fig. 2.1, shows the results of 100 tosses. Only one of the 11 outcomes did not occur. It was the case of only one head. The distribution is much smoother with the highest frequency being 5 heads (and 5 tails). If each outcome (heads or tails) is equally likely, you would expect 5 heads and 5 tails to be the most common event.

The dotted line connecting the circles is the theoretical value for 10 coins tossed an *infinite* number of times. Thousands of tosses should bring you *very close* to the theoretical values.

THE LESSONS FROM OUR MANUFACTURED DISTRIBUTION

What can we learn from this handmade series of distributions? The major lesson is in the caption of Fig. 2.1. Many tosses are required for a smooth distribution. Let's say it another way. In tossing pennies, a few tosses can produce results markedly different from the average (theoretical) curve generated by many tosses. As we shall see later, a mathematician would say our experience shows that a small *sample* can vary considerably from the total *population*.

Later in this book we are going to relate this idea to wildcat drilling. We will say that in an area with a given success rate, a small number of wildcat wells can produce a number of discoveries that differ markedly from the average success rate.

Note also that even after 100 tosses we don't have actual data that would duplicate a curve of thousands of tosses. The outcome of 5 heads occurred 35% of the time when ultimately it would only be slightly over 24%. The significance of the number of tosses related to the end result should be apparent from the three illustrations.

Were you surprised that in a large number of tosses 5 heads would occur only one-fourth of the time? Try this idea on a friend or two. Ask them in a large number of tosses of 10 coins what percent of the time you would get 5 heads! You will be surprised at the range of answers you will get.

Later we have an entire chapter on binomial theorem. There you will learn how to calculate and prove the concepts we just reviewed. It is important to know a little about distributions before we get into the mathematics involved.

OTHER VALUES OF PROBABILITY (P)

What if P is not 0.5? Suppose you have a condition where the two outcomes are not equally likely? Such a condition is very common in drilling. Development wells usually do better than 0.5 successful, and wildcat wells seldom have a probability of success as high as 0.5.

Fig. 2.2 was drawn to show the theoretical shape of distributions for values of

$$P = 0.2$$
$$P = 0.4$$
$$P = 0.6$$
$$P = 0.8$$

Test tosses were not used here; a large number of tosses is assumed so the resultant distributions are smooth.

In each case the number of coins (wells) is 10. Graph A of Fig. 2.2 shows the theoretical frequency distribution of heads if $P = 0.2$. Here

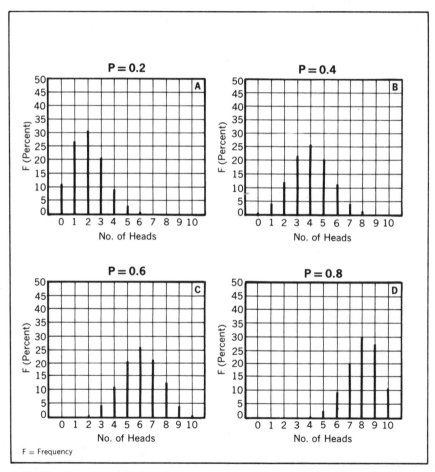

FIG. 2.2   Frequency if heads and tails are not equally likely

the highest frequency, about 30%, is at two heads as you would expect if $P = 0.2$. Note the similar but reversed shape of Graph A to Graph D, where $P = 0.8$. If Graph D were folded over on top of Graph A it would be the same graph! For $P = 0.8$, the most common occurrence is 8 heads with a frequency of about 30%.

Note also the reverse similarity of Graphs B and C. They show the same shape, same frequency distributions, but for different values of heads.

One further observation may escape your eye because of the scales used in the graphs of Fig. 2.2. When $P = 0.5$, a binomial distribution is exactly symmetrical. It is almost symmetrical at $P = 0.4$ and 0.6. This lack of symmetry is barely discernible in Fig. 2.2; but when $P = 0.2$ and 0.8, you can easily distinguish the lack of symmetry. Later a lack of symmetry will be called *skewness*.

In Chapter 7 we will learn how to calculate the frequency for a value of P or n (n equals the number of things being measured—in our manufactured example 10 coins were used, so $n = 10$). For now we shall just illustrate the principle.

One more fact. It should be obvious that as n increases, the relative frequency of a specific event decreases. For example, if n is 20 ($P = 0.5$), one would not expect 10 heads to occur as frequently as did 5 heads when n was 10. The answer for the probable frequency of 10 heads when $n = 20$ and $P = 0.5$ is 17.6%. Logic confirmed! As the number of possible events increases, the chance that any specific event will occur decreases. One might think of an increase in n as an increase in competition among possible occurring events—by virtue of more competitors (events).

THE PRACTICAL VALUE OF COIN-TOSSING

You may say at this point that we have spent a lot of useless time on coin-tossing. Yet there are some very practical applications of a binomial distribution in the real world.

Suppose you have a two-outcome condition:

- a defective part
- death from a disease
- birth of a boy or a girl
- hitting or missing a target

A manufactured part is either good or defective. The outcome from a disease is either life or death. The birth of a child is either a boy or a girl. We have lots of two outcome situations in human life. They all have binomial distributions.

Suppose a change in the assembly line is introduced to reduce defective parts. The new distribution compared to the old will tell you if the change is working and to what extent. Furthermore, you can tell from a sample rather than a long-term run if the new procedure is effective. However, the accuracy of a sample increases with the square root of the sample size. Thus to double the accuracy of a sample, it must increase fourfold.[1] We saw the importance of sample size in our coin-tossing!

Binomial distributions form the basis for testing the effectiveness of vaccines as well as other types of medical treatment. It also forms the basis for the law of Gambler's Ruin, which has certain philosophical applications in exploration (see Chapter 8).

In truth, however, when n is large (20 or more) and P is not small, the binomial distribution begins to equate to a *normal distribution*. Remember our comment about the lack of symmetry when P was small. We shall save examples of practical uses of distributions until after discussing the *normal distribution*.

THE NORMAL DISTRIBUTION

The ancient Greeks gave us the first abstract concepts involving numbers. They were the first to divorce numbers from their physical counterparts. They could add 5 + 3 to get 8 and not worry about what physical things were being added. The Greek concepts of Euclid were involved in absolutely irrefutable concepts. They glorified in proofs seemingly inviolate.

Although some pioneering work was started in the 1600s, statistical concepts and their usefulness did not significantly enter the social sciences until the 1800s. The late introduction was partly the result of clinging to the historical tradition, stemming from the Greeks, of deductive reasoning. In the 1800s many observations about people and their characteristics were found to have a consistent distribution, and some statistical concepts had already been employed in the physical sciences.

Statistical work initiated by John Graunt (1620–1674), DeMoiore (1667–1754), and Sir William Petty (1623–1675) was revived by a Belgian, L.A.J. Quetelet (1796–1874) in application to the social sciences.[2] Quetelet found, for example, that all mental and physical characteristics of human beings follow a consistent frequency distribution. We now call this distribution the *normal distribution*. Quetelet's measurements of human characteristics included height, size of a limb, weight, head size, and intelligence. The physical characteristics of plants and animals also exhibit a normal distribution.

The normal distribution also reproduces the measurements of other physical quantities. Measurements that tend to cluster around a central value exhibit a normal frequency curve or shape. A marksman's variations from a bull's-eye show this tendency. Variations in precise measurements of length, temperature, etc., form such a curve. Because the curve shape shows deviations from a central value, it often illustrates the errors from exact measurements. The relationship occurs so frequently that the normal frequency curve is often called the standard error curve—or the normal law of error. It is a most interesting fact: variations of error in measuring physical characteristics do not have some haphazard relationship or chance form—they *always* exhibit the bell-shaped form of a normal distribution.

Fig. 2.3 illustrates a normal distribution. The curve is bell-shaped; the left half is exactly the opposite of the right half—an important relationship we shall use later.

No units are shown in Fig. 2.3 for either scale. The reason is important. The height and width of the curve may vary, but as long as the left area (shaded) equals the right area and is the exact opposite in shape, we have a possible normal distribution. So you can have squatty curves, tall ones, or anything in between, yet still possibly have a normal distribution. We say possibly because not all bell-shaped frequency distributions are normal distributions; but the normal distribution is the most common. That's where it gets its name— normal! This characteristic is important. As we shall soon see, two simple measurements about a normal distribution—the mean and the standard deviation—enable us to describe any normal distribution.

We shall come back to the normal distribution in a later chapter. Next we must learn about some important definitions or characteristics of a distribution.

REVIEW

A particular distribution, the binomial distribution, can be constructed by tossing coins. From this distribution some of the characteristics of a continuous distribution can be inferred and understood.

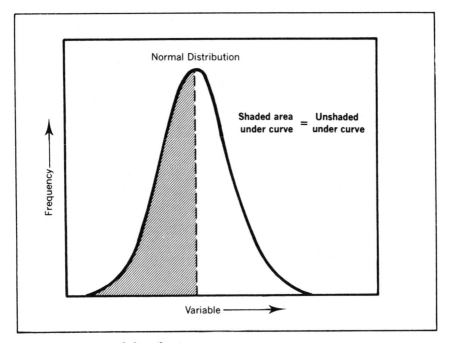

FIG. 2.3   A normal distribution

Many human characteristics when measured give results forming a normal distribution. Under certain conditions the binomial is almost the same as the normal distribution. The normal distribution also illustrates the errors in measurements of physical items, including physical characteristics of human beings.

References

1. Richard, Robert S. *The Figure Finaglers.* New York: McGraw-Hill, 1974, p. 109.
2. Kline, Morris. *Mathematics for Liberal Arts.* Reading, Mass.: Addison-Wesley Publishing Co., 1967, p. 501.

CHAPTER 3

Defining characteristics of a distribution

U p to this point we have learned a little about distributions. We have glimpsed an application or two that imply usefulness. Before we can proceed, we need to establish and define a few terms indispensable to future chapters.

If you already understand the meaning of the terms *mode, median, mean, standard deviation,* and *variance,* move to Chapter 4.

Many times when faced with lots of data points, we want to learn something about the spread or scatter of the points about some average. The distribution of points about some measure of central tendency is often described by the term *dispersion.*

The most important measures of the dispersion of a distribution are the *variance* and its square root, the *standard deviation.*

However, before defining and illustrating these terms, certain others must be reviewed. These other terms define something about a particular location in a set of data points. They are the building blocks for understanding variance and standard deviation.

MEASURES OF CENTRAL TENDENCY

The words *sample* and *population* are used by mathematicians to describe two fundamental concepts. The points or values that have been observed from some larger set of data are called a *sample.* The larger data set is called the *population.* It is the use of a sample to learn about the population (often unknown) that makes statistical concepts such valuable tools. Also, there are powerful but simple mathematical techniques that enable us to learn much about an entire population from a relatively small sample.

We can use three terms to describe a sample.

1. Median. In any set of data, or a population, there is one point whose value is such that half of the remaining points are above and half are below. The point whose value exceeds half the data points and is itself exceeded by the other half is called the *median.* Sometimes our data points are observations in an experiment. The median is the middle point of all observations.

2. Mode. In a group of observations, the one value that occurs more frequently than the other values is called the *mode.* The mode is the value of the item measured where the concentration of points is the greatest. We often refer to the measured item as the *variable.*

3. Arithmetic Mean. The mean is what most people call "the average." It is the sum of all measured values divided by the number of measurements. It is written in mathematics as

$$\text{Mean} = \frac{\text{sum of values}}{\text{total number of measurements}} \quad \text{or} \quad \overline{X} = \frac{\Sigma(X)}{N} \qquad 3.1$$

If you have 12 watermelons and the sum of their weight is 264 pounds, the arithmetic mean is 22 pounds; i.e., when the weight of each is measured and all are totaled, the total divided by the number is the mean

$$\overline{X} = \frac{\Sigma(X)}{N} = \frac{264}{12} = 22$$

In statistics the Greek letter Σ (sigma) is always used to mean "sum of." Also $\overline{X}$ is used to represent the arithmetic mean.

There are other types of means (geometric, harmonic, quadratic, root mean square). One can find references to these in any standard text on statistics. The so-called "weighted average" is in truth a weighted mean. If the word "mean" is used without a qualifying adjective, it is assumed to be the *arithmetic mean.*

The characteristics of frequency distribution just described are shown graphically in Fig. 3.1. Each characteristic tells a different fact about the data plotted. In general, the mean has many useful properties not possessed by the mode or median.

The distribution shown in Fig. 3.1 is skewed to the right, i.e., it has more values to the right of its highest frequency (mode) than to the left.

Skewness is a measure of the "lopsidedness" of a distribution. This type of curve best illustrates the relationship between mode, median, and mean for a non-normal distribution. Under what conditions

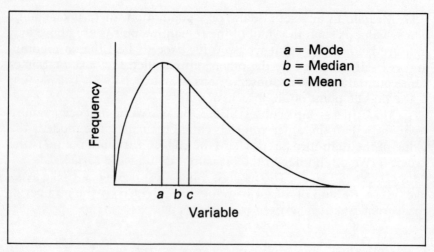

FIG. 3.1 A lognormal distribution

would the median and mean be on the left side of the mode? In a left-skewed distribution the mean and median would be to the left of the mode. The more skewed the distribution, the greater will be the mean from the mode. Thus, the difference between mean and mode can be used as a measure of dispersion.

A mean can be larger or smaller than a mode. In the right-skewed distribution the mean is greater than the mode. In a left-skewed distribution the mean will be smaller than the mode.

In a normal distribution the mode, mean, and median all have the same value. For this reason it does not illustrate the relationship between the three terms.

VALUE OF THESE TERMS

Of what value are these terms? They are quite useful in risk analysis. To be able to understand clearly and quickly the important relationships about key parameters, expressed as distributions, we need to know, understand, and be able to use these terms. For example, some geologic data enter risk simulation programs as triangular distributions. This type of distribution is so important we will have an entire chapter devoted to its use, significance, advantages, and limitations.

In a triangular distribution (see Fig. 3.2) you submit three points: a minimum, a maximum, and a most-likely. Frequently the resulting

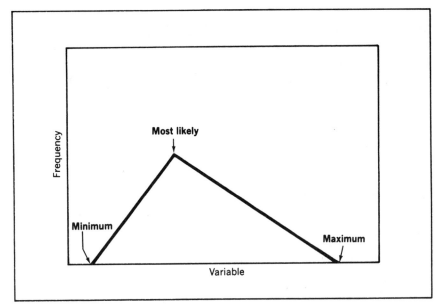

FIG. 3.2   A triangular distribution

distribution is skewed to the right. In this case the most-likely value is a *mode*, not a mean or median. In other words the most-likely value will occur more frequently but will not be the average of all values or the middle point. We shall discuss this in much more detail later—and with practical examples. For now you need the assurance that a good understanding of the terms mean, median, and mode *is essential.*

MEASURES OF VARIANCE

Sometimes you want to know more about a set of data than just some characteristics of central tendency (mode, mean, median, etc.). In such instances other statistical concepts can tell more about the data as a whole. One such concept involves the measurement of variation.

Range of Values. A common measure of variation is the range of values (for example, used to describe sand thicknesses). Ranges express variation with the extremes of the data—the maximum and minimum—as a descriptive device. Knowing only the complete range of values may not give a very satisfactory description of your data. So we have other descriptions of variation.

The Mean Deviation. The mean deviation, a measure of dispersion, is the sum of the deviations of the individual data points from the mean divided by the number of points. It is thus the average deviation from the mean of all data.

Since the sum of the deviations about the mean is zero, ignore signs when summing the deviations. The formula for mean deviation is written

$$MD = \frac{\Sigma(X_i - \overline{X})}{N}$$
3.2

where:

    X_i = specific data point, i.e., each of the data points
    $\overline{X}$ = arithmetic mean
    N = total number of data points

If you calculate a mean deviation, it gives you the average difference between all data points and the mean. A large MD means wide dispersion—a lack of clearly marked central tendency. A small MD shows closely grouped data—not far from the average in value.

The mean deviation illustrates another calculation to give you an insight into a characteristic of a mass of data.

The MD may be computed about either the mean or the median. It is most commonly computed about the mean. When the MD is computed about the median, the value will be smaller because the average deviation from the median is a minimum. Remember, the median divides a distribution into two equal areas and is less distorted by unusual values.

The Variance. In mathematics the word "variance" is a statistical term, not a descriptive word. The formula for variance (V) is

$$V = \frac{\Sigma(X_i - \overline{X})^2}{N}$$
3.3

In other words, the variance is

$$\frac{\text{the sum of the squares of the differences between individual values and the mean value}}{\text{the number of data points}}$$

Note the similarity to the mean deviation. The only difference is the *squaring* of each deviation. The squaring causes problems in using the variance. It measures dispersion in squares units, and most of us don't think in squared units. For example, the variance for a set of pay thicknesses would have units in feet squared. Heights of men would have variances in inches squared. A more convenient measure is our next measure of central tendency.

The Standard Deviation. A more convenient unit is the square root of the variance, called the standard deviation. By taking the square root of variance, we will end up with units in feet, inches, acres, etc. The formula for standard deviation is written as follows:

$$\sigma = \sqrt{\frac{\Sigma(X_i - \overline{X})^2}{N}}$$ 3.4

Two symbols are found in textbooks to denote standard deviation.

1. The lowercase sigma (σ) is used for standard deviation when all data points are included—that is, the entire population is represented.
2. If less than the entire population is included, you are dealing with a sample. In this instance the lowercase "s" is sometimes used and $n - 1$ (lowercase n) instead of N. Both the use of s and ($n - 1$) denote *less than* the total population.

Because all values are squared, in the variance the standard deviation is larger than the mean deviation. In a normal distribution the MD is about 80% of the standard deviation

$$MD = 0.798\sigma \text{ (for a normal distribution)}$$ 3.5

For moderately skewed distributions this rough relationship still holds approximately true.

The standard deviation is the most popular of all measures of dispersion when dealing with distributions. It gives us a measure of how far data spread on both sides of the mean. As the mean is the most important single "describer" of most sets of simple data, so the standard deviation is the most important describer of continuous distributions. Remember, both the mean and the standard deviation provide significant characteristics about a set of data. If you know these two facts, you can accurately describe the *distribution* of the data. Most present-day computer programs dealing with any type of distribution will automatically calculate and print the standard deviation and the mean.

Like the MD, the standard deviation is affected by every single data point. Its values are squared, however. It thus provides greater influence from the maximum and minimum values than the MD; even though you eventually take the square root of squared values, the standard deviation produces a value greater than the MD.

CALCULATING A STANDARD DEVIATION

The steps in calculating a standard deviation are illustrated using the data in Table 1.1. This table, however, has data that are grouped in depth intervals, which complicates matters. We need a simpler example first. For this example we will use the data in Table 3.1. Again, wells and well depths are the basic data set. Please check Table 3.1 carefully. Start with the well depths and see how each column is computed. The symbols (X_i, $\overline{X}$, etc.) refer to formula 3.4. Check it again for reference.

TABLE 3.1   Calculating the standard deviation

1		2 X_i	3 $(X_i - \overline{X})$	4	5
	Well		Dev. from		
No.	Depth		Mean	$(X_i - \overline{X})^2(10^3)$	$(X_i)^2(10^3)$
1	5,000		−4,200	17,640	25,000
2	6,000		−3,200	10,240	36,000
3	7,000		−2,200	4,840	49,000
4	8,000		−1,200	1,440	64,000
5	8,000		−1,200	1,440	64,000
6	9,000		− 200	40	81,000
7	10,000		800	640	100,000
8	12,000		2,800	7,840	144,000
9	13,000		3,800	14,440	169,000
10	14,000		4,800	23,040	196,000
Totals	92,000		24,400*	81,600	928,000

$$\overline{X} = \frac{92,000}{10} = 9,200$$

*Sum with signs ignored

We are now ready to calculate a standard deviation. If you are already familiar with this calculation skip to the next chapter.

First let's check the columns in Table 3.1. The first column lists the well number. The second lists the depth for each well—the measured variable. It is the X_i of the formula. The mean (9,200 ft) or $\bar{X}$ is calculated by dividing the sum of the X_i's by the number of wells (N).

The third column shows the deviation of each individual well depth from the mean of 9,200 ft. The fourth column is the square of Column 3. Column 5—$(X_i)^2$—will be used for another calculation later. It is obviously the square of Column 2.

Now we fit all of the pieces into Equation 3.4

$$\sigma = \sqrt{\frac{\Sigma(X_i - \bar{X})^2}{N}}$$

$$\sigma = \sqrt{\frac{81,600,000}{10}} = \sqrt{8,160,000} = 2,857 \text{ ft}$$

The standard deviation of our 10-well set of data is 2,857 ft. Another formula to check our answer is

$$\sigma = \sqrt{\frac{\Sigma(X_i)^2}{N} - \left(\frac{\Sigma X_i}{N}\right)^2} \qquad 3.6$$

This formula uses the sum of Column 5, $(X_i)^2$ from Table 3.1. It also uses the mean—both numbers are squared, but note the different position of N relative to the quantity squared. The latter quantity in the equation $\dfrac{\Sigma(X_i)}{N}$ is the mean, so one could substitute $(\bar{X})$ for this value. Our new formula becomes

$$\sigma = \sqrt{\frac{928,000,000}{10} - (9,200)^2} = \sqrt{92,800,000 - 84,640,000}$$

$$\sigma = \sqrt{8,160,000} = 2,857 \text{ ft}$$

How does the standard deviation differ from the mean deviation? The mean deviation is the sum of column 3, Table 3.1, divided by 10 or 2,440 ft (see formula 3.2). Remember we said that because the standard deviation used the square root of squared values, it was more sensitive to the extremes. The MD is thus normally less than the standard deviation.

Now we are ready to calculate the standard deviation for a group of wells. Because grouped data are used, the approach must be slightly different. For grouped data we do not have each individual well depth; we have the number of wells in a given depth bracket. With grouped data the steps to calculate a standard deviation are

1. Find the midpoint of each depth interval. It will be used as the average depth for all wells in the depth interval.
2. Calculate a mean for the entire set of data using the following formula

$$\overline{X}_g = \frac{\Sigma(n \cdot X_{mp})}{N} \qquad\qquad 3.7$$

where n is the number of wells in each group; X_{mp} is the midpoint of each depth interval; N is the total number of wells.

3. The mean is subtracted from each midpoint to find the mean deviation of each group, $X_{mp} - \overline{X}_g$.
4. Each group or average deviation is squared, $(X_{mp} - \overline{X}_g)^2$. This also conveniently gets rid of negative values.
5. The squared deviation of each group is multiplied by the number of wells (n) in the group, $n(X_{mp} - \overline{X}_g)^2$. This represents the total squared deviation of all wells in the group.
6. All columns are totalled *except* the wells and footage, which were previously summed to calculate the mean.
7. The standard deviation is then calculated by dividing the total number of wells, N, into the sum of all the group deviations, $n(X_{mp} - \overline{X}_g)^2$, and then taking the square root of the resultant number. The formula looks like

$$\sigma = \sqrt{\frac{\Sigma n(X_{mp} - \overline{X}_g)^2}{N}} \qquad\qquad 3.8$$

We can now construct a table to get a standard deviation from the 365 wells grouped by equal depth intervals.

Inserting our values in Eq. 3.8 we have the sum of column seven in Table 3.2 divided by the number of wells, or

$$\sigma = \sqrt{\frac{5,597,740,000}{365}} = \sqrt{15,336,273} = 3,916 \text{ ft}$$

The mean deviation from our 365 wells (using the sum of column eight, Table 3.2) is

$$MD_g = \frac{\Sigma n(X_{mp} - \overline{X}_g)}{N} = \frac{1,121,000}{365} = 3,071 \text{ ft}$$

Again the MD is less than the standard deviation. Most of us tend to think in terms of a mean deviation. To the mathematician, however, the standard deviation, although slightly larger, is more useful particularly for the normal distribution. As we shall see later, he likes it because it is a more powerful tool.

One final point: in grouped data we do not have each individual data point. Groups of data points and their approximately measured value are used (in this case depth of the well) with the midpoint of the class interval. Thus the calculated values for MD and standard deviation are not absolutely correct. They are, however, accurate enough for almost all uses. In general, the standard deviation and mean deviation will tend to be slightly larger from grouped data than from ungrouped data.

THE MEAN, THE STANDARD DEVIATION, AND THE NORMAL DISTRIBUTION

We have spent much time on the arduous calculations of mean, mean deviation, and standard deviation. We have explained the difference between the mean (or average) deviation and the standard deviation because most of us think in terms of averages. Why have we labored so long? For several reasons:

1. The standard deviation is common output from most computer programs whether summing several distributions or displaying a single distribution. Thus, you need to understand the term and how it is calculated.
2. The standard deviation is a vital measure of a normal distribution. With the mean it provides a way to describe and utilize data from any normal distribution. In nature and science so many measurements (or observations) are either normally distributed or nearly so. The mean and standard deviation alone

TABLE 3.2 Calculation of a standard deviation—grouped data

1	2	3	4	5 Dev. of Midpoint from Mean	6 Dev. of Midpoint from Mean	7	8
Class Interval	Midpoint (X_{mp})	No. of Wells n	Footage $(X_{mp} \cdot n)$ $\times 10^3$	Actual* $(X_{mp} - \bar{X}_g)$	Squared $(X_{mp} - \bar{X}_g)^2(10^3)$	$n(X_{mp} - \bar{X}_g)^2$ (10^3)	$n(X_{mp} - \bar{X}_g)$ (10^3)
0–2,500	1,250	20	25	−7,775	60,451	1,209,020	155
2,501–5,000	3,750	40	150	−5,275	27,826	1,113,040	211
5,001–7,500	6,250	60	375	−2,775	7,701	462,060	167
7,501–10,000	8,750	100	875	− 275	76	7,600	28
10,001–12,500	11,250	80	900	2,225	4,951	396,080	178
12,501–15,000	13,750	40	550	4,725	22,326	893,040	189
15,001–17,500	16,250	20	325	7,225	52,201	1,044,020	144
17,501–20,000	18,750	5	94	9,725	94,576	472,880	49
Totals		365	3,294	40,000†	270,108	5,597,740	1,121†

$*\bar{X}_g - \dfrac{\Sigma(X_{mp} \cdot n)}{N} = \dfrac{3,294,000}{365} = 9,025$

†Signs ignored.

can be used to describe the entire population of a variable or sample with as much accuracy as needed. No wonder the mathematician considers them two very powerful tools.
3. Furthermore many of the measures computed from samples of a population tend to be normally distributed even though the original data are not. The key word here is "tend," as exceptions do occur. The tendency, however, allows us greater power in extending the usefulness of the mean and standard deviation.

In employing the two terms, mean and standard deviation, the mathematician sets the area under the normal distribution equal to one. Since the sum of any set of probabilities concerning a single event must equal 1.0, portions of the area under the normal curve can be equated to probabilities. We will show how important this concept is when we discuss triangular distributions.

A STANDARD NORMAL DISTRIBUTION

A normal distribution (ND) is converted to a *standard* normal distribution by dividing all observations in the ND by the standard deviation. This division changes the mean of the ND to zero—making it a standard normal distribution. The standard normal distribution has two characteristics:

1. Its mean is zero
2. Its standard deviation is 1.0

The ability to convert all normal distributions to a common reference point allows further mathematical manipulation. It provides more answers about our distribution.

THE AREA UNDER A NORMAL DISTRIBUTION

How do we use the standard normal distribution and its area for probability determinations? First let's look again at a normal distribution.

Fig. 3.3 shows a normal distribution. The mean ($\overline{X}$) is the same as the median and mode. One standard deviation is shown on each side of the mean. One of the characteristics of a normal distribution is that the distance equal to one standard deviation measured from the mean includes 34.13% of the total observations. Stated another way, one standard deviation, measured from the mean, will include 34.13% of the area under a normal curve.

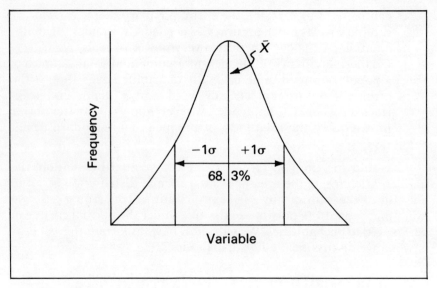

FIG. 3.3   A normal distribution

Fig. 3.3 shows a standard deviation measured from the mean going both right and left from the mean. Now the area equals 68.3% of the total. Two standard deviations measured off include 95.5% of the area under a normal curve. Three standard deviations would include 99.7% of the area.

Perhaps now you can begin to see the possibilities for our use. Because many natural phenomena and their measurements occur in normal distributions we can use them to help understand problems that have not a single answer but a distribution—i.e., a range of possible answers whose frequencies can be represented as a normal distribution.

How does one use a distribution for probability determination? Suppose we have a problem in which the answer is provided in the form of an ND. If two-thirds of the values lie within one standard deviation, plus and minus from the mean, then any value outside (larger than a standard deviation) these limits only has a 33% (one-third) chance of occurring.

Since the area under the normal curve is set equal to 1.0, then portions of that area can be used as portions of 1.0 or as probabilities whose total equals one. This is how the standard deviation, mean and normal distribution produce estimates of probability; and that is why we spent this chapter defining terms relating to distributions.

REVIEW

Estimates of probability often involve distributions. We need, therefore, an understanding of the terms used to describe the characteristics of a distribution. In this chapter the common terms describing a distribution were defined and illustrated. We shall use these terms in subsequent chapters.

Recommended Reading

Mosteller et al. *Probabilities and Statistics.* Reading, Mass.: Addison-Wesley Publishing Co. Inc., 1961.
Wallis, W.A., and Harry V. Roberts. *Statistics, A New Approach.* Glencoe, Illinois: The Free Press, 1956, Chapter 11.

CHAPTER 4

The lognormal distribution

O ne more distribution must be briefly described before we can proceed further: the lognormal distribution. In this chapter we will generate a normal distribution and show how the same basic data become a lognormal distribution. We will also begin our discussion of the relevance of this distribution to the search for oil and gas fields.

GENERATING A NORMAL DISTRIBUTION

In Chapter 2 we generated a binomial distribution from tossing pennies. From this manufactured distribution many of the important facts about distributions were observed.

Now we will develop another discrete distribution to illustrate additional aspects about distributions. The example used was suggested by King[1] and deals with tossing dice, not coins. Since each die has six possible answers from one toss, the number of possibilities exceeds that of a coin. King used four dice in the following way to develop a normal distribution. From each tossing of four dice he summed the faces. Suppose the face values were

$$3, 4, 2, 6$$

The sum of the four faces equals 15. This value is recorded, the dice are tossed again and again, and the sum of the faces is recorded. The tosses are continued until you have sufficient data to illustrate your example. King used 100 tosses.

What is the range of possibilities here? The lowest sum would be

$$1 + 1 + 1 + 1 = 4$$

The highest sum would be four faces of six, or 24. Our discrete distribution can have values *only* between 4 and 24.

The results of King's 100 throws of four dice are shown in tabular form in Table 4.1 and graphically in Fig. 4.1. The distribution is uneven as were our 100 tosses of ten pennies; but the resemblance to a normal distribution is indicated.

Note that neither a sum of 4 nor 24 appeared in 100 tosses of four dice, indicating a rarity of these events. From elementary probability rules we know why this is so. The probability of rolling a 1 from the six possible faces is one in six, or 1/6.[2] According to the multiplication rule the probability of rolling four ones is

$$1/6 \times 1/6 \times 1/6 \times 1/6 = \frac{1}{1,296}$$

One would expect to roll four ones or four sixes only one time in 1,296 tosses. So it is very normal or natural not to have a value of four in 100

TABLE 4.1   Values from tosses of dice, uniform distribution

Value	Sum	Value	Sum	Value	Sum	Value	Sum	Value	Sum
3 2 6 3	14	3 5 1 3	12	6 3 6 4	19	3 3 1 4	11	3 2 1 3	9
5 5 4 2	16	5 4 6 6	21	1 2 3 4	10	1 4 6 4	15	4 1 4 4	13
4 6 4 4	18	5 2 6 1	14	3 2 6 1	12	6 4 5 3	17	6 2 5 2	15
6 1 3 3	14	5 3 4 6	18	5 4 3 6	18	2 2 2 5	11	1 4 4 2	11
5 1 3 6	15	5 3 2 4	14	6 3 1 6	16	5 3 2 3	13	5 6 4 6	21
5 5 4 6	20	2 5 3 2	12	6 6 4 4	20	5 1 5 5	16	5 5 4 2	18
1 3 6 4	14	4 3 6 3	16	3 5 5 3	16	4 4 4 3	15	2 3 3 1	9
4 6 1 4	15	6 2 6 3	17	3 5 5 5	18	1 4 6 2	13	2 6 2 6	16
2 3 4 5	14	6 2 1 4	13	4 2 5 1	12	1 3 6 2	12	4 6 2 2	14
3 5 5 1	14	2 5 3 2	12	1 1 2 2	6	2 3 5 1	11	6 5 1 1	13
5 5 3 5	18	6 2 6 2	16	5 2 5 3	15	2 6 4 2	14	5 1 3 6	15
6 5 5 2	18	4 2 2 1	9	2 6 3 2	13	1 1 5 1	8	1 1 4 3	9
4 6 6 4	20	1 2 6 3	12	4 6 4 5	19	1 4 2 1	7	2 2 4 1	9
4 1 4 3	12	2 1 1 3	7	3 5 5 4	17	6 2 5 5	18	3 6 1 3	13
2 2 6 2	12	5 2 5 2	14	4 1 1 5	11	5 4 6 5	20	5 5 2 1	13
2 6 5 4	17	2 4 2 2	10	6 6 5 3	20	5 3 4 2	14	2 4 6 5	17
2 3 1 1	7	4 6 4 5	19	6 3 4 4	17	2 1 3 4	10	4 5 4 4	17
3 6 4 3	16	3 1 4 2	10	5 2 6 1	14	6 2 5 1	14	4 6 4 2	16
1 4 5 1	11	2 4 2 5	13	2 6 4 3	15	1 3 3 6	13	1 5 4 2	12
1 3 6 2	12	1 5 4 3	12	2 1 6 2	11	4 1 4 5	14	4 6 5 4	19

After JEK, with permission from Industrial Press Inc.[1]

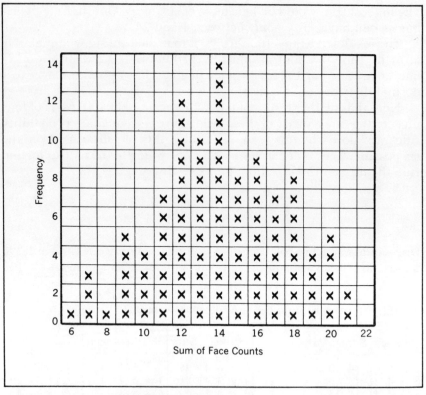

FIG. 4.1   An emerging normal distribution

tosses. You always have the possibility—it could even happen on the *first* toss. But it is not very probable with only 100 tosses.

THE SHAPE OF OUR DISTRIBUTION

Why do the values bunch in the middle ranges of sums? A little deductive thinking supplies our answer. We have shown that the sums of 4 and 24 would be rare—only one chance in 1,296 tosses. All other possibilities then lie between these two values.

Consider the sums of only *two* dice. It is easy to see that the most frequent sum will be seven since it has the greatest number of combinations of two faces, i. e., $1 + 6, 2 + 5, 3 + 4$, etc. Seven is the middle value between 2 and 12, the extreme values. Fourteen is the middle value for the combinations between 4 and 24 for four dice; there are more combinations of values that add to this sum than any other.

If 7 is the most common sum of the faces of two dice and 14 the most common sum for the faces of four dice, what does this suggest as the most common sum for faces of eight dice? You can see how a mathematician would take this empirical relationship and develop a formula to fit throws of any number of dice, but that is not our purpose.

GENERATING A LOGNORMAL DISTRIBUTION

You can take the same exact data—the raw data—and generate an entirely different distribution. Our raw data are the values on faces of four dice from 100 tosses.

If we take the raw data and *multiply* the four values instead of summing them, we get an entirely new distribution— a lognormal distribution (see Table 4.2).

We can show the reasons for our difference by Table 4.3.

TABLE 4.2   Products of face counts from tosses of four dice (raw data given in Table 4.1) the logarithmic normal distribution

108	45	432	36	18	375	144	150	96	90
200	240	24	96	64	300	16	72	5	12
384	60	36	360	120	576	48	480	8	8
54	360	360	40	32	48	6	300	300	54
90	120	108	75	720	48	100	20	600	50
600	60	576	125	200	240	24	540	120	240
72	216	225	192	18	6	480	288	24	320
96	216	375	48	144	216	24	60	60	192
120	48	40	36	96	20	80	144	54	40
75	60	4	30	30	36	60	24	80	480

After JEK, with permission from Industrial Press Inc.[1]

TABLE 4.3   The four faces

Sum	Product
$1 + 1 + 1 + 1 = 4$	$1 \times 1 \times 1 \times 1 = 1$
$2 + 2 + 2 + 2 = 8$	$2 \times 2 \times 2 \times 2 = 16$
$3 + 3 + 3 + 3 = 12$	$3 \times 3 \times 3 \times 3 = 81$
$4 + 4 + 4 + 4 = 16$	$4 \times 4 \times 4 \times 4 = 256$
$5 + 5 + 5 + 5 = 20$	$5 \times 5 \times 5 \times 5 = 625$
$6 + 6 + 6 + 6 = 24$	$6 \times 6 \times 6 \times 6 = 1,296$

The range of values for a sum was from 4 to 24; but for products the range is from 1 to 1,296—a much broader range of values.

The new range of values is so broad that we have to group our data to comprehend the results better. As we stated in Chapter 1, grouping data properly allows us to condense much information into small enough units for easier comprehension.

On Fig. 4.2 we have done just that. We have grouped the products into ranges of 100. The marked difference in the two relationships is apparent. The product values bunch at the low end of the distribution. Why? Examine Table 4.3 again. It is just as common to get face values of 1, 2, and 3 as it is to get values of 4, 5, and 6. Products with 1, 2, and 3 should have low values mostly below 100; and that is exactly what Fig. 4.2 says. In fact, 57 of the 100 tosses resulted in products of 100 or below. Note the sharp decrease in the number of products of higher values.

No product above 800 was rolled, even though the top range is 1,296. However, as shown for the normal distribution, the chance of getting four faces each with the value of six is rare.

A NATURAL LOGNORMAL DISTRIBUTION

Now let's look at some natural relationships that have a lognormal distribution. Many relationships involving money exhibit a lognormal distribution. Family income is one. Although the number of millionaires increases with time, percentagewise they are a small part of the number of income units.

Church pledges exhibit a lognormal distribution. On Table 4.4 the pledges from a suburban church are listed. The 296 pledges received were grouped by $100 class intervals—the interval representing the annual pledge. Column 2 lists the number of pledges in each interval. Column 3 is the percent each interval is of total pledges, and Columns 4 and 5 show the cumulative percentage, Column 4 beginning with the smallest building to 100% and Column 5 beginning with the largest. Columns 6 and 7 deal with plotting relationships used later. They contain the midpoints of the class interval and the logarithm to the base 10 of the midpoint value.

A quick glance at Table 4.4 shows most pledges bunched at the lower end—just exactly like the products of the four faces were in Fig. 4.2. We have an approximate lognormal relationship.

Looking at church pledges gives you a simplified definition of a lognormal distribution—

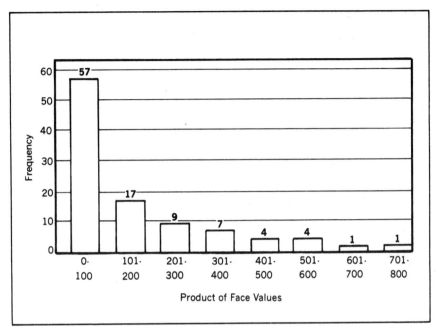

FIG. 4.2   A lognormal distribution

"Lots of little values and not many big ones!"

Column 4 is particularly revealing. Note these facts:

1. 45% of the individual annual pledges are less than $299
2. About 65% are less than $399
3. 80% are less than $599
4. Only 5% are greater than $1,100 per year

A linear plot of the pledges is shown in Fig. 4.3. Note the similarity in shape to Fig. 4.2. Now check Fig 4.4. The horizontal scale shows the *logarithm* of annual pledges, not the pledge value itself. Look at the change in shape. The pledges now have a shape about like a normal distribution—Fig. 4.1.

Herein lies the definition of a lognormal distribution. If the logarithm of a variable vs frequency plots as a normal distribution (assumes the shape of the normal curve), you have a lognormal distribution.

TABLE 4.4   A distribution of church pledges

	1	2	3	4	5	6	7
				Percent			
			Of Total	Cumulative*		Midpoint of Class Interval	
	Class						
Row	Interval, $	Actual		Small	Large	Midpoint	Log$_{10}$
1	0–99	18	6.1	6.1	100.0	50	1.70
2	100–199	74	25.0	31.1	93.9	150	2.18
3	200–299	41	13.9	45.0	68.9	250	2.40
4	300–399	57	19.2	64.2	55.0	350	2.55
5	400–499	26	8.8	73.0	35.8	450	2.65
6	500–599	22	7.4	80.4	27.0	550	2.74
7	600–699	11	3.8	84.2	19.6	650	2.81
8	700–799	14	4.8	89.0	15.8	750	2.87
9	800–899	6	2.0	91.0	11.0	850	2.93
10	900–999	7	2.4	93.4	9.0	950	2.98
11	1,000–1,099	6	2.0	95.4	6.6	1,050	3.02
12	1,100–1,199	1	0.3	95.7	4.6	1,150	3.06
13	1,200–1,299	3	1.0	96.7	4.3	1,250	3.10
14	1,300–1,399	4	1.4	98.1	3.3	1,350	3.13
15	1,400–1,499	—	—	98.1	1.9	1,450	3.16
16	1,500–1,599	3	1.0	99.1	1.9	1,550	3.19
17	1,600–1,699	—	—	99.1	0.9	1,650	3.22
18	1,700–1,799	—	—	99.1	0.9	1,750	3.24
19	1,800–1,899	—	—	99.1	0.9	1,850	3.27
20	1,900–1,999	1	0.3	99.4	0.9	1,950	3.29
21	2,000–2,099	1	0.3	99.7	0.6	2,050	3.31
22	2,100–2,199	—	—	99.7	0.3	2,150	3.33
23	2,200–2,299	1	0.3	100.0	0.3	2,250	3.35
Total		296					

*Class intervals of 100

LOG PROBABILITY PAPER

One of the easy ways to check for a lognormal distribution is through a special kind of graph paper called log probability paper. Data that plot on this paper as a straight line can be considered lognormal. In the most simple form you need individual data points because you must have the size associated with a particular (individual) percentage of the total sample. Data on Table 4.4 are grouped and do not lend themselves easily to such a plot.

Fortunately for a simple illustration alternate data are available. On Table 4.5 are listed the deposits in savings and loan institutions in

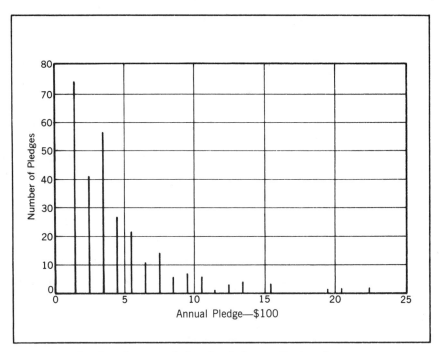

FIG. 4.3   The distribution of church pledges, a linear plot

Harris County, Texas. They are ranked by size and listed in decreasing order. The largest institution has almost $450 million in deposits. The cumulative fractile percentages are shown in Column 3. Fractile percentages are calculated by using the total sample plus 1 as the divisor.[2] In the data set a single fractile is $1/(27 + 1)$ or 0.0357 (3.6%), i.e., each data point is about 3.6% of the total sample.

Data from Table 4.5 are plotted in Fig. 4.5. The vertical scale for the variable is logarithmic; the horizontal scale for the percentages is a special one that stretches out the data points. We do not have an absolutely straight-line relationship for the data; therefore, the distribution is only approximately lognormal. Nevertheless, a general lognormal trend is visible.

A SHORTCUT

Suppose you have a large data sample—100 or more items. You may not want to plot all 100 items to check for lognormality. A shortcut exists.

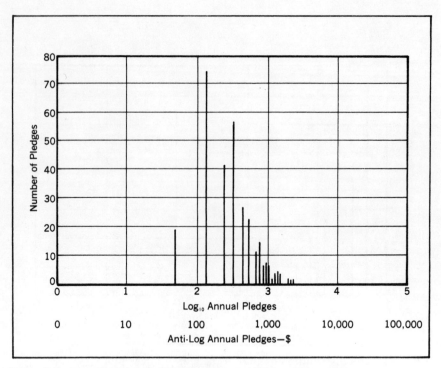

FIG. 4.4   Distribution of church pledges, a logarithmic scale

There were 136 banks in Harris County, Texas, on June 30, 1974. Their deposits were listed, ranked with fractiles calculated as in Table 4.5 for savings and loan institutions. The result is plotted on Fig. 4.6. You do not see all 136 points, however; only 12 are shown. Those shown represent the data from every thirteenth bank in descending order with one point added at 5% for further curve definition.

When faced with lots of data, plot every tenth, twentieth, etc., point. The number to plot depends on the population size—number of data points.

Note our data again do not form an absolutely straight line. There is a tail upward at the top, away from an otherwise good trend. So again we have only an approximate lognormal relationship.

Two banks had deposits above $1 billion. They do not appear on the graph paper, falling just outside the 2% line. This omission illustrates one fact about some types of log probability paper: much of it stops at 2% on the high side and 98% on the low side. For a large

TABLE 4.5 An approximate lognormal distribution

Bank rank	Deposits, $\overline{M}$* As of 6-30-74	Fractile %
1	448	3.6
2	301	7.1
3	158	10.7
4	122	14.3
5	95	17.9
6	92	21.4
7	84	25.0
8	83	28.6
9	80	32.1
10	71	35.7
11	61	39.3
12	52	42.8
13	46	46.4
14	35	50.0
15	33	53.6
16	30	57.1
17	24	60.1
18	23	64.2
19	18	67.8
20	10	71.4
21	10	75.0
22	7	78.5
23	6	82.1
24	5	85.7
25	3	89.3
26	2	92.8
27	1	96.4
Total	1,900	

*Savings and loan institutions, Harris County, Texas
$\overline{M}$ = millions of dollars

sample the extreme points are not shown. But frankly the extremes are not what you are usually interested in when using a distribution. They are the atypical, not the typical.

LOGNORMAL DISTRIBUTIONS AND OIL AND GAS FIELDS

An entire chapter has been devoted to the lognormal distribution—for sound reasons. It is the most important distribution in the search for hydrocarbons. It has been well documented that reserve sizes of oil and gas fields in a given play or basin form a lognormal

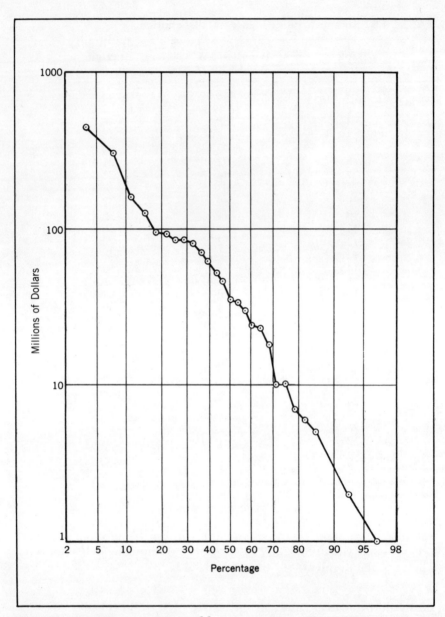

FIG. 4.5 Deposits in savings and loan institutions, Harris County, Texas, June 30, 1974

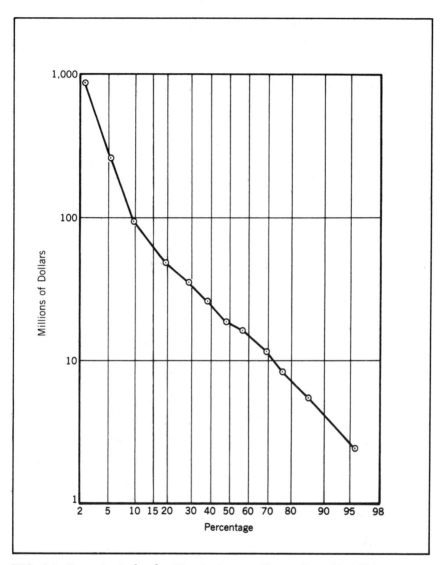

FIG. 4.6   Deposits in banks, Harris County, Texas, June 30, 1974

distribution.[3,4] There are few giant fields and many small ones. We therefore need to understand this particular size arrangement in nature so we can use it effectively.

Why should oil and gas fields show a lognormal distribution? Geologically speaking they do because of the rarity of the special conditions in nature required to produce large fields.

If you need a mathematical answer, the example of products (from the four die faces) forming a lognormal distribution should suffice. Estimates of the reserve size will almost always involve multiplication. The example used in *Exploration Economics* multiplied

$$\text{net pay} \times \text{recovery per acre} \times \text{area}$$

Logically, then, estimates of reserve sizes should line up in a lognormal distribution because they arise from multiplication rather than addition.

REVIEW

The same data that build a normal distribution can be used to construct a lognormal distribution. Adding random data produces a normal distribution; multiplying random data produces a lognormal distribution. Much statistical data involving money and its derivatives (incomes, deposits, etc.) show lognormality. Log probability paper offers a quick way to check a data set for lognormality. The lognormal distribution has special significance to the explorer. It illustrates the way the sizes of oil and gas fields are distributed. Our simplified description of a lognormal distribution is

"Lots of small values and not many big ones."

References

1. King, James E. *Probability Charts for Decision Making.* New York: Industrial Press Inc., 1971, pp. 66–68.,
2. Megill, Robert E. *An Introduction to Exploration Economics.* 2nd ed. Tulsa: Penn-Well Publishing Co., 1979, pp. 123–124.
3. Kaufman, Gordon M. *Statistical Decision and Related Techniques in Oil and Gas Exploration.* Englewood Cliffs, N.J.: Prentice-Hall Inc., 1963.
4. McGrossman, R.C. "An Analysis of Size Frequency Distributions of Oil and Gas Reserves of W. Canada." *Canadian Journal of Earth Sciences.* Vol. 6, 1969, pp. 201–211.

CHAPTER 5

The shape of distributions

W e have devoted four chapters to enhancing an understanding of distributions. We have checked a few of the mathematical properties of distributions and tried to convey meanings about some of their characteristics.

We need the ability to make a quick mental leap from a basic frequency histogram—a distribution—and its resultant shape in the cumulative form. Why? The cumulative frequency distribution is often used in risk analysis. Therefore, we need to be able to think both forward and backward—forward from a histogram to a cumulative frequency and backward from a cumulative curve to the input histogram. Seeing one, we need to be able to envision the other.

This chapter will help develop the transition to easy recognition of distribution shapes.

TWO METHODS OF DISPLAY

To begin with, let's review what we saw in Figs. 1.4 and 1.5, where we plotted a distribution for offshore wells. There we saw two different means of displaying a cumulative frequency distribution, each with the same vertical scale.

Fig. 5.1 repeats the general relationship for these two presentations. The earlier curves, referring to well depth, used two terms:

- equal to or shallower than
- equal to or deeper than

In other usage, with parameters other than well depth, we will see the terms "less than" and "greater than" with shapes as shown in Fig. 5.1. The data involved are the same, and the same information can be gleaned from each graph. For a given parameter size one curve "says" 25% are equal to or less than that value. For the same size the greater-

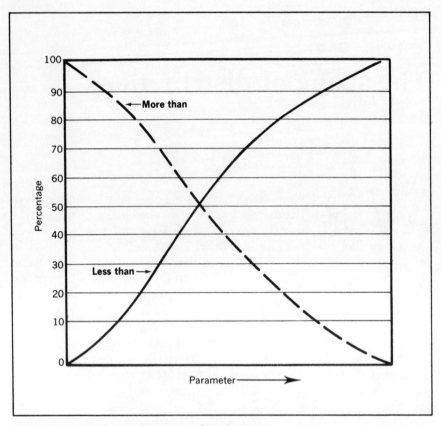

FIG. 5.1 Cumulative-frequency distributions

than curve says the same thing in different words: 75% of the parameter sizes are equal to or greater than that value.

DISTRIBUTION SHAPES

On Fig. 5.2 eight different frequency histograms are shown—A
through H. Each also has to its right the resultant cumulative frequency distribution. All numerical values are percentages. A brief
review of these shapes will vastly enhance our ability to recognize
frequency distribution shapes when viewing only the cumulative
curve. The cumulative curves are drawn in the greater-than shape.

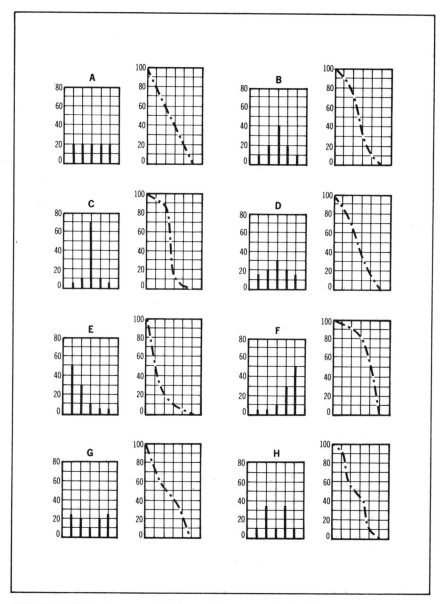

FIG. 5.2   Histograms and their resultant cumulative frequency distributions

Distribution A

We begin with A. It is a rectangular distribution. What is a rectangular distribution? A rectangular distribution is one in which each parameter value (of which there are five) has an equal frequency of occurrence. A typical rectangular distribution would be the frequency of rolling 1, 2, 3, 4, 5, or 6 with one die. Each face has an equal chance of occurring.

Now note the cumulative curve to the right. It is a *straight line. Thus, any straight line represents a rectangular distribution,* and a rectangular distribution occurs when each outcome or value has an equal chance of happening. Straight lines mean equal frequencies.

Distribution B

Distribution B has a shape similar to a normal or bell-shaped curve. It produces a curved cumulative frequency distribution. Note the steep slope in the center. It corresponds to the highest frequency of the B distribution. Here our second point emerges: *steep slope means high frequency.*

Distribution C

Our second point appears more pronounced in the C distribution. Note the very sharp, steep slope, again related to the highest frequency. Steep slope relates to your "most-likely" occurrence. Seventy percent of the parameter values in C fall within the middle value. You can see this in the C distribution. Can you see it also in the cumulative curve? If so, how? You see it in the cumulative frequency curve by noting that the steep slope occurs between 85% and 15%. Thus, 85 minus 15 shows 70% of the values occur in a very narrow range of frequencies, represented in the C distribution by the tall bar.

Distribution D

D is of special interest. Check its frequency histogram. The middle value is largest but not so pronounced as in B and certainly not like C. In fact, D is between A and B in shape. Its cumulative curve demonstrates this fact well. It is not a straight line but is less curved than B's cumulative. With no major parameter differences D has no detectable sharp slope on the cumulative curve. *No sharp slope means no sharply differing frequencies.* Do you begin to see the shapes and their relationships? Can you see D's cumulative curve and say, "That's almost a rectangular distribution." If so, you are getting the message on shape recognition.

Distribution E

As we shall see later, E is somewhat akin to a lognormal distribution. It is skewed to the right. If it were more right skewed, it would be approximately lognormal. It does show mostly small values and few big ones. The cumulative curve shows steep slope on the left, flattening to the right.

When N (the number of items) is large and P (the probability of occurrence) is small, the Poisson distribution has this shape. The Poisson distribution results in situations where an event can occur more than once, for example, automobile accident experiences over a period of time. The binomial distribution has this shape when P is small.

Cumulative distributions for oil and gas fields should always have their steep slope to the left. Nature made more small fields than giant ones. Remember the shape of E.

Distribution F

F is the opposite of E. As such it gives an upside-down cumulative curve relative to E. One would never expect to find F in a size distribution of oil and gas fields.

Distribution G

G is a peculiar distribution. It represents a situation where the highest values are at the extreme ends of the distribution. As you see, the steep slopes of the cumulative curve are there also.

Distribution H

Plot H shows a bimodal distribution: two peaks of about the same frequency. It is not uncommon in natural statistical gatherings. Again, steep slopes go with high frequencies. Can you read from H's cumulative curve the percentages associated with the highest frequencies? Use the same method employed in the review of C.

APPROXIMATE LOGNORMAL DISTRIBUTIONS

Now let's try to generate real lognormal distributions. We can begin by drawing histograms and showing the resultant cumulative frequency distribution. The next two distributions, I and J, begin our experiment.

Distributions I and J

Distributions I and J on Fig. 5.3 show shapes akin to E but more toward lognormality. Note the long tail on J. You would think it is surely lognormal. How can we check?

The easiest way is to plot the data on log probability paper. Remember, we said it is a special kind of paper deliberately set up so that lognormal distributions plotted on it will show as straight lines.

The following steps enable a plot on lognormal probability paper.[1]

1. Arrange the parameter values by size, starting with the largest value first.
2. Calculate the cumulative percentages for each observed point. In Table 5.1 (see curve J, Fig. 5.3) there are nine parameter values. Each is thus 11.1% (⅑ of 100%) of the total sample. These percentages are known are *percentiles*.
3. Find the midpoint of each percentile for each value on the cumulative distribution. This is done by taking half of the first percentile (11.1%/2 or 5.5%) for the first point and adding the full percentile (11.1) to the first point to get the second (11.1 + 5.5 = 16.6). The third point is obtained by adding 11.1 to 16.6, etc. Fractiles rather than midpoints were illustrated in the previous chapter. Both techniques are used and have essentially the same plot results for 10 or more points. Midpoints are probably easier to use and understand.
4. Plot the midpoints vs the parameter values.

Table 5.1 shows the raw data for curve J.

It takes Column 1 and Column 3 to plot a line on lognormal probability paper. The size (11) is plotted vs midpoint of the cumulative percentage (5.5). These two columns are plotted on Fig. 5.4 as the lower line J.

J does not form a straight line; therefore, it is not lognormal. The largest values for J would have to be larger for a straight line and a lognormal distribution.

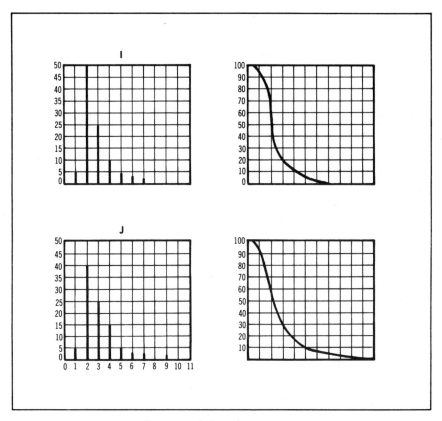

FIG. 5.3   Approximate lognormal distributions

TABLE 5.1   Raw data, curve J

(1) Parameter Size	(2) Cumulative Percent Actual	(3) Cumulative Percent Midpoint
11	11	5.5
9	22	16.5
7	33	27.5
6	44	38.5
5	55	49.5
4	66	60.5
3	77	71.5
2	88	82.5
1	99	93.5

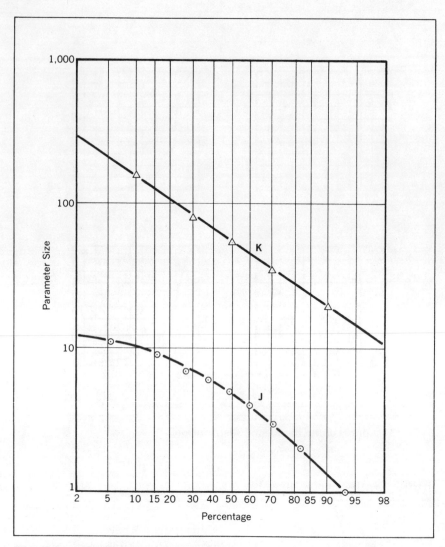

FIG. 5.4 A check for lognormality

Note the straight line K. It represents a truly lognormal distribution. Its raw data are shown on Table 5.2.

TABLE 5.2 Raw data, curve K

(1) Parameter Size	(2) Cumulative Percent	(3) Cumulative Percent
	Actual	Midpoint
160	20	10
80	40	30
55	60	50
35	80	70
20	100	90

The straight line, K, on Fig. 5.4 was plotted from Columns 1 and 3 as in the case of J. What would K look like on rectangular coordinate paper? The answer is on Fig. 5.5. Note the long tail—strong skewness to the right.

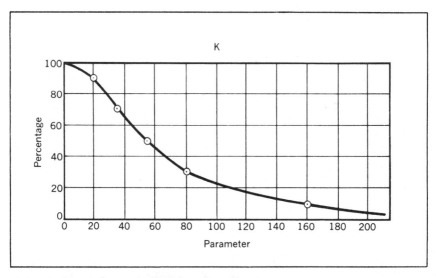

FIG. 5.5 Cumulative probability distribution

REVIEW

Risk analysis deals in probabilities, and probabilities often are expressed in the form of either frequency histograms or as cumulative frequency distributions. It is important, therefore, to be able to recognize the meaning of a given cumulative curve. Each distribution has its own particular resultant cumulative shape—from the straight line of a rectangular distribution to the sloping curve of the lognormal distribution.

Steep slope always means high frequency. Thus, for curves of cumulative probabilities, steep slope expresses a higher degree of certainty or occurrence. Flat slopes express uncertainty. These simple concepts will have value as we proceed further.

Remember, however, that the slope is a function of the scale of the abscissa. So when comparing cumulative frequency distributions, be sure to use a common scale for the horizontal axis. Also, our comments about steep slopes assume linear plots.

Reference

1. Megill, R.E. *An Introduction to Exploration Economics.* 2nd ed. Tulsa: PennWell Publishing Co., 1979, p. 124.

CHAPTER 6

Permutations and combinations

W e are well on our way to completing Part I. Yet there are still important mathematical concepts needed for an easy understanding of principles in risk analysis. One such concept involves permutations and combinations. There two words are building blocks to an understanding of binomial theorem which in turn allows an insight into the law of Gambler's Ruin. We shall develop an understanding of permutations first.

PERMUTATIONS

Permutation is a fancy word for the arrangement of things—but it is a special kind of arrangement where *order* counts. What do we mean when we say order counts? Each different order represents a different permutation.

For example, in how many ways can two books be arranged *in order* on a shelf? If we call the books *a* and *b*, the answer is

ab
ba

or two ways. We have the same two books, but they are arranged in two different orders and, therefore, count as separate permutations. Order counts.

Suppose we have three books, *a*, *b*, and *c*. How many ways can they be arranged in order on a shelf?

abc   *bca*
acb   *cab*
bac   *cba*

or six ways. Again, we can see the significance of order. Note that *abc* and *acb* count as two separate arrangements. Changing the order makes a different arrangement.

You can use a tree diagram to illustrate the arrangement of things. Such a diagram for the prior example would be

1st Space	2nd Space	3rd Space	Possible Arrangements

```
                    b ──────────── c        abc
         a <                                
                    c ──────────── b        acb
                    a ──────────── c        bac
  0 <    b <                                
                    c ──────────── a        bca
                    a ──────────── b        cab
         c <                                
                    b ──────────── a        cba
```

The zero point is shown so you have a common point to count from. Starting at this common point, you can move to the right and see all possible arrangements of three items when order counts.

Now suppose we have four items? In how many ways can four books be arranged *in order* on a shelf? If we call the books *a*, *b*, *c*, and *d*, we have the following possible arrangements

abcd	*bacd*	*cabd*	*dabc*
abdc	*badc*	*cadb*	*dacb*
acbd	*bcad*	*cbad*	*dbac*
acdb	*bcda*	*cbda*	*dbca*
adbc	*bdac*	*cdab*	*dcab*
adcb	*bdca*	*cdba*	*dcba*

There are 24 ways four items can be arranged if order counts. You can see that drawing tree diagrams or listing all possible combinations gets very tedious, if not impossible, for a large number of items.

Fortunately, mathematicians have developed a shortcut for this calculation. Mosteller et al. use squares to indicate the positions on the shelf—like this, for four items[1]

To fill in the spaces you consider some of the possibilities and limitations. In the first space we can put any one of the four books

4			

Once we do this we limit the possibilities in the second space. Any one book placed in the first space leaves only three possibilities for the second space.

4	3		

Following this logic, we see that for the third space we only have two books left—two possible choices

4	3	2	

For the last space, after the three other choices are made, there is only one book left and we fill in the last space with 1

4	3	2	1

Remember when we listed all possible arrangements for four items, it came out 24? We can get the same answer by multiplying the four numbers in the boxes times each other

$$4 \times 3 \times 2 \times 1 = 24$$

This number corresponds to the 24 branches that would appear on a tree diagram illustrating the example of four items.

Using this formula we can check the ways in which five things can be arranged in order

$$5 \times 4 \times 3 \times 2 \times 1 = 120$$

Trying to show how five things could be arranged in order by a tree diagram would be very time-consuming. We can be grateful to the mathematicians for giving us this shortcut.

A FORMULA FOR PERMUTATIONS

In developing a formula for permutations, mathematicians use a special symbol called the *factorial symbol*. The factorial symbol denotes the product in declining order of whole numbers *beginning with* the number shown. The symbol is indicated by the exclamation point. For example

$1! = 1$
$2! = 2 \times 1! = 2$

$$3! = 3 \times 2 \times 1 = 3 \times 2! = 6$$
$$4! = 4 \times 3 \times 2 \times 1 = 4 \times 3! = 24$$
$$5! = 5 \times 4 \times 3 \times 2 \times 1 = 5 \times 4! = 120$$
$$6! = 6 \times 5 \times 4 \times 3 \times 2 \times 1 = 6 \times 5! = 720$$

. . .

$$7! = 5,040$$
$$8! = 40,320$$
$$9! = 362,880$$
$$10! = 3,628,800$$

You can see that a factorial number can express a large number

$$10! = 3.6 \times 10^6$$
$$26! = 4 \times 10^{26}$$

The numerical value of factorials increases at a tremendous rate.

Perhaps you have already guessed why we introduced the factorial symbol. It is the formula for simple permutations. We have seen that the permutations of four different things, taken all together (order counts), is 4!. The general equation has the form of

$$_4P_4 = 4!$$

The number of permutations (arrangements) of n things taken all together is $n!$. This expression is usually written

$$_nP_n = n! \qquad\qquad 6.1$$

It is read as the permutations of n things taken n at a time (all together) equal $n!$.

But suppose we don't use all n items, i.e., we don't take them all together. As an example, imagine that we want to know the number of arrangements that can be taken from six things taken three at a time. Our equation is written

$$_6P_3 = \frac{6!}{(6-3)!} = \frac{6!}{3!} = \frac{720}{6} = 120$$

Another way to evaluate $_6P_3$ is to begin with 6 and proceed for three numbers

$$_6P_3 = 6 \times 5 \times 4 = 120$$

This method is even more simple for this illustration than the use of factorial numbers. Why does it work? It works because 6! is really $6 \times 5 \times 4 \times 3!$, and therefore

$$_6P_3 = \frac{6 \times 5 \times 4 \times 3!}{3!}$$

The 3! in the numerator and denominator of the fraction cancel each other and

$$_6P_3 = 6 \times 5 \times 4 = 120$$

The equation that expresses this relationship for all values of n and x is

$$_nP_x = \frac{n!}{(n - x)!} \qquad 6.2$$

It is read the number of permutations of n things taken x at a time equals $n!$ divided by $(n - x)!$

Another example would be the number of arrangements of five things taken two at a time

$$_5P_2 = \frac{5!}{(5 - 2)!} = \frac{5!}{3!} = \frac{5 \times 4 \times 3!}{3!} = 5 \times 4 = 20$$

Again, to use the short form of $_5P_2$ you begin with 5 and proceed two factors

$$_5P_2 = 5 \times 4 = 20$$

Just to show that our equations still represent the world of reality, let's construct an example of $_5P_2$ (i.e., the permutations of 5 things taken 2 at a time). We can again assume books for our physical items and indicate them by the symbols a, b, c, d, and e. Remember, however, that our number of arrangements can only involve two books at a time even though there are five books available. Under this constraint our arrangements are

ab	bc	cd	de	ca
ac	bd	ce	da	eb
ad	be	ca	db	cc
ae	ba	cb	dc	ed

Thus we have shown by our example that five things taken only two at a time ($_5P_2$) can make exactly 20 possible arrangements; we have confirmed that $_5P_2 = 20$.

REPETITIONS

The game changes slightly if you can have repetitions. In a prior example of four books arranged in order, we had 24 possible arrangements. Suppose you had four copies of each of the four books and could make repetitions. Then in each space you could always put one of each book and one possible arrangement would be all four of the same book—*aaaa*. The possible arrangements with repetitions would be

$$4 \times 4 \times 4 \times 4 = 256$$

Repetitions Expand the Possibilities. One can also use permutations with repetitions to consider different things arranged together. A common example used in textbooks is auto license plates. Most states use two things on their plates—numbers and letters. When cars were not so plentiful, numbers were sufficient. If you assume you don't want a zero in the first space, a five-number license could show the maximum different arrangements for the 10 possible numbers (0 through 9) as follows

$$9 \times 10 \times 10 \times 10 \times 10 = 90,000$$

With letters, however, you can expand the number of different arrangements since 26 different letters can go into the first space as follows

$$26 \times 9 \times 10 \times 10 \times 10 = 234,000$$

Just the addition of a letter in the first position, in a five-position license, changes the possible arrangements from 90,000 to 234,000. Two letters and three numbers expand the possible arrangements even further

$$26 \times 26 \times 9 \times 10 \times 10 = 608,400$$

Three letters and two numbers produce

$$26 \times 26 \times 26 \times 9 \times 10 = 1,581,840$$

We can illustrate the effect of repetitions a different way when numbers and letters are not mixed. Consider

$$_4P_2 = 4 \times 3 = 12$$

We illustrate the formula with a, b, c, and d as follows

$$\left.\begin{array}{cccc}
ab & ba & ca & da \\
ac & bc & cb & bd \\
ad & bd & cd & dc
\end{array}\right\} = 12$$

But with repetitions we can add aa, bb, cc, and dd or four more possibilities

$$12 + 4 = 16$$

or 4 items taken 2 at a time ($_4P_2$)

But with repetitions $= 4 \times 4 = 16$. Then n items taken x at a time *with repetitions* equals n^x.

COMBINATIONS

Our next building block involves combinations. A combination is an arrangement (or subset) in which *order does not count*. It thus differs from a permutation where order does count.

In a previous example, we saw that

$$_5P_2 = 20$$

Now suppose we say that order does *not count*. How many combinations do we have? Assume that we have five things, a, b, c, d, and e. Then possible combinations are

$$\begin{array}{cccc}
ab & bc & cd & de \\
ac & bd & ce & \\
ad & be & & \\
ae & & &
\end{array}$$

There are ten combinations. Note, we cannot have ba because it is the same as ab *if* order does not count.

Let's take another previous example. We saw that

$$_6P_3 = 120 \text{ permutations}$$

How many combinations are possible from six things taken three at a time? Remember, order does not count. Consider our things to be a, b, c, d, e, and f. Our combinations are

abc	bcd	cde	def
abd	bce	cdf	
abe	bcf	cef	
abf	bde		
acd	bdf		
ace	bef		
acf			
ade			
adf			
aef			

There are 20 combinations. Again, we cannot count *efa* as a separate combination because it is the same as *aef*, since order doesn't count.

It seems obvious that under *most* circumstances there will always be fewer combinations (order is ignored) than permutations (order is everything). We might also suspect that there is some relationship between a combination and a permutation—and there is. Our general formula for permutations was

$$_nP_x = \frac{n!}{(n - x)!}$$

The general equation for combinations is

$$_nC_x = \frac{n!}{x! \, (n - x)!}$$ 6.3

The difference is just an $x!$ in the denominator, and we can prove it by calculating the two samples we counted.

Combinations of five things, taken two at a time, are

$$_5C_2 = \frac{5!}{2! \, (5 - 2)!} = \frac{5!}{2! \, 3!} = \frac{5 \times 4 \times 3!}{2! \, 3!} = \frac{5 \times 4}{2!} = \frac{5 \times 4}{2 \times 1} = 10$$

Combinations of six things taken three at a time are

$$_6C_3 = \frac{6!}{3! \, (6 - 3)!} = \frac{6!}{3! \, 3!} = \frac{6 \times 5 \times 4}{3!} = \frac{120}{6} = 20$$

Now we have a new formula for determining combinations. To understand its relationship to permutations, consider what happens to the equation for combinations

$$_nC_x = \frac{n!}{x! \, (n - x)!}$$

if we multiply the equation times $x!$. It then becomes

$$_nC_x(x!) = \frac{n!}{(n - x)!}$$

The right side is now the formula for permutations. Thus, the number of combinations (C) times the factorial (!) of the number taken at a time (x) equals the number of permutations (P).

Some authors use a different notation for combinations. Instead of writing $_nC_x$ they simply write $\binom{n}{x}$. So if you see $\binom{5}{2}$ or C_2^5 or $C\binom{5}{2}$ these are not fractions but expressions meaning the same as $_5C_2$. Springer et al. use an even different notation.[2] They use a lowercase c followed by (n, x); for example

$$c\,(n, x) = {}_nC_x = C_2^5$$

Mathematicians need a bureau of standardization to encourage all to use the same symbols.

There are many practical uses for combinations and permutations. License plates were mentioned earlier, but one of the most ancient and still useful application of permutations is in the construction of locks. In fact, Jean Borrel wrote about the significance of permutations and locks as early as 1559.

Suppose you have a cylinder for a lock with five pins. How many different key combinations are possible? You have to make an assumption about the number of different positions an individual pin in the lock's cylinder can assume. The usual number is five. Using your knowledge of permutations, determine the number of possible combinations for a five-pin lock. Calculate the number of different permutations of six pins in a cylinder, and you can see why more pins mean more security. One additional pin increases the number of possible combinations severalfold.

REVIEW

Permutations and combinations represent key building blocks as we move toward concepts in risk analysis.

In later chapters an understanding of these concepts will open the door to uses of binomial theorem. They also provide an understanding with binomial theorem of the law of Gambler's Ruin—a useful concept in understanding oil and gas exploration.

References

1. Mosteller, Fredrich, et al. *Probability and Statistics*. Reading, Mass.: Addison-Wesley Publishing Co. Inc., 1961, p. 20.
2. Springer, Clifford H., et al. *Statistical Inference*. Homewood, Illinois: Richard D. Irwin Inc., 1966, p. 131.

CHAPTER 7

Binomials and binomial coefficients

I t's hard to believe that the round-about route of Chapter 6 leads to binomials. Yet you must understand permutations before you can comprehend combinations; and combinations are very important to the binomial theorem and binomial expansion.

From binomial expansion stem concepts and knowledge about:

1. Risks in multiple well programs (either exploratory or development)
2. The significance of success ratios
3. The value of multiple exposure
4. The number of wells needed to achieve a reasonable degree of success

THE BINOMIAL

Our next mathematical building block is the binomial. What is a binomial? *Bi* means two and *nomial* stands for number, so a binomial is an algebraic expression with two terms.

$$x + y = 0 \text{ or } (a + b)^1 = 0$$

In these expressions, x and y or a and b are the two terms. A binomial expansion is the algebraic expression we get when we multiply a binomial by itself once or more; this is the same as raising it to a power of one or more. For example

$$(x + y)(x + y) = (x + y)^2 = x^2 + 2xy + y^2 \qquad 7.1$$

Most people remember the last expression automatically, but you can derive it by multiplying as follows

$$
\begin{array}{r}
x + y \\
x + y \\
\hline
xy + y^2 \\
x^2 + xy \\
\hline
x^2 + 2xy + y^2
\end{array}
$$

$\leftarrow$ (multiplying by y)
$\leftarrow$ (multiplying by x)

$\leftarrow$ (summing)

Binomial expansion becomes complex when you have powers greater than two. For example, $(a + b)^3$ and $(a + b)^4$ expand to

$$(a + b)^3 = a^3 + 3a^2b + 3ab^2 + b^3 \qquad 7.2$$

$$(a + b)^4 = a^4 + 4a^3b + 6a^2b^2 + 4ab^3 + b^4 \qquad 7.3$$

As you go to larger and larger exponents, binomial expansion becomes very tedious. Calculating the exponents for each number is simple: as one gets smaller, the other gets bigger. However, calculating the coefficients—the values in front of each expression—quickly becomes *quite* difficult. Again, mathematicians have figured out a shortcut that reduces the work.

It is the coefficients, the numbers in front of each expression in the binomial expansion, that have our interest; and it just happens that the formula for combinations derives the coefficients. Just why combinations derive the coefficients will be shown later (Eq. 7.6). In the preceding expansion of $(a + b)^3$, the coefficients were 1, 3, 3, and 1. To show all coefficients, they are enclosed in parentheses as follows.

$$(1)a^3 + (3)a^2b + (3)ab^2 + (1)b^3 \qquad 7.4$$

Let's see if the formula for combinations really does produce these coefficients. (First you need to know that 1! and 0! are both defined as having a value of 1.) The general formula is

$$_nC_x = \frac{n!}{x!(n - x)!} \qquad 7.5$$

Our coefficients, then, are

$$_3C_0 = \frac{3!}{0!(3-0)!} = \frac{3 \times 2 \times 1}{1 \times 3 \times 2 \times 1} = \frac{1}{1} = 1$$

$$_3C_1 = \frac{3!}{1!(3-1)!} = \frac{3 \times 2 \times 1}{1 \times 2 \times 1} = \frac{3}{1} = 3$$

$$_3C_2 = \frac{3!}{2!(3-2)!} = \frac{3 \times 2 \times 1}{2 \times 1 \times 1} = \frac{3}{1} = 3$$

$$_3C_3 = \frac{3!}{3!(3-3)!} = \frac{3!}{3!} = 1$$

Our answer is 1, 3, 3, and 1; these *are* the coefficients of any binomial expanded to the third power. So the formula for combinations *does* produce the coefficients for binomial expansion.

Now, if we consider n the exponent, then a general equation for the binomial theorem is

$$(a + b)^n = {}_nC_0a^n + {}_nC_1a^{n-1}b + {}_nC_2a^{n-2}b^2 + {}_nC_3a^{n-3}b^3 \ldots {}_nC_xb^n$$

7.6

By using a slightly different method of display, mathematicians abbreviate this formula as follows

$$(a + b)^n = \sum_{x=0}^{n} {}_nC_x\, a^{n-x}b^x$$ 7.7

You would read this expression as

The expansion of $(a + b)$ to the nth power is equal to the sum of the values of all combinations (from $x =$ zero to $x = n$) of n things taken x at a time, times a to the n minus x, times b to the x.

Note from Eqs. 7.6 and 7.7 that x is always the exponent for b, the second number of the binomial. Perhaps this relationship will further explain how combinations relate to the coefficients.

This formula is very useful in discussing binomial probability. It is from binomial probability we derive ideas about probabilities for success and failure in exploratory drilling.

PASCAL'S TRIANGLE

Before moving to binomial probability, however, an important shortcut will be reviewed. A mathematician named Blaise Pascal

(1623–1662) was one of the beginning thinkers about probability. He found an extremely simple method of finding the coefficients for the variables in binomial expansion. It is so simple, in fact, that you can construct a triangle (called Pascal's triangle) from the binomial expansions just reviewed. We have discussed $(a + b)^1$, for which the coefficients are 1 and 1. For $(a + b)^2$ the coefficients were 1, 2, and 1; for $(a + b)^3$ they were 1, 3, 3 and 1. Arranging these in ascending order

Binomial	Coefficients					
$(a + b)^0$				1		
$(a + b)^1$			1		1	
$(a + b)^2$		1		2		1
$(a + b)^3$	1		3		3		1

Let's stop here and see what is shaping up. Notice the 2 in the third line of coefficients? It is the sum of $1 + 1$, the numbers to the right and left *above* it. Isn't this also true of the numbers 3 in the fourth line? From this simple beginning you can construct Pascal's triangle merely by adding the two numbers above to form the one below.

Expanding the previous illustration we have Table 7.1. You could carry this experiment out as far as you like. What marvelous time-savers come from shortcuts! Pascal really found a valuable shortcut to values for $_nC_x$. We shall come back to this table several times to take advantage of the shortcut.

TABLE 7.1 Pascal's triangle

Binomial	Coefficients										
$(a + b)^0$						1					
$(a + b)^1$					1		1				
$(a + b)^2$				1		2		1			
$(a + b)^3$			1		3		3		1		
$(a + b)^4$		1		4		6		4		1	
$(a + b)^5$	1		5		10		10		5		1
$(a + b)^6$	1		6	15		20		15	6		1
$(a + b)^7$	1	7		21	35		35	21		7	1
$(a + b)^8$	1	8	28	56		70		56	28	8	1
$(a + b)^9$	1	9	36	84	126		126	84	36	9	1
$(a + b)^{10}$	1 10	45	120	210	252		210	120	45	10	1

Just to refresh your memory as to the meaning and significance of Pascal's triangle, an illustration follows. Check the last line of Table 7.1. Here n equals 10 and, for the sixth figure in that line, x equals 5; so the coefficient should be $_{10}C_5$. The proof is

$$_{10}C_5 = \frac{10!}{5!\,(10-5)!} = \frac{10 \times 9 \times 8 \times 7 \times 6 \times 5!}{5!\,(5!)}$$

$$= \frac{10 \times 9 \times 8 \times 7 \times 6}{5!} = 252$$

The future use of $_nC_x$ will involve concepts of *drilling* and *success*, where n will be the number of wildcats drilled and x the number of successes (or discoveries).

Before leaving Pascal's triangle another arrangement deserves a review. The figures from Pascal's triangle can be arranged on their "side," so to speak, to illustrate another point. For example

$(a + b)^0$	1					
$(a + b)^1$	1	1				
$(a + b)^2$	1	2	1			
$(a + b)^3$	1	3	3	1		
$(a + b)^4$	1	4	6	4	1	
$(a + b)^5$	1	5	10	10	5	1
etc.						

Note the second column in the new arrangement. It represents the exponent in the binomial expansion. If you refer to Table 7.1, you will see that the column above is equivalent to the second diagonal column in Pascal's triangle. Now you can easily locate the exponent of the binomial expansion.

We next move from binomial expansion to binomial probability.

BINOMIAL PROBABILITY

In making the change from binomial expansion to binomial probability, it is necessary to change notation in the following manner

Binomial Expansion		Binomial Probability	Meaning of the Term
a	becomes	q	probability of failure
b	becomes	p	probability of success

So $(a + b)^n$ becomes $(q + p)^n$, or preferably $(p + q)^n$. If you come across binomial probabilities elsewhere, the $(p + q)^n$ notation is what you will most likely find.

If p is the probability of an event occurring in any single trial (you can call this the probability of *success*) and $q = 1 - p$ (the probability of a dry hole), then the probability that the event will happen exactly x times in n trials (i.e., x discoveries and $n - x$ dry holes) is given by

$$p(x) = {_nC_x}p^xq^{n-x} = \frac{n!}{x!\,(n-x)!}\,p^xq^{n-x} \qquad 7.8$$

This equation is called the *binomial probability function*. Note how similar it is to Eq. 7.7. Now you can see the value of all our work to this point. The lengthy discussion of binomial expansion and binomial probability has been the groundwork necessary to get to this one important equation.

You can substitute D and S in the binomial probability formula (Eq. 7.8) to indicate the probability of a dry hole or a successful well

$$p(x) = {_nC_x}S^xD^{n-x} \qquad 7.9$$

In Eq. 7.9

$p(x)$ = probability of *exactly* x successes
x = number of successful wells
n = total number of wells
S = probability of success
D = $(1 - S)$ or probability of each well being dry
${_nC_x}$ = a coefficient that is our familiar formula for *combinations*, or the number of combinations of n things taken x at a time

Before using this newly found formula, let's go back to a simple illustration.

Suppose you are dealing with several things that might happen and you want to relate these to what will happen. One might say this as

Lots of things *can* happen, but only one thing *will* happen.

A mathematician would say that an equation for this idea would read

The sum of the probabilities of all things that can happen must equal what does happen (which must be one of the things that can happen)

More succinctly

The sum of the probabilities of all possible outcomes = 1.0.

Let's now bring this knowledge to bear on an example involving wildcat wells. As shown in Eq. 7.9 we will use symbols D and S to indicate dry hole (D) and successful well (S). An easy way to begin is with a three-well program. This example could, however, also be used to illustrate the possible outcomes in a development well with three potential pay zones.

In drilling only three wells, there are eight possible sequences of events that can occur. A mathematician would state this relationship as 2^3 or $2 \times 2 \times 2$ or 8. These eight outcomes are shown in Table 7.2. The outcomes range from all dry to all successful. Three possible combinations include two dry holes and one success; and three combinations could produce only one dry hole and two successes.

TABLE 7.2   All possibilities in a three-well program

DDD	All 3 dry
DDS	2 dry—3rd successful
DSD	2 dry—2nd successful
SDD	2 dry—1st successful
SSD	2 successful—3rd dry
SDS	2 successful—2nd dry
DSS	2 successful—1st dry
SSS	All 3 successful

D = dry; S = success

If we assume that D and S are *equally* probable, then this simple arrangement shows us that each event has a chance of occurring once in eight times, or we could say each event has a probability of 0.125. However, there are three events that produce one discovery; therefore, the chance for one discovery (if D and S are equally probable) is three in eight or 3/8. We would say one discovery has a probability of 0.375. The same probability of 0.375 applies to two discoveries since there are also three events that could produce that result. Only one chance in eight exists for three successes—the same as three dry holes.

THE OUTCOMES FROM BINOMIAL EXPANSION

We will now use our knowledge of binomial expansion on this illustration. We can express in binomial expansion the same illustration shown in Table 7.2. The eight outcomes just discussed for our three-well program can be expressed algebraically as shown in Table 7.3.

TABLE 7.3   Binomial expansion

$$(D + S)^3 = 1$$

D^3	$+ 3D^2S$	$+ 3DS^2$	$+ S^3$	$= 1$
DDD	DDS	SSD	SSS	
	DSD	SDS		
	SDD	DSS		
1	3	3	1	

Note the expansion of $(D + S)^3$. It yields the same set of outcomes listed in Table 7.2. This time, however, they have been derived from binomial expansion. The eight possible outcomes are listed below their appropriate algebraic expression. Here again we see the higher probabilities (if D and S are equally probable) of one or two successes.

The expression $(D + S)^3$ was set equal to one. We do this to acknowledge the fact that only one event can occur and that the sum of the probabilities of all possible outcomes must equal one.

Note also that the sum of the coefficients equals the total number of events, i.e., $1 + 3 + 3 + 1 = 8$. Remember these numbers from Pascal's triangle? We now have another important fact to use later:

The sum of the coefficient in Pascal's triangle for a specific binomial expansion equals the total number of possible events.

Here's how we put this relationship to use. We now know that if D and S are equally probable, the chance of all three wells being successful (SSS) is only one in eight, or

$$\frac{1}{1 + 3 + 3 + 1} = 0.125$$

We could develop this same data from the binomial probability function as follows

$$p \text{ (for 3 successes)} = {}_3C_3 \, (0.5)^3 \, (0.5)^{(3-3)} \qquad 7.10$$

$$= {}_3C_3(0.5)^3(0.5)^0 = {}_3C_3(0.5)^3$$

$$= \frac{3!}{3!(3-3)!} \, (0.5)^3 = 1(0.5)^3$$

$$= (0.5)(0.5)(0.5) = 0.125$$

Perhaps now you can see why Pascal's triangle provides such a convenient and time-saving shortcut if D and S are equally probable. Although the outcomes from the two events (D and S) can be determined by the equation, it becomes more cumbersome as the number of wells (n) in a drilling program increases. A four-well program has (2^4) events, or 16. A five-well program has (2^5), or 32. (Remember, we can also get the number from Pascal's triangle; for a five-well program, $1 + 5 + 10 + 10 + 5 + 1 = 32$.) So as the number of wells drilled increases, we have more difficulty in easily getting at the probabilities for specific successes unless we can use the coefficients in Pascal's triangle.

Some authors use different symbols for the prefix of the binomial probability function (Eq. 7.9). One such prefix starts with b (or B) indicating binomial probability function, followed by the three key factors

$$x = \text{number of successes}$$
$$n = \text{number of trials}$$
$$p = \text{probability of success}$$

The prefix of the equation thus becomes $B(x, n, p)$ and is read as "the probability of getting exactly x successes from n trials given a chance of p for one trial." Using this format we would rewrite our prior illustration as

$$B(3, 3, 0.5) = {}_3C_3(0.5)^3(0.5)^{(3-3)} = 0.125 \qquad 7.11$$

This expression is identical to Equation 7.10 except that our prefix gives us the three key parameters of x, n, and p.

As is so often the case in exploring for oil and gas fields, D and S do not have an equal chance of occurrence. What happens in our three trials to the probability of three successes if the chance of success is not 50% but only 20%? Using the format of Equation 7.11, we have

$$B(3, 3, 0.2) = {}_3C_3(0.2)^3(0.8)^{3-3} \qquad 7.12$$

$$= (0.2)(0.2)(0.2) = 0.008$$

If the chance of success is only 20%, then the probability of three successes in only three trials is 1 in 125 or 0.008. Remember, when p is 0.5 (50% chance), the probability of three successes in three trials is one in eight (0.125).

You should be off and running now; you can use this new formula for any set of conditions. Before you do, let's work another example.

Given:

We will have a 10-well program $n = 10$
The success rate has averaged 30% $p = 0.3$

Question:

What are our chances of exactly two successes in 10 wells with an average success rate of 30%?

Answer:

$$B(x, n, p) = {}_nC_xp^xq^{(n-x)} \qquad 7.13$$

$$B(2, 10, 0.3) = {}_{10}C_2(0.3)^2(0.7)^8$$

$$= \frac{10!}{2!(10 - 2)!} (0.09)(0.0576)$$

$$= \frac{10 \times 9 \times 8!}{2!8!} (0.09)(0.0576)$$

$$= 45 \times 0.005188$$

$$= 0.233$$

The probability of exactly two successes in 10 trials, where the chance of success is 0.3, is only 0.233. Let's work one more example.

In this example we are asking what are the chances of exactly three successes in seven wells at $p = 40\%$.

Answer:

$$B(3, 7, 0.4) = \frac{7!}{3!(7 - 3)!} (0.4)^3(0.6)^{(7-3)} \qquad 7.14$$

$$= \frac{7 \times 6 \times 5 \times 4!}{3! \times 4!} (0.4)^3(0.6)^4$$

$$= \frac{210}{6} (0.064)(0.1296) = 35 \times (0.00829)$$

$$= 0.290$$

For exactly three discoveries in seven wildcat wells in a trend where our chance of success is 40%, the probability is 0.290.

CUMULATIVE PROBABILITIES

Now let's pose a slightly different problem. Suppose someone asks you the probability of getting four *or more* heads in six tosses of a coin. Remember, in coin tossing p is always 0.5. The question posed differs substantially from the chance of exactly four heads in six tosses. To answer 4 *or more* you must consider the probabilities of getting 4 heads, 5 heads, and 6 heads because each condition would satisfy four or more. Now the formula takes a different shape

$$B(4 \text{ or more}, 6, 0.5) = B(4, 6, 0.5) + B(5, 6, 0.5) \\ + B(6, 6, 0.5)$$

$$B(4 \text{ or more}, 6, 0.5) = {}_6C_4(0.5)^4(0.5)^2 + {}_6C_5(0.5)^5(0.5)^{6-5} \quad 7.15 \\ + {}_6C_6(0.5)^6 = 0.344$$

$$B(4 \text{ or more}, 6, 0.5) = 0.234 + 0.094 + 0.016 = 0.344$$

The probability of four or more heads in six tosses is 34.4%. The expression "four or more" is mathematically the same as saying "at least four."

To refresh your memory, let's look at the coefficients from the expansion of $(a + b)^6$ (Table 7.1). We shall list them and then state what they stand for in terms of success or dry.

Coefficient	Meaning
1	All dry
6	5 dry—1 successful
15	4 dry—2 successful
20	3 dry—3 successful
15	2 dry—4 successful
6	1 dry—5 successful
1	All successful
64	Total possibilities

Remember, these coefficients represent the number of possibilities for each meaning; they can be used directly if $p = 0.5$ (D and S are equally likely). Thus, B (4 or more, 6, 0.5) can be calculated as follows from the coefficients from Pascal's triangle

$$B \text{ (4 or more, 6, 0.5)} = \frac{15}{64} + \frac{6}{64} + \frac{1}{64}$$

$$= 0.324 + 0.094 + 0.016 = 0.344$$

The answer is produced again by a different method.

You can see how cumbersome it would be to calculate the binomial probability of an outcome for a large number of trials. It is even worse to calculate the cumulative binomial probability (*x or more* successes). Fortunately, another shortcut exists in the form of tables from which we can read probabilities directly. Using tables is much faster than having a large Pascal's triangle for binomial coefficients ($_nC_x$), and the tables require no calculations—just an understanding of how they are constructed.

Table 7.4 contains an excerpt from such tables. Note it lists *cumulative*, not individual, probabilities. That means the probabilities are for *x or more*, not just *x*. Tables have been constructed for both B (x, n, p) and B (*x or more*, n, p). In Table 7.4 the data listed for the conditions where $p = 0.2$—20% chance of success. Values of x go to 7 and values of n are shown to 10. In Appendix C are several tables of both individual and cumulative probabilities.

To use tables such as Table 7.4, locate the number of trials (n) and the corresponding values of *x or more* listed to the right of the value of n. For example, the probability of one or more successes in 10 trials is 0.89; for 4 or more successes in 10 trials, 0.12; etc.

AN APPLICATION

A brief example on wildcat drilling can illustrate the useful insights to be gained from binomial expansion. You have often heard that many companies and individuals try to spread their risks in trends or plays where little is known and the money involved is large. Just why is a one-half interest in two wells less risky than a full interest in one well? Why is a one-fourth interest in four wells less risky than a full interest in one well?

You may feel intuitively that these questions are answered by inspection. Binomial expansion, however, can show us exactly why individuals may wish to spread the risk.

TABLE 7.4 Cumulative binomial probability B (x or more, n, 0.2)

n	1	2	3	4	5	6	7
			Values of x				
2	0.36	0.04					
3	0.49	0.10					
4	0.59	0.18	0.03				
5	0.65	0.26	0.06				
6	0.74	0.34	0.10	0.02			
7	0.79	0.42	0.15	0.03			
8	0.83	0.50	0.20	0.06	0.01		
9	0.87	0.56	0.26	0.09	0.02		
10	**0.89**	0.62	0.32	0.12	0.03	0.01	

The demonstration of the answer is shown on Table 7.5. It uses the payoff-table concept to illustrate monetary gain and exploratory risk. A one-well, two-well, and three-well program are illustrated. The assumptions for the example follow:

1. Only 10% chance for a successful wildcat
2. A large inventory of prospects similar in size and risk

The payoff tables show:

1. The possible outcomes from each well program
2. The probability of their occurrence
3. The economic reward (actual value profit—AVP); it can also be an actual value *loss*
4. The risk-weighted profit, which is the actual value profit times its probability of occurrence
5. The expected value, which is the sum of the risk-weighted values for all possible outcomes

What does our example show? In the one-well program the expected value for two possible outcomes is $10,000. The dry hole, which will occur 9 out of 10 times, represents a risk-weighted loss of $90,000. A successful well would produce $1,000,000; but since it will occur only once in 10 wells, the risk-weighted profit is only $100,000. Thus, the expected value, the sum of the two risk-weighted values, is $10,000.

TABLE 7.5   Reducing the risk with multiple wells

One-Well Program			
Outcome	Probability	AVP(L), $M	Risk-weighted AVP, $M
D	0.9	−100	−90.0
S	0.1	1,000	100.0
	1.0		10.0

Two-Well Program			
Outcome	Probability	AVP(L), $M	Risk-weighted AVP, $M
DD	0.81	−200	−162.0
DS	0.09	900	81.0
SD	0.09	900	81.0
SS	0.01	2,000	20.0
	1.00		20.0
		One-half interest in 2 wells =	10.0

Three-Well Program			
Outcome	Probability	AVP(L), $M	Risk-weighted AVP, $M
DDD	0.729	−300	−218.7
DDS	0.081	800	64.8
DSD	0.081	800	64.8
SDD	0.081	800	64.8
SSD	0.009	1,900	17.1
SDS	0.009	1,900	17.1
DSS	0.009	1,900	17.1
SSS	0.001	3,000	3.0
	1.000		30.0
		One-third interest in 3 wells =	10.0

$M = thousands of dollars

The two-well and three-well programs show that one-half of the expected value in a two-well program and one-third of the expected value in a three-well program are also $10,000. The monetary gain *remains the same* under the conditions set forth!

What does change? The probability of all wells being dry changes. For a one-well program the chance of it being dry is 90%; for a two-well program the chance of all being dry is 81%; and for a three-well program the chance of all being dry is 72.9%. The chance of losing everything *decreases* with a lower participation in a larger number of wells. In this way risk is *reduced*.

A firm with a strong risk aversion willingly sacrifices the likelihood of above-average outcomes for a reduction in the likelihood of below-average chances of losing everything.

One other factor also changes. The more wells in which you have an interest, the better your chances of getting one of the larger fields in a lognormal distribution. This condition was not allowed in our original set of conditions, as we assumed prospects of similar size and risk. Large fields are rare; so the only way you increase your chances of participating in the larger finds—in a statistical sense—is to participate in a greater number of exploratory wells.

Mathematically, the preceding statement can be illustrated by calculating the mean of an increasingly larger sample of fields from the *same* lognormal distribution. Table 7.6 shows 5, 10, and 20 field samples from the lognormal distribution in Fig. 7.1. Here the assumption is made that all are fields that will align themselves along the line of the parent distribution, i.e., the five-field sample was read from the curve of Fig. 7.1 at the midpoints indicated; the 10 fields were read from the midpoints shown as were the 20 fields. Thus, each sample of fields was spaced equidistant (percentagewise) along the one lognormal curve.

Note how the mean values of the distributions increase with field sample. The five fields have a mean of 7.9 million barrels (bbl); the 10 fields have a mean of 9.4 million bbl; and the 20 fields have a mean of 10.4 million bbl. The median, however, remains the same. The incremental increase in mean size gets smaller and smaller as the number of fields increases. You can see how rapidly this occurs by the curve in Fig. 7.2. Note also how critical the curve is up to about the sixth discovery. Since from 20 to 50 wildcats would have to be drilled to get 5 to 10 discoveries, the sharply breaking early part of the curve is the most critical.

Just precisely why the mean increases can be seen from Fig. 7.3, which shows the increase in the size of the largest field with sample size. Again, the curve rapidly decreases in slope after the twentieth discovery.

All of these relationships reveal another of the practical values of binomial expansion. Spreading the risk enhances your possibilities of getting a larger mean reserve; and as we have seen, it reduces your chance of them all being dry.

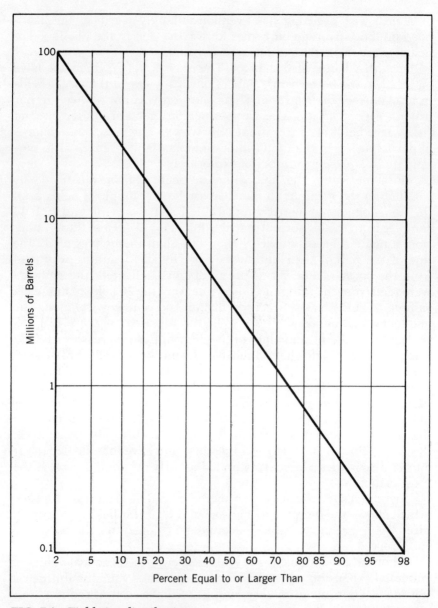

FIG. 7.1   Field-size distribution

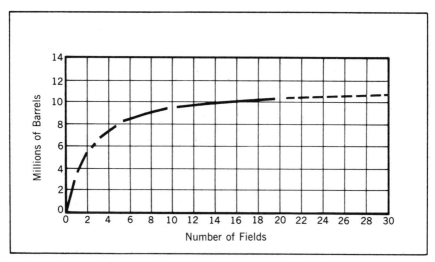

FIG. 7.2   Mean value increases with sample size, lognormal distribution

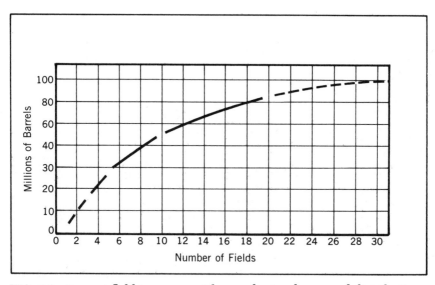

FIG. 7.3   Largest field increases with sample size, lognormal distribution

TABLE 7.6   Mean increases with number of fields

No.	5 Fields Value*	5 Fields Midpoint	10 Fields Value*	10 Fields Midpoint	20 Fields Value*	20 Fields Midpoint
1	27.0	10	50.0	5	85.0	2.5
2	7.6	30	18.0	15	35.0	7.5
3	3.2	50	10.0	25	22.0	12.5
4	1.3	70	6.0	35	15.0	17.5
5	0.4	90	3.9	45	11.3	22.5
6			2.6	55	8.6	27.5
7			1.7	65	6.5	32.5
8			1.0	75	5.4	37.5
9			0.5	85	4.3	42.5
10			0.2	95	3.5	47.5
11					2.8	52.5
12					2.3	57.5
13					1.8	62.5
14					1.4	67.5
15					1.1	72.5
16					0.9	77.5
17					0.7	82.5
18					0.5	87.5
19					0.3	92.5
20					0.2	97.5
Totals	39.5		93.9		208.6	
Mean	7.9		9.4		10.4	
Median	3.2		3.2		3.2	

*Millions of barrels

REVIEW

Following an introduction to permutations and combinations, this chapter introduced the binomial theorem, binomial expansion and Pascal's triangle. Any two-event system benefits from knowledge about binomial theorem. The exploratory well with its outcomes of dry or successful fits into a two-event system. Probabilities of success or failure can be derived for any level of drilling from binomial theorem. Pascal's triangle gives shortcuts to these calculations for the special case where the probabilities of the two events are equally likely. For success rates (values of p) other than 50%, tables from statistical reference books can be used to determine probabilities of outcomes.

Binomial probabilities also help illustrate the benefits of spreading risks. The next chapter will show how binomial probabilities can help determine the number of wells needed to achieve a desired degree of success.

PART II

APPLICATIONS

C hapter 8 begins Part II. The following chapters build upon the base of the first seven chapters. They assume you understand the importance of lognormality and the significance of binomial theory to the two-event system of drilling for oil and gas. These chapters will provide simple illustrations of risk analysis concepts, some of which are recommended and some that are not. Those concepts not recommended are included only because you will run across them in the literature. You need to know their limitations.

Wherever possible new concepts are explained in nonmathematical terms. In a few chapters, because of the proprietary nature of the state of the art, only the available published literature is reviewed. However, the important conclusions about risk analysis are almost all available from the literature. Risk analysis has been around a long time. What has changed is that more and more explorationists are becoming aware of its value to their exploration programs. To a large degree the sealed bid sales in the Outer Continental Shelf have done more than anything else to advance the use of risk analysis. The limited geological knowledge and high monetary commitments have necessitated the consideration of every possible useful technique.

CHAPTER 8

Gambler's Ruin

S earching for hydrocarbons may well be the world's biggest gambling game. The stakes are high, and the results are uncertain. In gambling, the odds favor the house. In the search for oil and gas, nature represents the house, and she wins much of the time. It is as if the house is drilling development wells with its money and your money goes for wildcats. Even in the simple toss of a coin (which has the high probability of success of 1/2), you can have a long run of either heads or tails. If the stakes are high and your capital is minimal, you can be ruined.

For this reason gamblers have toyed with a fundamental concept called Gambler's Ruin. This rule, based on binomial theory, says that the higher the risk (that is, where the chances of success are small), the greater the chance of going broke from a normal run of bad luck. The concept holds regardless of long-run expectations of a profit.

There is no way to avoid this risk absolutely, but you can reduce it by making sure that your exposure—when related to your capital— has only a small chance of loss. This really means you need enough capital to ride out the inevitable runs of bad luck. When a business fails due to Gambler's Ruin, we say it was "undercapitalized."

NORMAL RUNS

What are "normal" runs of bad luck? How do we determine them? How does this knowledge help us? The answer to the first question can never be answered with absolute exactness. Yet normal runs of bad luck can be inferred from binomial probabilities, and that's what we've been talking about.

Concepts involving Gambler's Ruin have some distinct limitations that will be discussed. Nevertheless, the term Gambler's Ruin appears in the literature frequently, and a few authors still espouse its usage.[1] Thus, even with its limitations it needs discussion.

In a figurative sense an insurance company places so many bets that it is not affected by Gambler's Ruin.[2] But an oil company does not have the luxury of thousands of bets (wells). Therefore, information on Gambler's Ruin has value. For example, if you drill 10 wells in an area where the success rate has averaged 10%, the law of Gambler's Ruin would tell you that you had a 35% chance that all 10 wells would be dry. The purpose in this chapter is to show you the exact basis for the preceding statement.

GRAPHING CUMULATIVE BINOMIAL PROBABILITY

We saw in Table 7.4 that tables exist that display cumulative binomial probabilities—showing the probabilities for various successes (x or more) for varying numbers of wells (n). In Table 7.4 the heavy blocked number was the answer to

$$B(1 \text{ or more}, 10, 0.2) = P(1) + P(2) + P(3) + P(4) \ldots P(10)$$

$$= 0.27 + 0.30 + 0.20 + 0.07 \ldots$$

$$= 0.89$$

The probability of one or more (sometimes read as "at least one") discoveries for 10 wells in a trend with 20% success rate is 0.89, or 89%. Note that the highest individual probability (0.3) is nearest the average probability ($P = 0.2$) or at exactly two successes. A review of the nature of the formula for binomial probability will show you that this will always be true. The series $P(1) + P(2) + P(3)$, etc., is not a progression numerically downward from $P(1)$.

On Fig. 8.1 a plot of cumulative binomial probabilities is shown for the special case where $P = 0.2$ (20% chance of success). The top curve is labeled "at least one." It can be shown also as $\leq$, which means "equal to or less than." Thus, the top line in Fig. 8.1 shows the case of one or more discoveries at various numbers of wildcats (values of n), these values being the horizontal axis. Note the intersection of the top curve on the line for $n = 5$. This intersection says that if $n = 5$, there is a 65% chance of at least one discovery. For 10 wells there is an 89% chance of at least one discovery. Thus, we can show graphically the numbers contained on tables of cumulative binomial probability.

The Case of x = 0

There is a special case of individual probability that has a direct bearing on Gambler's Ruin. That case is the one where $x = 0$. It rep-

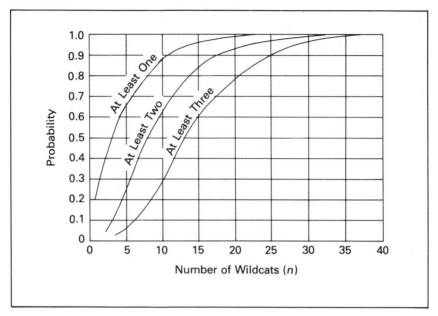

FIG. 8.1   Chance of at least one, two, or three discoveries, 20% success rate (p)

resents the situation where all wells were dry—none were successful. The reason this special case occupies our interest for Gambler's Ruin is this: The basic question answered by Gambler's Ruin is, "What is the probability that all wells are dry?" The effective use of Gambler's Ruin concepts comes when you utilize the answer to this question to make investments such that potential losses are minimized.

Fig 8.2 was generated by plotting from tables of individual binomial probabilities the values for $x = 0$ for various values of n. In the figure n is the horizontal axis, and probability is the vertical axis. The probability that all wildcats will be dry is shown for three success rates (3 values of p)—namely 10%, 20%, and 30%.

First, let's examine the 20% line. Remember from Table 7.4 and Fig. 8.1 the chance of *at least one* discovery was 89%. Therefore, the chance that **all** would be dry is one *minus* the chance of at least one discovery

$$B(0, 10, 0.1) = 1 - 0.89 = 0.11 \text{ or } 11\%$$

Now read the 20% line on Fig. 8.2 at the value of $n = 10$. You see that it shows a chance of 11% for all wells being dry. The 30% line shows

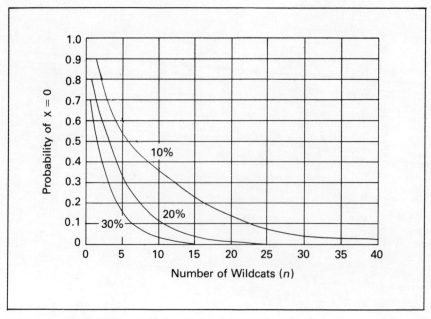

FIG. 8.2   Probability of all dry holes, binomial probability

only a 3% chance of all being dry at $n = 10$; the 10% line shows a 35% chance of all 10 wells being dry (if $p = 0.1$).

Remember the statement made in the sixth paragraph of this chapter: You have a 35% chance of all dry holes in a 10-well program where the success rate averages 10%. Now you see exactly how that statement was derived.

USING CONCEPTS DERIVED FROM $x = 0$

The law of Gambler's Ruin is one extension of the use of curves or data from individual probabilities of $x = 0$. There are very simple uses of the concept, and there are more complex usages. One referred to earlier was by Arps and Arps ("Prudent Risk-Taking," *JPT*, July 1974). The authors stated that prudent risk-taking involves two concepts:

1. Successive risk-taking ventures should be undertaken only under a break-even situation over the long term
2. The money risked on a single venture should not exceed that which would increase the risk of Gambler's Ruin beyond *acceptable limits*

Note the term "acceptable limits" in the second concept. The investor must determine *for himself* what his acceptable limits are. The maximum would be the limits for *total loss*.

Let's now use a very simple example to illustrate these concepts.

Assumptions:

1. There are 10 prospects
2. The drilling capital is $1,000,000
3. Dry cost per wildcat well is $100,000
4. Expected average success rate is 20%
5. A 95% assurance of at least one discovery is desired

Given these facts as input, we seek answers to the following questions:

1. What are the chances of all 10 prospects being dry?
2. With 10 prospects is there 95% assurance of one or more discoveries?
3. If not, how much larger must n be (how many more wells)?
   or
4. With 10 wells what will the success rate be to have 95% chance of at least one discovery?

The answer to question one has already been provided from a prior illustration. When $p = 0.2$ and $n = 10$, there is still an 11% chance that all wells would be dry. This answer comes from the 20% chance curve in Fig. 8.2.

If there is an 11% chance of all being dry, then obviously the answer to question two is **no.** We cannot be 95% sure of at least one discovery. Thus, if 95% is the "acceptable limit," we would reject this series of prospects.

On the other hand, Fig. 8.2 shows that if 14 wells are drilled instead of 10, there is a 95% chance of at least one discovery. The answer to question three is 14 wells.

However, there is only enough capital to drill 10 wells, not 14. Suppose the estimate of *average* success is conservative. How much would the success rate have to be to give the 95% assurance of one or more discoveries? The answer to this question requires interpolation between the 20% and 30% curves in Fig. 8.2. A success rate of approximately 26% is needed to have a 95% chance of one or more discoveries with only 10 wells.

Notice we have only dealt with the chance of success, not the chance of profit. Profit must be worked into the solution of this problem. A small discovery might not return the $1 million of invested capital. The assumption here is that all 10 wells are drilled. One possibility is that the first two or three holes could be dry and could also disprove the basic geologic assumptions upon which the prospects were isolated. You could stop drilling then. On the other hand, that first well could be a discovery and finance the whole play.

A NORMAL RUN OF BAD LUCK

One important point needs special comment: If you drill 14 wells, are you *guaranteed* at least one discovery in our example above? The answer is **no.** There is no guarantee. Binomial probability is based on long-term averages, but short-term variations are possible. Remember the coin tosses in Chapter 2? Even 100 tosses did not reproduce the long-term average frequency of heads.

The values of $x = 0$ are mathematical expressions of a normal run of bad luck in a two-event system. Normal, then, is the long-term expected average from many coin tossings or many well programs. In the example of 10 and 14 wells, it is still possible to drill even 20 wells all dry; but if $p = 0.2$, the probability is low. However, even low probabilities can and do occur. If it can happen, it will happen sometime. Even at 10,000 to 1 odds, an event could happen the first time!

Before discussing some limitations of binomial probability, let's illustrate another simple example.

Given:

1. Drilling capital is $5,000,000
2. Dry cost per wildcat well is $250,000
3. A 90% assurance of at least one discovery is desired

Solution:

Success Rate (p)	Prospects (n) for Only 10% Dry Chance
10	23
20	11
30	7

Without posing questions, the table tells us:

1. A total of 23 prospects are required to satisfy the acceptable limits at 10% success rate

2. The capital is not sufficient for this type of play
3. At 20% success rate only 11 prospects satisfy the acceptable limits
4. At 30% only seven prospects are needed

These answers were derived from binomial probability tables as in the previous example. From these simple examples you can see the types of applications made from the law of Gambler's Ruin. However, this concept has some severe limitations that must be considered.

LIMITATIONS
1. First of all, not all runs of bad luck are normal. The estimate of the number of wells it takes to achieve acceptable limits is itself an average based on the results of many events.
2. Second, the probabilities are assumed constant with time, i.e., they do not change as we drill each prospect. This assumption doesn't fit most plays where each new well adds significant data.
3. Third, binomial theorem assumes each event is independent of other events, which may not be the case. If one well is related to the outcome of another, the events are *not* independent.
4. The law of Gambler's Ruin has no application to a single event (one prospect). This realization reaffirms the geologic common sense of trying to higrade prospects—to drill the best ones first.
5. For exploration, binomial theorem assumes a constant supply of prospects—sampling *with* replacement, a mathematician would say. However, the population diminishes with each new discovery. Newly discovered fields are not replaced but represent one less reservoir left to find.
6. Finally, success is not quantified. The size of discoveries is ignored, and this factor must enter your decision process. The average success rate is related to the chance of getting *anything*, the minimum size or more. At least one discovery doesn't guarantee a field large enough to make a profit.

THE USES

With all of these limitations, what value is the law of Gambler's Ruin? What good is it to know what constitutes a normal run of bad luck?

1. Gambler's Ruin concepts reemphasize important aspects about success ratios. They remind us that success ratios are averages based on many events.
2. Because success ratios are long-term averages, any small group of prospects can vary considerably from that average.
3. Gambler's Ruin shows how far a given number of wells would normally vary from the average by illustrating a normal run of bad luck.
4. Concepts about Gambler's Ruin can foster an understanding of the probabilities associated with exploration drilling, development drilling, and multiple-pay field wells.
5. The dimensions of a particular deal can be expressed in the number of wells or success ratios needed to achieve a desired goal.
6. Concepts of Gambler's Ruin can demonstrate for the nonexplorationist that in a 10-well program, a 20% success rate does *not* automatically mean *two* discoveries—even though that is the most probable outcome.
7. You can augment concepts of Gambler's Ruin by reducing your working interest in one or more prospects. Such an action keeps your exposure to the same number of geologic prospects but lowers your overall financial risk to acceptable limits.[3]

When the risks are great, there is no absolute rule; but any insight that helps us more fully understand an opportunity is of value. It is in this sense that binomial theorem and Gambler's Ruin have value and meaning to the explorationist.

REVIEW

A concept of the chances of ruin has meaning to a company with limited capital. The meaning is general and philosophical in nature. The geology of a prospect still is its most important aspect. For the company that is not capital limited, understanding Gambler's Ruin adds a philosophical dimension to the array of data about an investment. Even after considering the geology, geophysics, and economics, you still need to consider the probabilities of a completely unsuccessful play.

An understanding of Gambler's Ruin can help explain some of the mysteries others see in the petroleum industry. Never has there been a more important time to help the public understand the industry. A little math, a table, or a chart may help explain the difficulties faced even under the best of nature's circumstances.

References

1. Arps, J.J., and J.L. Arps. "Prudent Risk-Taking." *Journal of Petroleum Technology,* July 1974, p. 711.
2. Slichter, L.B. "The Need of a New Philosophy of Prospecting." *Mining Engineering,* June 1960, p. 570.
3. Quick, A.N., and N.A. Buck. *Strategic Planning for Exploration Management.* IHRDC, 1983.

CHAPTER 9

Opinion analysis or the case for subjective probability

"Even when all the experts agree, they may well be mistaken."
—*Bertrand Russell*

". . . the greatest error in forecasting is not realizing how important are the probabilities of events other than those everyone is agreeing upon."
—*Paul Samuelson*
    Bus. Week 12/21–74, pg. 51

"The man who insists upon seeing with perfect clearness before deciding never decides."
—*Henri Fredric Amiel*

Almost every human activity involves decisions that must be made where proper information for assuring the right decision is lacking. These activities can be global or individual. On a global basis mankind perpetually seeks solutions to famine, inflation, resource shortages, and war. The uncertainties here seem obvious, but there are equally difficult decisions to be made in an individual human life. Choosing between job opportunities, buying an automobile, or even selecting a spouse entails decisions that often have an inadequate base of data.

WHAT IS PROBABILITY?

Whenever the number of possible outcomes for an event is numerous, we can only surmise what is probable. Some events can have their probabilities depicted in distributions, as illustrated in Chapter 4. In that chapter we learned that some distributions are discrete, i.e., only a certain, limited number of outcomes is possible. Rolling two dice represents a discrete distribution. Only 36 possible combinations of two dice can occur. Furthermore, some outcomes can be shown to be more probable than others. A distribution with an unknown number of possible outcomes is commonly called a continuous or nondiscrete distribution. Many situations exist where the number of possible outcomes is unknown. Obviously, in these instances the data base is obscure. Probability and probability concepts are attempts to assign the frequency of possible happenings to the happenings. There are two types of probability: objective and subjective.

Objective probability is based on either a discrete set of outcomes or upon data obtained from reasonable, empirical experience. *Subjective probability* must be utilized when all of the outcomes are unknown and when even the frequency of those recognized outcomes cannot be estimated with certainty. Objective probability helps in understanding the choices in gambling. Subjective probability is what explorationists use in the search for oil and gas fields. For the explorationists neither the number of fields to be found is known nor is their size. Furthermore, the explorationist has no guarantee for a small number of wildcats (a small sample) of an average success rate. He may not think of it as subjective probability, but the explorationist uses his past experience and judgment to make decisions about future events. He uses subjective probability or, as some persons like to think of it, opinion analysis.

THE KNOWLEDGE CURVE

The relationship between subjective probability and objective probability is shown by Fig. 9.1. Knowledge or information is plotted against the range of opinion. When knowledge is large (when there are many facts) factual analysis is possible. We can use objective probability. However, when knowledge is limited (when the facts are few) we must rely upon an analysis of opinion or subjective probability.

The knowledge curve shows an important fact about subjective probability. With few facts, the range of opinion is broad. Therefore, *expect* broad differences of opinion in risk analysis.

IMPORTANT REFERENCES

Within the last two decades an increasing number of writers have sought to explain and espouse the value of subjective probability in

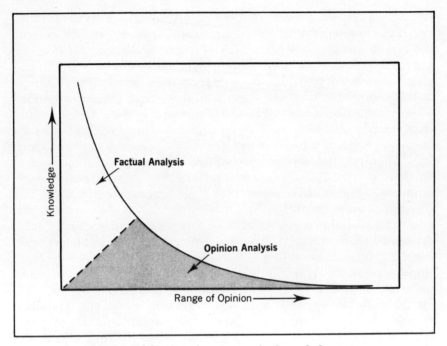

FIG. 9.1   Separation of facts and opinion; the knowledge curve

risk analysis. Several of these references will be reviewed in the paragraphs to follow.

Hertz

One particular paper is a constant reference in most articles or books dealing with risk analysis. That paper, published in a 1964 issue of the *Harvard Business Review*, was written by David B. Hertz.[1] Much of the substance of the article was later published in a portion of a book on management science.[2]

Hertz's initial article is a classic. Its succinct articulation of an approach to dealing with uncertainty—as well as its lucid clarity—probably account for its popularity. Many managers would be utilizing subjective probability if the literature contained more articles with the simplicity and ease of understanding present in Hertz's *HBR* article.

Hertz begins the article with a discussion of the impact of assumptions on any answer in capital investments. The printed page from computer-generated calculations looks so deceivingly formal and precise. Yet behind the printed page lie data that are anything but precise. The calculation of investment yardsticks (rate of return, profit, payout, etc.) involves numerous variables, each of which has a large degree of uncertainty. Most managers recognize that assumptions determine an answer and the answer is no better than the accuracy of its underlying assumptions. Nevertheless, there are managers who, faced with vast uncertainty in basic assumptions, still insist on a single answer.

Hertz illustrates the fallacy of a "most-likely" answer using five variables. Each variable has only a 60% chance of being right. Thus, the most-likely probability would be 0.6 (60%) for each variable. However, the chance that each variable will be exactly right to produce the most-likely answer is very low—in fact, only 8%. This number is calculated by taking $0.6 \times 0.6 \times 0.6 \times 0.6 \times 0.6 = 0.08$. So the most-likely answer really becomes a very *unlikely* occurrence. Hertz calls it an "unlikely coincidence." You might wish to call it the "unlikely most-likely" case. The most-likely case as a single answer is seldom what a decisionmaker really needs. The principal reason is that a single answer obscures the full spectrum of possible occurrences. Thus, the true, total range of possibilities is hidden. Most-likely estimates, then, seldom tell the manager the extent of the risk he is taking.

Hertz lists five attempts made to improve forecasts or investment analysis and lists the flaws in each. He presents his own suggestions for sharpening the picture, which are:

1. Estimate the range of values for each key variable
2. Sample at random from the distributions of each variable. (With computers to help, from 500 to 5,000 iterations will usually produce an adequate final distribution reflecting the forecast or investment opportunity)

Estimates for each variable are obtained from the most knowledgeable persons. In this book frequent reference is made to the triangular distribution because of its simplicity—both in using and in extracting information from the experts. As Hertz points out, guessing about a range is usually more accurate than guessing at a single number. A range—and particularly a three-point range of minimum, most likely, and maximum—provides better basic data about the experts' beliefs involving a particular uncertainty. Such an estimate is far superior to an average. Even though an average represents the mean of your expectations, it does not fully describe the full suite of outcomes.

Hertz closes with ". . . to understand uncertainty and risk is to understand the key business problem and the key business opportunity."*

Hanssmann

A 1968 publication of John Wiley and Sons by Fred Hanssmann is entitled *Operations Research Techniques for Capital Investments.* Of particular interest in this volume is Chapter 6 on "Techniques for Subjective Estimation and Forecasting," page 211.[3] Hanssmann makes the following points relative to subjective probability:

1. Subjective probability is denoted by the absence of a model that produces the desired answer from existing data
2. Gaining data from experts (a key ingredient in any investment decision involving vast uncertainties) requires standardized and unambiguous questions
3. Single estimates (most-likely) should be used *only* if you think uncertainty is either negligible or unimportant
4. The most simple form of illustrating uncertainty is the distribution. It is a probabilistic approach that corrects the defects of other techniques that mislead the decisionmaker

Reilly and Johri

A third reference by Park M. Reilly and Hari P. Johri[4] deals with the extraction of data from experts. The authors review the many real-life situations where subjective probability exists. One example is the physician and a single patient. For the patient, no repeats of an illness are possible to help understand the odds for a cure. (An explorationist faces the same problem with only one prospect. No two oil or gas prospects are exactly alike, and past experience is usually not precise enough to guide with absolute accuracy his decision to drill.)

In extracting odds, Reilly and Johri remind us that equal odds imply *no* ability to distinguish between alternates. Long odds imply considerable knowledge of the outcome.

Opinion analysis, say Reilly and Johri, can cover the entire range of outcomes plus indicate the degree of belief in the occurrence of

*This classic article is recommended reading for students of risk analysis.

each possible event. It is the combination of the two factors—range and probability—that helps the decisionmaker.

SOME DISSENT

Not all managers approve of quantifying opinion. A few scientists even question its use—not because of the validity of the concept, but from errors in using the technique. A good example of these reservations is an article by Tversky and Kahneman[5] of the Psychology Department of Hebrew University, Jerusalem. Their major point is that heuristic (the self-discovery process of learning, i.e., experience-related learning) principles are useful, but they can lead to either distortions from biases or systematic errors. Their reservations include the following:

1. Lack of sensitivity of heuristics to prior probabilities of outcomes; ignoring others' experience
2. Insensitivity to sample size; small samples can and do vary more from the mean of a large population (Remember our penny-tossing experiment?)
3. Misconceptions about chance; ignoring the fact that a run of heads has no relationship to the next coin toss—it still remains a probability of 1/2 for heads
4. Insensitivity to predictability and misconceptions about correlations
5. Misunderstanding the question asked or the goal sought

Kahneman and Tversky have written another interesting article that deals with the psychology of choices or preferences.[6] In part it is a good review of utility theory (a theory that states we are more prone to avoid risk than to seek a gain of similar amount), but it is much more than that. It covers not only risk aversion and risk-seeking but also the following major points.

1. Risk-seeking preferences are common when we choose between an absolute loss or a substantial probability of an even larger loss, i.e., given a sure loss, we will gamble (we are influenced to choose) on something with an even larger possible loss but with some chance for little or no loss.
2. On the other hand, when gains are involved we prefer the sure thing to a gamble.
3. As expected from utility theory, the threat of a loss affects our choice more than the possibility of an equivalent gain.

4. Our concept of loss or gain is affected by the basic reference point. Some identical problems, in terms of result, can cause different preferences because of different reference points.
5. Important to the explorer is the finding that we are more sensitive to changes in low probabilities (e.g., 0 to 10%) than to the same percent change in intermediate or high probabilities (50% to 60%, for example). This means that low probabilities are commonly overweighted (underrisked) but intermediate or higher probabilities are underweighted (overrisked) relative to certainty. The authors claim the inflated effect of small probabilities accounts for the attractiveness of such risks as aviation insurance and lottery tickets.
6. Preferences are affected by how we define or frame the consequences. Again, this concept relates to whether we see the opportunity as a loss or a gain.
7. Our choices are also affected by the amount of money involved. We are less disturbed by a price increase in an item from $1,410 to $1,420 than by an increase from $10 to $20 in another item, even though the amount of increase in absolute dollars is the same. (Our income level may seem good or most inadequate, depending upon whether our salary has recently increased or decreased.)
8. The regret associated with failure of an act is felt more intensely than the regret of failing to act, so anticipation of regret favors inaction over action.

Tversky and Kahneman are helping to demonstrate to all of us that although we must often employ subjective probabilities, conditions exist that make our decisions less than logical. These two researchers have done much to aid our understanding of the foibles of human judgment.

WHY SUBJECTIVE PROBABILITY?

With these posed limitations one might well ask, "Why subjective probability?" The answer is because there is nothing better. In spite of seeming limitations, opinion analysis is used and will continue to be used for this basic reason. Opinion analysis also has several positive factors working for it.

1. It can or should consider all critical factors bearing on the final judgment. At least all factors contemplated can be shown by documentation. It is of real value to know what *was* considered

a key variable. Seat-of-the-pants intuitive judgments leave no tracks. This does not mean that they are not often right—it is just that no one knows what went into making the decision.

2. In considering several related events, investments, or risks, it helps to have the consistency that well-documented opinion analysis can provide.
3. Up-side and down-side risks and relationships are better illustrated and handled. The complete spectrum of possibilities (beliefs) can be shown by documenting an analysis of opinion properly.
4. The degree of unknownness can be fully exposed—or expressed.

In a complex problem, intuitive judgments have a greater chance for error and inconsistency. Some methodology is needed to document fully the vital factors. It is for this reason that managers turn to opinion analysis to help them make the right decisions under great uncertainty. The proper analysis of opinion is not an absolute guarantee of success, but in the long run it is a better way than unrecorded, inconsistent, intuitive judgment.

To demonstrate the usefulness of well-documented analysis of opinion and what it can do to help in making decisions, two examples follow. Each deals with subjective probability in a simple, straightforward manner. Both examples will involve prospect evaluation—the most perplexing problem facing the explorationist.

All prospect evaluations are a search for better understanding, a clearer meaning to a problem involving much uncertainty. Most explorationists would agree that the search is laudable even though they must use subjective probability (or some variation thereof) to arrive at their decision.

One example will deal with the chance of hydrocarbons existing; the other will deal with the possible sizes of a prospect if it is productive.

CHANCE OF SUCCESS

First, let's deal with the chance of success. This part of risk analysis has many names. It is sometimes referred to as geologic risk, geologic success, existence risk, or the chance of adequacy (of hydrocarbon presence). Whatever the name, it is an attempt to assess the risk of hydrocarbon presence when the facts for assessment are *few*.

How do you go about estimating geologic risk? First, you must decide what factors control the existence of hydrocarbons. In *Exploration Economics* three factors are used:

- structure
- reservoir
- environment

The three factors ask these questions:

1. Are structural or stratigraphic conditions adequate for entrapment?
2. Are good reservoir conditions present?
3. Was the paleo-environment appropriate for hydrocarbon accumulation?

Few prospects allow three such simple questions. You may think of eight or ten or more factors influencing hydrocarbon presence. Fine. Remember, however, you must have data or experience for estimating each factor; otherwise, you are just grabbing numbers from the air. The way to solve the dilemma of too many factors for which no data are available is to combine factors for probability estimation. The term "environment" obviously includes many geologic variables important to hydrocarbon generation. However, it might be easier to think of these variables in their entirety than to make individual estimates. The three factors will suffice for the examples in this chapter.

How Many Factors?

The number of factors critical to hydrocarbon formation, entrapment, and preservation can be numerous. However, when the facts are few, we are better off dealing with as few variables as possible; otherwise, the tendency is to overwork the problem.

In addition there is a mathematical reason for limiting the number of variables. Since we are using the multiplication rule in probability, the greater the number of factors, the smaller will be our composite success estimate. In fact, the number of variables can be so large that the success estimate can become unrealistic. This result occurs even though the risking is not severe. Consider the following two examples where each factor is risked at 0.9 or 0.5, i.e., 90% or 50% chance of adequacy.

In the multiplication rule of probability, the probability of two or more independent events having specific outcomes is the product of their separate probabilities. In our simple example of Table 9.1, we have assumed that we are dealing with independent variables and that each variable has the same chance of occurrence, i.e., either 90% or 50%. As the number of factors increases, the composite geologic success estimate decreases, even at such low levels of risk for each factor as 90%. Too many factors, then, can produce an answer well below empirical experience. Ten variables or factors each risked at 50% produce a final product of only 0.1%—probably an unrealistic number. Four factors each risked at 70%, not shown on Table 9.1, yield a geologic success estimate of 0.24.

TABLE 9.1   The effect on geologic success estimate (GSE) of an increasing number of factors

Number of Factors	Composite GSE	
	@ 0.9	@ 0.5
3	$(0.9)^3 = 0.729$	$(0.5)^3 = 0.1250$
4	$(0.9)^4 = 0.656$	$(0.5)^4 = 0.0625$
5	$(0.9)^5 = 0.590$	$(0.5)^5 = 0.0313$
6	$(0.9)^6 = 0.531$	$(0.5)^6 = 0.0156$
7	$(0.9)^7 = 0.478$	$(0.5)^7 = 0.0078$
8	$(0.9)^8 = 0.430$	$(0.5)^8 = 0.0039$
9	$(0.9)^9 = 0.387$	$(0.5)^9 = 0.0020$
10	$(0.9)^{10} = 0.349$	$(0.5)^{10} = 0.0010$

A reality check will thus be necessary for setting up the basis for a geologic success estimate. If you are in a trend where the average success rate is 30%, your composite geologic success estimate (GSE) should yield about 30% for a series of prospects. If the series will not average this amount, you are either dealing with a set of prospects different from the discoveries to date (a possibility), or you are out of touch with reality. You must decide.

If the trend average is 30%, why risk each prospect? The reason is simple. Always remember that a success rate is an average. An individual prospect is one event; it cannot be an average. You should risk each prospect so that a series can be developed for an average. Geologic judgments should enable you to sharpen your estimates about a particular prospect. You must decide if this prospect or that prospect has the best chance of being productive.

Not to believe that you can select, on the average, the best prospects for drilling is to agree that the trend average will automatically apply to your prospect or that your geologic judgments cannot isolate the better-than-average prospects. Either approach can lead to a high cost of finding and a large possibility of going broke. Risking individual prospects, whether intuitively or formally, is an important part of managing an exploration program.

Gehman, Baker, and White propose a technique similar to that just described in a paper given at an AAPG Research Symposium.[7] In this book a thorough discussion of prospect risking is given in Chapter 16.

The Results of More than One Estimate

The data on critical geologic parameters in the search for hydrocarbons, illustrated in *Exploration Economics*, were based on an assumed sample of 50 exploratory wells.[8] These wells present an empirical base for future reference in estimating geologic success in the same play for the remaining undrilled prospects.

Using the three parameters from *Exploration Economics*, one person can calculate a geologic success estimate for a prospect. You then have a single opinion. Suppose, however, that you want more than one opinion. Such a desire would be expected if the money involved in a decision were large. How would you gather, assemble, and handle several estimates, and what would they indicate?

On Table 9.2 the results of 10 separate estimates are shown for the three parameters with the composite geologic success estimate calculated for each.

TABLE 9.2   Geologic risk factors prospect A

Geologist	Risk Factors[a]			Composite GSE[b]
	Structure	Reservoir	Environment	
Able	0.5	0.3	0.9	0.135
Baker	0.7	0.5	0.8	0.280
Charlie	0.4	0.7	0.7	0.196
David	0.6	0.2	0.9	0.108
Edgar	0.8	0.9	0.8	0.576
Frank	0.7	0.5	0.7	0.245
George	0.6	0.5	0.6	0.180
Hector	0.7	0.4	0.7	0.196
Ignatio	0.8	0.7	0.6	0.336
Julius	0.7	0.7	0.7	0.343
Average	0.65	0.54	0.74	0.260

[a]Estimated chance of favorable occurrence
[b]GSE = geological success estimate

For example, Able estimates as follows:

	%	Prob.
The chance of the structure being as he sees it	50	(0.5)
The chance of getting good reservoirs	30	(0.3)
The possibility of an optimum depositional environment	90	(0.9)

Able's composite geologic success estimate (GSE) is the product of the three independent parameters

$$(0.5) \times (0.3) \times (0.9) = 0.135$$

He estimates only a 13.5% chance for success for Prospect A.

Able's estimate is not the lowest, however. That honor goes to David with a GSE of 0.108. David's estimate is low because he places a high risk (only 20% chance of adequacy) on getting good reservoir conditions.

The estimates of Able and David illustrate an important point: The smallest estimate of risk *controls* the answer. You can easily understand this point by considering what happens if the estimate of success for any of the three parameters is zero. Then the GSE is also zero because if you think there is no chance for good reservoir conditions, you have no prospect and the GSE should be zero. So the lowest estimate of adequacy *controls* the GSE.

Edgar wins the prize as the optimist; he has high values for each parameter

0.8 for structure
0.9 for good reservoirs
0.8 for optimum environment

Edgar's probabilities, when multiplied, yield an answer of only 0.576. Even relatively high estimates for the parameters will produce a lower composite because you are saying *each* must happen favorably for the final outcome to be successful; therefore, the risks compound whenever you have two or more events in which all must occur for your desired outcome. Remember, rolling two sixes with a pair of dice has a much lower probability than rolling one six from two dice.

If you want to summarize the 10 estimates, you can add the 10 GSEs and divide by 10. The average of all 10 GSEs is 0.260; you can

get the same result by summing the 10 estimates under each parameter, averaging each, and multiplying the averages

$$(0.65) \times (0.54) \times (0.74) = 0.26$$

The consensus of our 10 geologists is a 26% chance—about one in
four—of the prospect being productive.

Our Favorite Distribution

A closer examination of the data reveals some other interesting
facts. Seven of the 10 values are 0.28 or lower—many low estimates
and few large ones. That statement immediately makes you suspect a
lognormal distribution. Sure enough, we have a rough approximation
of a lognormal distribution from the data (see Fig. 9.2). Once again we
have shown that a series of products from several factors will yield a
lognormal distribution.

To refresh your memory on the construction of a distribution plot
on lognormal probability paper, the plotting points are shown in
Table 9.3.

TABLE 9.3   GSE plotting points for Figure 9.1

GSE Value	Cumulative Probability Midpoints, %
0.576	5
0.343	15
0.336	25
0.280	35
0.245	45
0.196	55
0.196	65
0.180	75
0.135	85
0.108	95

Other Observations

Six values are less than our mean of 0.26 and four are larger, again
demonstrating that the mean of a lognormal distribution is skewed
(toward larger values) from the median, which on our figure is
0.23.

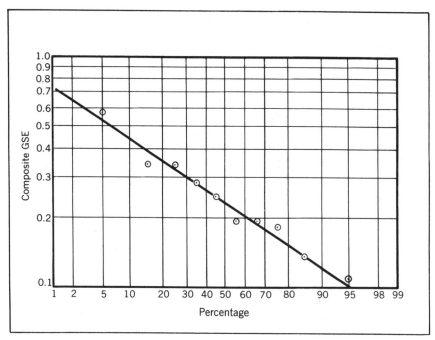

FIG. 9.2   Composite geologic success estimates, Prospect A

The sum of the estimates for the 10 geologists shows the highest value for environment, 0.74. There is the least divergence of agreement for this parameter. Wide divergence produces the lowest average for estimates of reservoir condition. For each parameter the average and range are shown:

	Average of Ten	Range of Values
Structure	0.65	0.5–0.8
Reservoir	0.54	0.2–0.9
Environment	0.74	0.6–0.9

Again, the low values, not the range per se, produce the low average.

The Meaning

Suppose you decided to use the consensus of several exploration-ists to arrive at your final GSE. What should you expect, and what is its meaning? Is any further action required?

The biggest value of considering each parameter separately is that you can see where the differences are, i.e., you can see where your estimators agree that the uncertainty is the greatest.

The first check you would make is a reexamination of the factor on reservoir conditions. Obviously, some of the estimators have concerns here. The range of opinion is the most broad and the average chance of favorable conditions is the lowest. The consensus, then, is that res-ervoir conditions are the most critical—the most uncertain. Addi-tional work may need to be done in this area, including a review of all data for possible further definition.

You would also want to make a reality check for the consensus against the average success rate of the trend or play. Although the same number would be coincidental, this reality check should alert you to consider further if the result is widely divergent from the trend average; that is, are your prospects *really* that different?

FIELD SIZE

Our first example dealt with a simple method for estimating *if* hydrocarbons are present. This question is the first that must be answered by the explorationist.

His next logical question, after a favorable answer on hydrocarbon presence, would involve size. He would ask "How big is it?"

This question is of vital importance. Why? Because of the unusual distribution that ensures many small fields and few large ones. The next phase of risk analysis should deal with methods for determining or estimating size. After all, you want to look only for the larger fields, if possible, so a documentation of your concept of size is most impor-tant.

The example will be drawn from *Exploration Economics* and will show, again in simple fashion, how to document a range of opinion to show the full spectrum of reserve sizes possible for a prospect.

Reserve Estimates and the Three Factors

Every oil or gas field has a certain areal size, a thickness of the producing formation, and a recovery per foot of pay. For a single-reservoir field the reserve could be calculated by net pay (ft) × recovery per acre-ft (bbl) × area (acres)

The result is a reserve estimate in barrels, often expressed as a single number. Subjective probability is used in prospect evaluation because we do not have absolute answers for the three factors of pay, recovery, and area.

Under such circumstances consider what values appear reasonably possible. In the example from *Exploration Economics*, a three-value suite was estimated for each parameter and a probability of that value occurring assigned.

Parameter	Value	Probability
Net pay, ft	50	0.3
	100	0.5
	190	0.2
Rec/ac-ft, $\overline{\text{Mcf}}$	0.7	0.3
	1.0	0.6
	1.5	0.1
Prod. area, acres	800	0.3
	1,000	0.5
	1,400	0.2

The various combinations of these parameters produce 27 separate estimates, each of which has its own specific probability of occurrence. Plotted on lognormal probability paper (Fig. 9.3), the 27 cases show the relative chance of occurrence of fields of a given size or greater.

Subjective probability was used here—not on the final answer but on the key ingredients producing the answer. The opinions about the possible range of values for each parameter were taken into account. The result is a full suite of values showing the complete spectrum of possible cases plus their possibility of occurrence. These two facets give increased dimensions of opportunity to the decisionmaker. They are far superior to a single answer, which for a given prospect has almost no chance of occurring.

The brief review of the use of subjective probability from *Exploration Economics* illustrates another way to document the opinion of experts. We described a needed quantity where a single answer would not disclose the range of possible answers, much less their possibility of occurrence. In this last example, the three values for each parameter could be converted to a triangular distribution. Triangular dis-

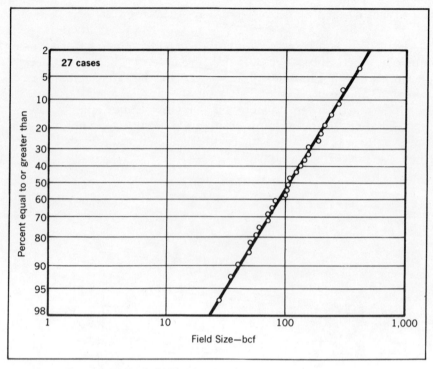

FIG. 9.3   Prospect size distribution

tributions produce the opinion of the experts *without* asking them for a guesstimate of probability. Just how this can be accomplished is the subject of the next chapter on triangular distributions.

REVIEW

Whenever an event has many possible outcomes, a single answer hides much from the decisionmaker. The analysis of expert opinion is a method that helps the decisionmaker by showing him both the full range of possibilities and their probability of occurrence. These two products of subjective probability enable better and more consistent decisions. Furthermore, the documentation possible will allow an after-the-fact analysis of a series of decisions to aid future choices. Intuitive judgments are often right, but they have a much greater chance for error; they can be inconsistent relative to complex problems and they leave no tracks.

References

1. Hertz, David B. "Risk Analysis in Capital Investment." *Harvard Business Review*, January–February 1964, p. 95.
2. Hertz, David B. *New Power for Management.* New York: McGraw-Hill, 1969.
3. Hanssmann, Fred. *Operations Research Techniques for Capital Investments.* New York: John Wiley & Sons, 1968.
4. Reilly, Park M., and Hari P. Johri. "Decision Making Through Opinion Analysis." *Chemical Engineering*, April 7, 1969, p. 122.
5. Tversky, Amos, and Daniel Kahneman. "Judgment Under Uncertainty: Heuristics and Biases." *Science*, Vol. 185, September 17, 1974, p. 1124.
6. Kahneman, Daniel, and Amos Tversky. "The Psychology of Preferences." *Scientific American*, January 1982, pp. 160–173.
7. Gehman, H.M., R.A. Baker, D.A. White. "Prospect Risk Analysis" *in* J.C. Davis, J.H. Doveton, and J.W. Harbaugh, convenors. *Probability Methods in Oil Exploration.* Amer. Assoc. of Petroleum Geologists, Research Symposium, August 20–22, Stanford University Preliminary Report, 1975, pp. 16–20.
8. Megill, Robert E. *An Introduction to Exploration Economics.* 2nd ed. Tulsa: PennWell Publishing Co., 1979, pp. 110–118.

CHAPTER 10

What you need to know about triangular distributions

A ssigning probabilities to the possible range of values of pay, recovery, and area may make some experts uncomfortable. Yet you still need to quantify the experts' opinions in a usable form. The triangular distribution often represents the answer to this problem. It automatically assigns probabilities, as will be shown in the following chapter, yet the word "probability" need not be mentioned.[1,2]

THE INPUT

All you need for a triangular distribution are three values:
- a minimum
- a most-likely
- a maximum

These three values must be carefully defined as they are often misunderstood.

For triangular distributions the minimum is the absolute number below which no value can exist. The frequency for the minimum is zero. If you ask a geologist what the minimum thickness is expected to be, make sure he *knows* he is saying no value can exist below the minimum. The reason this definition is stressed is simple. Many experts will give a value for a minimum and will mentally think that the value could occur, but rarely (i.e., has a low probability of occurrence). However, in a triangular distribution the minimum means *zero* probability, so the minimum will *never* occur. If the expert thinks his minimum can occur, *choose* a lower *minimum*.

The most likely is the value that should occur most frequently. It is the mode of the distribution—not the mean. Since we deal with lognormal relationships, the most-likely value will be nearer the minimum than the maximum.

The maximum value, as in the case of the minimum, is an absolute ceiling. No value larger than the maximum can exist. Likewise, the probability of the maximum value itself is zero. So, if an expert thinks of his maximum as some value that could occur, set a higher maximum. In other words, make sure that he knows the maximum can *never* occur.

A TRIANGULAR DISTRIBUTION

Let's suppose that you are asking an explorationist to estimate the possible productive area for a prospect. You ask him to pick an absolute minimum, an absolute maximum, and a most-likely size. His answers might be 500, 2,000, and 1,000 acres. He would most probably have geologic reasons for his choices or empirical ones based on experience. For example, he might say:

1. One structure in the trend was filled to the spill point (the last closing contour). On this prospect that would mean 2,000 acres
2. On the other hand, a few are only 20 to 25% filled. If the prospect is like that, it will be only 500 acres
3. However, I really think the field will be contained in 1,000 acres. That's the most-likely estimate of size

Fig. 10.1 is a drawing of the triangular distribution for his opinions. For reasons that will be clear in the next chapter, no values are assigned to f, the frequency associated with estimates. They are automatically determined when the value for the minimum, maximum, and most-likely sizes are set.

Note the ease with which the information was extracted from the explorationist. No probabilities were mentioned. Just his opinions were requested in relation to his experience. The same process can be used to estimate the range of values for recovery per acre-foot and net reservoir thickness. The ease of extraction makes the triangular distribution one of the most popular of all opinion-defining distributions.

ASSIGNING PROBABILITIES

Suppose the expert does wish to assign probabilities? Then you have other factors to consider. Many pitfalls can occur in assigning

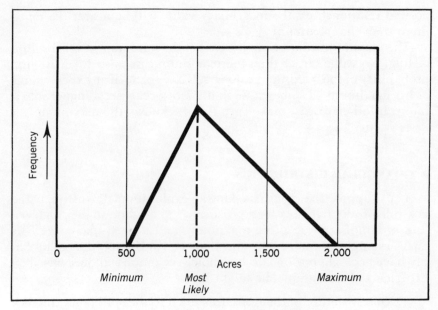

FIG. 10.1   Triangular distribution of productive area

probabilities if you are not careful in the selection of values or probabilities.

To begin with, since the minimum and maximum in a triangular
distribution have, by definition, values of zero, you cannot use these
terms. New terms, such as low side and high side or low value and
high value, must be used to distinguish between those terms assigned
a given probability and the maximum-minimum values.

One commercial evaluation program, POGO (an acronym for Prof-
itability of Oil and Gas Opportunities), uses the terms *minimum
expected value* and *maximum expected value*.* The point to remember is
simple: If you assign probabilities to the low or high value in a three-
point triangular distribution, avoid the terms minimum and maximum. In true triangular distributions they must have the value of
zero probability.

Nevertheless, you will not always see this terminology used; therefore, despite the pitfalls, some discussion of assigning probabilities to
the lowest and highest expected values is warranted.

What if a geologist or geophysicist thinks there is a 20% chance of
the area being as large as 2,000 acres and a 20% chance of the field

*POGO is a computer program authored by PSI Energy Software.

being as small as 500 acres? As you will see in Fig. 10.2, we now have a totally different distribution. Why?

First of all, in assigning probabilities to the low and high values, we have assigned a definite probability to the most likely, i.e., 100% − 20% − 20% = 60%.

Second, only by extending the 20% points to the horizontal base line are the true values of the maximum and minimum known. The maximum is now 2,500 acres and the minimum is 250 acres.

As we shall see later, Fig. 10.2 still does not describe the right probability, but most programs for Monte Carlo simulation correct for this type of input.

Triangular distributions set up in the manner of Fig. 10.2 are sometimes called weighted distributions. The points to remember are:

1. Assigning probabilities for lower- and upper-range values does *not* give the same frequency distribution as saying the lower and upper values represent the minimum and maximum
2. Having assigned two probabilities in a triangular frequency distribution, we have automatically determined the third probability since the three must add to 100

You can combine the two techniques and assume a value for either the minimum expected or the maximum expected value but *not* both.

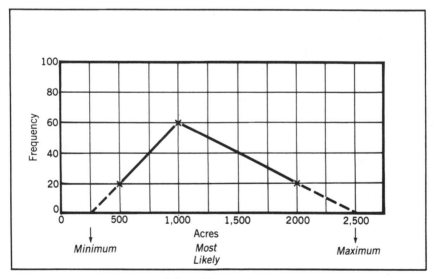

FIG. 10.2   Assigning probabilities for productive area

You would get a triangular frequency distribution such as shown in Fig. 10.3 if you assigned a 20% probability to the chance of 2,000 acres.

Note that since *zero* probability is assigned to our minimum value and 20% is assigned to our maximum value, the most-likely value becomes 80%. Projecting the line through the 20% chance for 2,000 acres, we arrive at a maximum value of 2,325 acres.

Now compare Figs. 10.2 and 10.3. It may surprise you to know that the mean of the distribution in Fig. 10.3 is greater than the mean of Fig. 10.2. Even though the maximum value in Fig. 10.3 is less than the 2,500 of Fig. 10.2, the mean value is 1,274 for Fig. 10.3 compared to 1,251 for Fig. 10.2.

Normally, increasing the maximum value will increase the mean, but in Fig. 10.2 we *lowered* the minimum value also.

CHANGING THE MAXIMUM VALUE

We will have more to say about mean values in the next chapter; first, however, let's show for our base frequency diagram the effect of changing the maximum values.

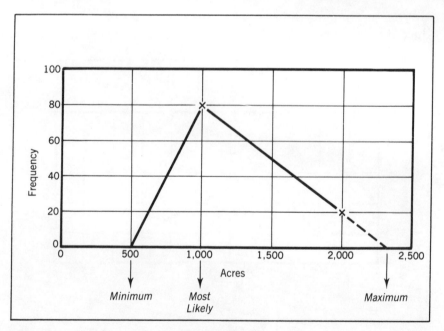

FIG. 10.3   Weighing only the maximum value

On Fig. 10.4 our base distribution is shown as maximum value ①. For reasons to be shown later, it is marked "lognormal." The mean value of this triangular distribution is 1,170 acres. A maximum value of 4,000 acres (max. ②) increases the mean to 1,830 and a maximum value of 6,000 (max. ③) increases the mean to 2,490 acres.

Thus, increasing the maximum value (leaving the minimum and most-likely values the same) increases the mean value.

CHANGING THE MOST-LIKELY VALUE

Changes in the most-likely value, leaving the minimum and maximum values the same, also changes the mean—in the direction of change of the most-likely value. On Fig. 10.5 the base distribution is shown with ① at the base case most-likely value of 1,000 acres. Lowering the most-likely value ② lowers the mean. Raising the most-likely values ③ and ④ increases the mean value.

TRIANGULAR DISTRIBUTIONS AND HISTOGRAMS

In Chapter 1 we reviewed the basic bar-type frequency distribution called a histogram. You can also describe the variables in histo-

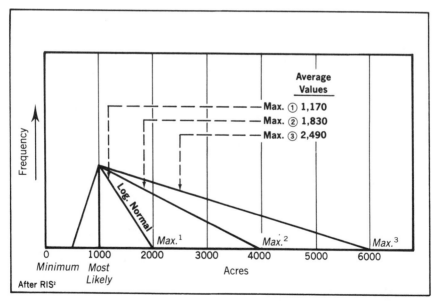

FIG. 10.4   Effect of changing maximum value

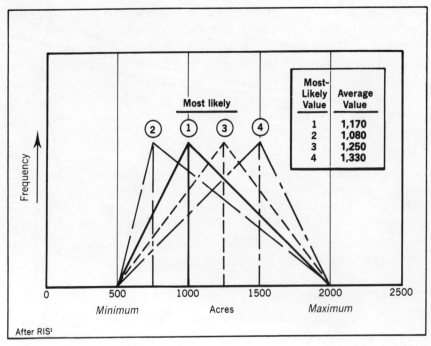

FIG. 10.5   Effect of changing most-likely value

grams with the same data extracted from the expert for the triangular distribution. However, you must carefully observe one of the rules of constructing bar distributions or histograms—namely, to keep the class intervals equal or constant.

Fig. 10.6 illustrates the area of a prospect in the form of a histogram. The class interval is 500 acres. We begin by assigning the midpoints of the first two intervals probabilities of 20% and 60%. However, we cannot arrive at a probability for 2,000 acres and a probability of 20% until we account for the class interval with the 1,500 midpoint, which as drawn would have a probability of 40%.

By now, you have noticed that something is amiss. The probabilities add up to more than 1.00. Their sum is 1.40—an impossibility since three-point probabilities (larger than the minimum and maximum for the extremes) must sum to 1.00. We solve this dilemma easily by dividing each probability by 1.4 (or multiplying it by the ratio of (1.00/1.40). We now have a new probability for each class interval.

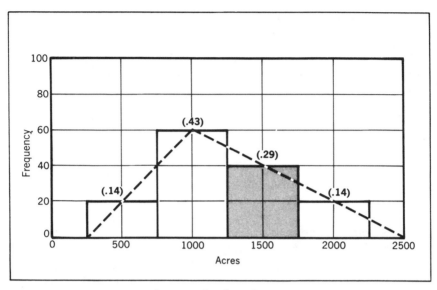

FIG. 10.6   Histogram and triangular distribution

These are shown in parentheses above each class interval, and they sum to 1.00. This process is much more cumbersome than the minimum, maximum, and most-likely estimate of a triangular distribution, but it achieves about the same answer.

Actually, we had this same problem in Figs. 10.2 and 10.3, but most computer simulation programs that accept three points and their probabilities will automatically correct to the proper histogram.

One other pitfall possible with assigning probabilities for a triangular distribution is to choose a probability for the minimum expected value that results in the projection of the true minimum (zero probability) as being *negative*.[3] You can avoid negative (unreal) values for your minimum by specifying the minimum only with no probability assigned. That value becomes zero and cannot be negative.

If three values are adequate for gathering an expert's opinion, the triangular distribution with *no* probabilities assigned is recommended. You can then avoid the problems that can accompany assigned probabilities. The triangular distribution is simple, quick, and easily converted by computer programs into a cumulative probability distribution—to be thoroughly reviewed in the next chapter.

APPROXIMATION OF LOGNORMALITY

A good rule-of-thumb ratio will help you achieve or check for log-normality. In a normal distribution the distance between the minimum and most-likely values is equal to the distance between the maximum and most-likely values. For a lognormal distribution the *log* of the two intervals is equal. So you can get an approximately lognormal relationship for your triangular distribution by satisfying this ratio for the three values

$$\frac{\text{minimum}}{\text{most likely}} = \frac{\text{most likely}}{\text{maximum}}$$

You can also see from the relationship that the most likely squared $(ML)^2$ is equal to the minimum value × the maximum value.

This relationship is not intended in usage to encourage you to force fit all of your triangular distributions to this ratio. Rather, the value lies in its use as a reference point. If your parameter tends to be lognormal, you can check your three-value triangle to see if you are thinking lognormally. It's a simple, useful ratio relationship.

REVIEW

One of the characteristics of the triangular distribution is that the values entered for maximum and minimum are *absolute* values.[4] The maximum cannot be exceeded, and nothing can be less than the minimum. Furthermore, statistically, neither will ever be reached, and values near the minimum and maximum will be rare. Many explorationists falsely assume that the triangular distribution allows for some small probability of occurrence of the minimum and maximum values.

As a result of reading this chapter, you should know the pitfalls in using triangular distributions as input for computer simulation models, particularly those where probabilities are assigned the low and high values. You can now avoid them.

The triangular distribution today ranks as one of the simplest and most effective ways of extracting data from an expert—if the number of possible answers is broad and the best guesstimate is underlain by much uncertainty. The triangular distribution is one of the tools that helps show the full spectrum of possibilities.

References

1. Megill, R.E. *An Introduction to Exploration Economics.* 2nd ed. Tulsa, PennWell
   Publishing Co., 1979, pp. 172–174.
2. Swanson, R.I. *"More on Triangular Distributions."* Unpublished memo, October
   1972.
3. Megill, 1979.
4. Swanson, 1972.

CHAPTER 11

Converting triangular distributions to cumulative frequencies

T riangular distributions are increasingly used as input in Monte Carlo simulation programs to express estimates of the limiting and most-likely values of a variable. Such programs convert triangular input into cumulative frequency distributions.[1] From these cumulative frequency curves we can read probabilities for a specific value of the variable—yet the explorationist did not consider probabilities as part of his input. How is this possible?

Let's restate this question another way. You input into a simulation program three values for a variable, e.g., pay thickness. You say (see Fig. 11.2):

- the minimum value is 10 ft
- the most-likely value is 50 ft
- the maximum value is 250 ft

The simulation program converts these three values into a cumulative frequency curve that expresses probabilities of occurrence. The nearest word to probability used by the explorationist was "most likely"! How, then, does "most likely" become a specific probability? What process is used in the computer program to convert three simply stated values into specific probabilities?

THE LOGIC OF CONVERSION

The manner in which this conversion is accomplished first starts with the entire triangle and equates the area of the triangle to 1.0. You must now recall another fact. The sum of all of the probabilities of occurrence of an event must also equal 1.0. If this is true, the sum of all of the probabilities of net pay (Fig. 11.1) must equal 1.0. Each value of net pay will have some frequency of occurrence, such as points P and f, where

> P represents any pay thickness
> f represents its corresponding frequency of
>   occurrence

We started our discussion by stating that we assign values only to P but derive f on a cumulative basis.

Any histogram can be converted into a cumulative frequency distribution. We did this in Chapter 1. You simply convert each class interval to percentage of the total and then add the class interval percentages of the histogram cumulatively. A triangular distribution is a form of histogram. The area under the triangle represents the frequency of all of the events that can occur. Greater frequencies have greater area. Just imagine a large number of class intervals, each drawn to the upper line of the triangle, and you can visualize how larger frequencies have larger areas. One can use area, then, to express frequency, and that is the key to the mathematical conversion.

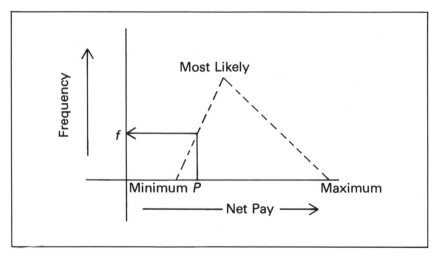

FIG. 11.1   Triangular distribution

THE MATH OF CONVERSION

If you are not interested in the mathematical concepts behind the logic of conversion, you may wish to move immediately to the section in this chapter headed "Practical Applications."

To covert P into cumulative values of f requires the introduction of another concept. A *small* triangle is formed by drawing a line perpendicular to the base of the larger triangle. The area of the small triangle represents some proportion of the area of the entire triangle. By prior logic it then also represents some value less than 1.0. Since P values with larger frequencies will have larger triangles, the area of the triangles can be used to simulate cumulative probabilities.

To do this and involve only base-line values requires some awkward but simple math, and it so happens that the ratio of any *portion* of the total area to the total area can be expressed as a function of values of the base line. This means you can develop a cumulative frequency curve for the distribution of possible pay thicknesses using only *three* values of pay thickness, namely:

- the minimum
- the most-likely
- the maximum

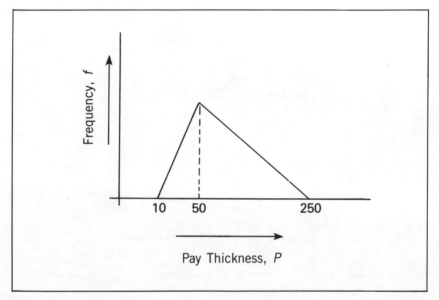

FIG. 11.2   Base case values

The actual mathematical proof for this premise is detailed in Appendix A. We shall use the end result to show what it can teach us about the three values of minimum, maximum, and most likely.[2]

THE EQUATIONS

Please begin this section by referring to Fig. 11.3, which is the reference triangle for the first equation.

Number One—To the Left of the Most Likely

Two equations are needed to develop our cumulative frequency curve. The first deals with those values of net pay to the left of (smaller than) the most-likely value. The equation is

$$\mathop{\mathrm{CF}}_{\substack{x' = x \\ x' = 0}} = \frac{\dfrac{(x')^2}{x}}{(x + y)} \qquad \qquad 11.1$$

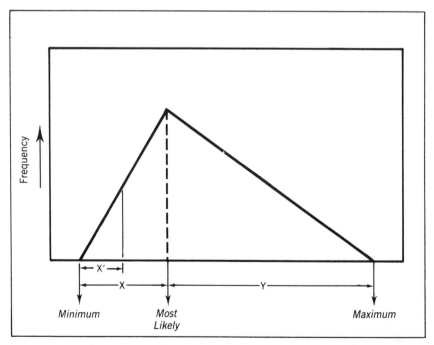

FIG. 11.3   Reference triangle

where:

    CF = cumulative frequency
    x' = any value of net pay along the base line from the minimum
        to the maximum value. Numerically, x' starts from *zero* at
        the extreme left of the triangle, i.e., from the minimum
        value. For example, in the specific case (Fig. 11.2) at the
        most-likely value of 50, x' has a value of 40, i.e., 50 minus
        10
    x = the value between the minimum and most-likely values (the
        most-likely value minus the minimum)
    y = the value between the most-likely and the maximum (the
        maximum minus the most-likely value)

Putting the mathematics of this equation into words we would say, for a triangular distribution, the cumulative frequency from $x' = 0$ to $x' = x$ is equal to x' squared, divided by x, and that quantity divided by $(x + y)$.

Note what happens when $x' = x$. The numerator reduces to x, and the equation becomes

$$\underset{x'=0}{\overset{x'=x}{CF}} = \frac{x}{x+y}$$
11.2

In Fig. 11.2 (for values 10, 50, and 250)

$$x = 40 \quad y = 200 \quad \text{and therefore} \quad x + y = 240$$

Using the values from this example, note that the value of x (most likely minus the minimum) divided by $(x + y)$ is

$$\frac{40}{240} = \frac{1}{6} = 0.167$$

The number 0.167 is valid only for our special case of input (10, 50, 250).

This ratio tells us that 16.7% of the values are equal to or less than the most-likely value and 83.3% are larger. The significance of this statement is (even though the value of 50 is our most-likely value, the range of values is so great and the distribution skewed so far to the right that 83.3% of the values of net pay are *greater than* the most likely—greater than the one value said to occur with the greatest frequency.

You can illustrate this point by drawing small rectangles along the triangle (keeping the class intervals equal); you will see visually that most cases lie to the right of the most-likely value. You can also prove it by considering only class intervals of value 10. There are four such intervals to the left of the most likely and 20 to the right. There are five times as many class intervals to the right as to the left!

The first significant point is this: When the most-likely value is much nearer the minimum than the maximum (when the distribution is skewed to the right), the most-likely value will have a small cumulative frequency. Mathematically, we are saying if x is small relative to y (where $x' = x$), the ratio $x/(x + y)$ will also be small. (The value of y relative to x is a measure of skewness. Values of y much larger than x mean greater skewness.)

This significant point sounds strange, doesn't it: the most-frequent value being in the smaller end of the cumulative frequency distributions. The cause is, of course, the wide range from the minimum to the maximum. The broader this range, the smaller likelihood of occurrence of any single value, including the most-likely value. Even though the most-likely value will occur more often than the other values, a broad range makes all individual frequencies small.

We can show this another way by looking at an isosceles triangle. Under these conditions $x = y$, so $x/(x + y) = 0.50$. Thus, our most-likely value occurs at a cumulative frequency of 50%, i.e., half the values are smaller and half are larger.

Perhaps these illustrations and examples will help you begin to understand some of the interesting aspects about triangular distributions. Remember, however, that lognormal distributions—those most commonly found in field-size distributions and other reserve-related parameters—are *always* skewed to the right; that is, the most-likely value (the mode) is always nearer the minimum than the maximum.

Number Two—To the Right of the Most Likely

The next equation is more complex. For values of the parameter to the right of the most likely (net pay in our case), the cumulative frequency can be calculated by the following equation

$$\text{CF}_{\substack{x' = (x + y) \\ x' = x}} = 1 - \frac{\left[1 - \dfrac{x'}{(x + y)}\right]^2}{1 - \dfrac{x}{x + y}} \qquad 11.3$$

This equation looks very formidable. However, in use it is not. The denominator of the fraction $1 - [x/(x + y)]$ is a constant for any three values, so it need be calculated only once.

For the base illustration of net pay (Fig. 11.2), the denominator becomes

$$1 - \frac{40}{240} = 1 - 0.167 = 0.833$$

Eq. 11.3 represents the area to the right of the most-likely value *out to* x' plus that to the left (i.e., areas $a + b$) as shown on Fig. 11.4. Note the entire fraction subtracted from one. It represents any small triangle (DEF) created by a value of x' less than $x + y$ (area c). As x' approaches $x + y$, the area of the small triangle approaches zero. When $x' = x + y$, the area equals zero.

What happens when $x' = x$? In words, when $x' = x$ our expression (ratio) represents the entire triangular area to the *right* of the most-likely value, or areas $b + c$ in Fig. 11.4. Again, looking at the ratio only (the part subtracted from 1) and substituting x for x', our ratio reduces to $1 - [x/(x + y)]$. From our first equation we remember that $x/(x + y)$ is the area of the entire triangle to the left of the most-likely value (area a). We now know that $1 - [x/(x + y)]$ is the area of the entire triangle to the right of the most-likely value ($b + c$). With just a little intuition, you may have guessed that the area to the right of the most-likely value is also equal to $y/(x + y)$. If that is so, then

$$1 - \frac{x}{x + y} = \frac{y}{x + y}$$

Rearranging, we have

$$\frac{x}{x + y} + \frac{y}{x + y} = 1.0$$

In words, this statement says that the area to the left of the most-likely value plus the area to the right are equal to the area of the whole triangle. By definition, at the outset, we set these areas equal to one.

One can also see from this relationship that the denominator of the ratio in Eq 11.3 could be replaced by $y/(x + y)$.

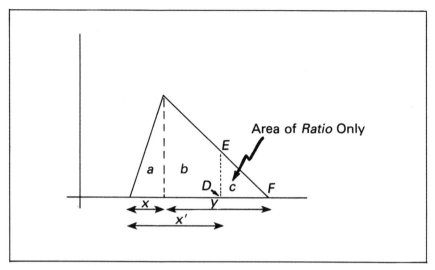

FIG. 11.4   Reference diagram

PRACTICAL APPLICATIONS

Changing the Input.   Up to this point we have demonstrated that areas (cumulative frequencies) of the triangle can be expressed as values of the base line alone. Now let's put this information to some practical use.

Fig. 11.5 is the first of several illustrations from which we will learn more about triangular distributions. Three curves appear on the figure. They are adapted from ideas of E.T. Lewis covering this particular point.[3]

Curve 1 represents the cumulative frequency distribution for the base case (Fig. 11.2).

Curve 2 represents the cumulative frequency distribution of the same range of data but a *different* most-likely value. This distribution is shown in Fig. 11.6.

From a comparison of curves 1 and 2, three observations can be made

1. A doubling of the most-likely value, from 50 to 100, did not produce a drastic change in shape of the cumulative curves
2. Since the minimum and maximum values did not change, the major effect is in the lower and middle values of the cumulative

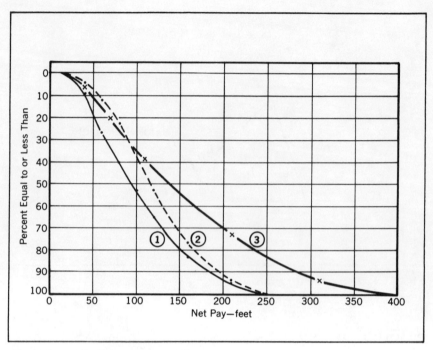

FIG. 11.5   Cumulative frequency from triangular distributors

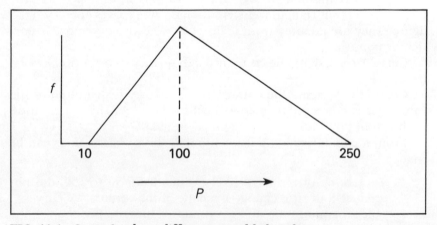

FIG. 11.6   Curve 2 values, different most-likely value

frequency. In a right-skewed distribution one would expect the change here, since we are changing the locale of the most-likely values.

3. At the 50th percentile (the median—not the most likely) the most probable thickness changed from 95 ft to 115 ft, an increase of 21%. At the 90th percentile there is only a difference of 10 ft, an increase of only 5%.

Curve 3 is a third triangular distribution in which the maximum value has been increased. (see Fig. 11.7). The maximum value is now 400; the minimum and most-likely values stay the same. Pertinent observations here are the following.

1. We see no steep slope on Curve 3, which means no dominant frequency. Remember, steep slope on a cumulative curve means high frequency.
2. We affirm point one by observing our triangle. The wide range of values (class intervals) allows no single value or class interval to occur at a very high frequency.
3. Percentagewise the change in the most-likely value was greater than the change in the maximum value. Doubling the most-likely value changed the 50th percentile to 21%. We did not even double the maximum value, but it changed the 50th percentile by 47%. At the 90th percentile, the change was significantly greater. We would expect this trend since we changed only the maximum value.

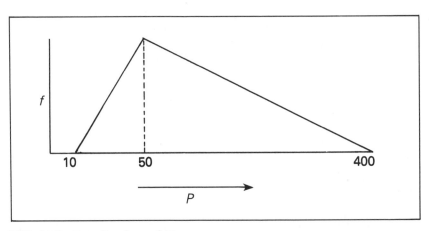

FIG. 11.7   Case 3 values of *P*

In summary, changing our input demonstrates that changes in the maximum or minimum value produce greater variance in the cumulative frequency curve than an equivalent change in the most-likely value. This is an important point to remember if you use triangular distributions as input for a computer program using Monte Carlo simulation. The extremes (maximum and minimum) exercise the greatest control over the cumulative frequency curve.

The changes outlined have the same effect on the mean (average) value for the curves. The means are, then:

Curve	Mean (Feet)	Change from Curve 1, %
1	99	—
2	114	15
3	147	48

The Locked-In Frequency. Now that we have shown that frequency can be calculated from base-line values alone, we can review both verbally and visually another aspect about triangular distributions. Setting the three values—minimum, maximum, and most likely—*locks in the frequency.* Visually, this observation produces the surprising conclusion that the height of the triangle has no bearing on the cumulative frequency distribution (see Fig. 11.8).

We have just said that the cumulative frequency distribution for triangle ABC is identical to that for *ABD*. Surprises you, perhaps; but it's true. Remember, we have proved mathematically that the areas (which represent frequencies) resulting from any value along the base line (between minimum and maximum values) can be calculated from values along the base line alone.

How is this possible? Mathematically, we show in Appendix A that all values of h (height) drop out of the equation. Visually, however, we can see that each triangle produced by a value of x' will represent the same identical proportion of the total area of the triangle of which it is part. Granted, triangle *ABC* has a larger area than triangle *ABD;* but it also has larger proportionate triangles (areas) produced by the same values of x' so that *the ratio remains constant.*

One other important fact comes from this analysis. You set the frequency of the most-likely value when you set the extremes—the minimum and maximum values. Once set, you have a locked-in maximum frequency. You can change the distribution shape by moving

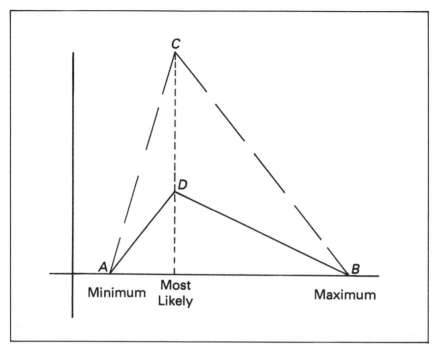

FIG. 11.8   Locked-in frequency

the locale of the most likely, but its maximum frequency remains the same. Thus, we have another important point.

Triangles Are Not the Real World.   We must not forget one important point before we leave this subject: Triangles do not give precise representations of either normal or lognormal distributions. For example, note the following comparison (Fig. 11.9).

In this comparison the triangle misrepresents both sides but particularly the right side of the real-world distribution. Why do we use it? Because it's the only way to approximate a distribution from only three points—minimum, maximum, and most-likely. In areas of great uncertainty, estimating even three values cannot be done with accuracy. So we still use triangular distributions, and they are accurate enough as computer input for uncertain parameters.

For most of the applications we have reviewed, these distortions are not serious. They become so if y becomes very large relative to x. Thus, if any of the input triangles show large skewness to the right (large values of y), keep this distortion in mind.

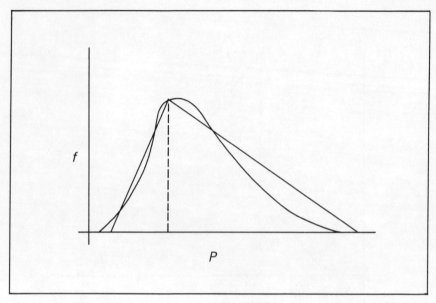

FIG. 11.9   Triangular vs continuous distribution

WHAT DOES THIS MEAN TO THE EXPLORATIONIST?

Triangular distributions are very useful mechanisms for input into Monte Carlo simulation. They allow an approximation of a real distribution from only three points. However, they tend to distort the real world when the data are heavily skewed to the right. When the potential range of values can be great, the distortion will be greatest.

Such a fact may be disturbing. Remember, however, that a wide range of possible events also expresses our own uncertainty of what might occur. Thus, the distortion may be less than the accuracy of the input. It is not serious for lognormal relationships.

REVIEW

We use many tools that have limitations. As long as we understand those limitations, we can make wise use of the tool. Perhaps this chapter has helped you understand the limitations of triangular distributions. You should have a new appreciation of the importance of the minimum and maximum values; you should have an awareness of what a large y value means to the answer. Above all, you should have a basic understanding of why base-line values alone describe a cumulative frequency distribution.

References

1. Megill, Robert E. *An Introduction to Exploration Economics.* 2nd ed. Tulsa: Penn-Well Publishing Co., 1979, p. 123, Fig. 17.
2. Newendorp, Paul D. *Decision Analysis for Petroleum Exploration.* Tulsa: PennWell Publishing Co., 1975, p. 274.
3. Lewis, E.T. "Triangular Distribution." Exxon Co. USA, Houston, memo, February 25, 1972.

CHAPTER 12

An example of subjective probability

Perhaps in no other industry does subjective probability play as important a role as in the oil and gas industry. Yet its role goes unrecognized by many who employ it, derive solutions from it, or make decisions based on its use.

As shown in Chapter 9, subjective probability goes by many names. In the search for new oil and gas fields, it assumes terms like "technical opinion" or "geologic judgment." But the principles are the same regardless of the name.

THE CONDITIONS

The simplest cases of subjective probability involve decisions where very little information exists. As more and more information becomes available, you move closer toward objective probability.

Let's set the conditions for an example of the use of subjective probability. It will be an example common to the search for oil and gas fields and will involve subjective judgments about the following:

1. The presence or absence of hydrocarbons and thus judgments about the factors for or against such occurrence
2. Your ability to find any oil and gas fields that may exist
3. Whether the fields found will be economic

When much information exists, each of these three facets of subjective probability can be examined in considerable detail. In the example to follow, fortunately or unfortunately, all three facets must often be compressed into one single judgment. Here are the conditions:

1. Four tracts are available for acquisition
2. Very little is known about these tracts except they are on trend with other, possibly similar, tracts that produce oil and gas
3. Several explorationists have some geologic knowledge of the general area surrounding the tracts
4. We may or may not be bidding competitively against other companies

The problem is to place a value on the tracts so that negotiations can begin for acquisition.

ESTABLISHING A RELATIVE RANKING

If only one geologist or geophysicist has any knowledge about the area, then the problem is greatly simplified. One person makes all evaluative judgments before the proposition goes to management. Since several explorationists have some general knowledge of nearby tracts, they can help with the evaluation. We are, of course, making the assumption that "two heads are better than one." Where the available information is extremely limited, this assumption can be correct—but it is an assumption. Nevertheless, in the example we shall use the judgments of all knowledgeable personnel. In the long run this action should be the wisest.

The first step is to establish a relative ranking of the properties. The ranking involves both rank *and* value. We do this because of the extremely limited amount of information. Five explorationists are given the following question

"For the four tracts, how much from a *total value* of 10 would you assign to each of the four tracts?"

The question involves not only which is the best tract but how much better is it than the other tracts. The answer involves both rank and value. It also allows the question to be answered in a simple manner—a subjective judgment that, for each explorationist, includes all of the factors he considers relevant. Each explorationist is to answer the question independently.

Suppose the five explorationists gave answers as shown on Table 12.1. Before we decide what these experts have told us, let's calculate another table. Table 12.1 gives us the exact values from the experts; Table 12.2 provides a sort of summary of the estimates. We shall concentrate on Table 12.2, but our comments will relate to both tables. Here are the judgments these estimates point toward:

1. The average ranking puts tract two first, followed by tract four, tract one, and tract three
2. All experts judged tract two to be the best
3. Although tract four averaged second in ranking, it was rated equal or below tract one by *four* of the evaluators. By one concept, then, tract one should be ranked ahead of tract four
4. Tract four had the smallest range of estimates. Tracts one and three had the largest. Large ranges of values mean less certainty

TABLE 12.1   Tract evaluations

| | Tract Number | | | | Total |
Explorationist	1	2	3	4	Value
Ames	2.5	4.0	1.5	2.0	10.0
Baker	2.0	3.9	2.1	2.0	10.0
Church	2.9	4.3	0.5	2.3	10.0
Douglas	1.0	4.2	2.3	2.5	10.0
Emerson	1.9	5.5	0.7	1.9	10.0

TABLE 12.2   Tract average and range

| Tract Number | Average Value | Range of Values | |
		Range	Amt. (Δ)
1	2.06	1.0–2.9	1.9
2	4.38	3.9–5.5	1.6
3	1.42	0.5–2.3	1.8
4	2.14	1.9–2.5	0.6

FIRMING THE RANKING

The next step involves firming the ranking, i.e., resolving the major differences so that a clearer ranking will emerge. The five explorationists are brought together to review their differences. You might wish to concentrate only on tracts one and four, since the relative rank and value of two and three should probably remain unchanged by a recycling of ideas.

What should the geological and geophysical experts try to resolve in the firming of the ranking?

1. The most obvious difficulty is tract one. Four explorationists ranked it ahead of tract four, but it averaged less than tract four because of Douglas's ranking. His ranking and reasoning should be reviewed. A very modest change in his values between tracts one, four, and three would shift tract one to second average ranking.
2. Douglas also ranked tract three, the lowest average, higher than the other four.
3. You might also want to review the differences on tract two, even though all rated it the best.

Firming the rankings may be regarded as an unnecessary step, particularly if you have very little information. After all, the real information your experts have told you is quite simple. Tract two is the best; tracts one and four are of about equal value, and tract three has the lowest value. On the other hand, firming often takes place coincident with the act of committing the money. Even after firming rankings, you should realize that the most diverse opinion could be right. Douglas's opinions could ultimately be the most accurate.

AFTER RANKING VALUE

After obtaining the ranking, which also gives a value concept, the next step involves assigning money for the acquisition. Several considerations now enter the evaluation:

1. A more definite concept of field size; it may be little more than a feeling at this point, based on surrounding tracts. You already have a reflection of this in your values assigned
2. A possible further refinement of risk
3. The maximum value you feel can be spent on the tracts for your minimum rate of return
4. Whether your value breaks any traditional land value concepts. You may not wish to offer $500 per acre where acreage has traditionally been only $100 per acre. Such a break with traditional values might ruin several future plays by establishing lease precedents that would put them beyond economic reasonableness
5. A judgment as to whether your first offer will be near the owner's as to concept of value

We will not go into any of these points as our main purpose has been to review a simple example of subjectively placing value on investment opportunities. The economic and strategy considerations are another story beyond the scope of this chapter. A completely new element enters if you are faced with competitive bidding rather than negotiation. Competitive bidding will be dealt with in a subsequent chapter.

WHAT DID WE GAIN?

You should always consider what was gained by an exercise in subjective probability. In our example the positive aspects were the following:

1. If we are really interested in the tracts, we have obtained an estimate of value—on an average—from knowledgeable experts
2. Furthermore, the answers were constructed in such a way as to give both a relative ranking and a value reference
3. The relative certainties and uncertainties of the tract values show where opinions were similar or essentially undecided

On the negative side:

1. Until the tracts are drilled, we will have no concept of validity. At this point we don't know if we have quantified ignorance or knowledge

We do know that the best judgments have been brought to bear on an opportunity with little information and much risk.

REVIEW

Acquiring tracts of land for oil and gas exploration often involves subjective judgments. Quantifying the opinions of experts may shed light on the relative rank and value of similar tracts in an area. Decision concepts about any investment where vast uncertainty is involved benefit from gathering the knowledge of the experts.

CHAPTER 13

Converting uncertainty to a cumulative frequency distribution

A ny uncertainty that can be quantified can also be converted to a cumulative frequency distribution, and cumulative frequency distributions can be used in Monte Carlo simulation to be merged with other uncertainties to check interrelationships.

In exploring for oil and gas fields, uncertainty exists in the assessment of potential, field size, and economic considerations. An economic evaluation, in reality, represents a series of forecasts merged to give an overview of an investment. In the search for new fields on the Outer Continental Shelf (OCS), special uncertainties exist. In addition to the uncertainty associated with the presence of hydrocarbons, there is the uncertainty as to sale schedule and your ability to participate in each sale. The Department of the Interior publishes a schedule of OCS sales periodically. That schedule is affected by other groups both inside and outside government. Some groups seek delay; others seek acceleration. Thus, sale dates can change, and even the amount of acreage offered can change. A change in the amount of acreage would change the amount of oil and gas potential offered at the sale.

Participation at a sealed bid sale is anything but certain. Large variations can and do occur for most operators in their participation from sale to sale.

In this chapter we shall demonstrate how the uncertainty of sale schedule can be quantified and converted to a distribution for further use. The method used is *not* the only method by which the distribution can be compiled, nor is it necessarily the best way. The point is not to show *the* method, but *a* method to illustrate the conversion of an uncertainty to a distribution.

THE BASIC INGREDIENTS

The model involves three basins where sales are pending. The names of these basins shall be the Bay of Zenith (BOZ), the Gulf of Apogee (GOA), and the Banks of Nadir (BON).

For simplicity's sake we shall assume that our base case is for one sale each year in each area. We desire to test the sensitivity of a one-year delay or a one-year speedup of the sale schedule during a two-year period. In the two-year period a one-year delay would remove one sale in each area. An acceleration of one year would put one additional sale into each area during the two-year period.

Our reserve assessment for each sale and for the two-year period in each area is

	Millions of bbl	
Area	Estimated Potential at Each Sale	Two-Year Potential
BOZ	100	200
GOA	150	300
BON	50	100

The two-year potentials are the base case in our illustration. They include the potentials for two sales, one each year. To check the sensitivity to delay and acceleration, we set up Table 13.1

TABLE 13.1   Potential change from timing uncertainties, two-year period

	Millions of bbl		
Area	One Year Early	Base	One Year Delay
BOZ	300	200	100
GOA	450	300	150
BON	150	100	50
Totals	900	600	300

Examine the first line of this table. The base case for BOZ is 200 million bbl. If our schedule is accelerated one year, then we put one more sale in the two-year period to make BOZ have an offering of 300 million bbl. Conversely, if sales are delayed one year, we have one *less* in our two-year period and the exposed oil potential drops to 100 million bbl. Similar cases are set up for GOA and BON. The amount of potential per sale is the same, but the amount exposed during the two-year period varies from the base case, depending upon either delay or acceleration.

As you have probably surmised, the outcomes set up the results from three different conditions. The base case contains two sales per area; three sales represents acceleration; and only one sale represents delay for each area. The example could include possibilities of a two-year delay, but for the sake of simplicity only, one-year delays were used. We must now assign probabilities to each outcome. How probable is delay or acceleration for each area? Here we are using our judgment as to the influence of all types of delay, regardless of the cause. The cases for each area and their probabilities are shown on Table 13.2.

In Column 1 of Table 13.2 the potential for each area under the three different outcomes is shown. Column 2 lists the probability assigned to each outcome. Column 3 is the product of one times two and represents the risk-weighted potential for each outcome. Note, as always, that the probabilities for each area add up to 1.0; only one outcome can actually occur.

TABLE 13.2   Assigning timing probabilities

Area	1 Possible Potentials, M bbl	2 Probability of Occurrence	3 Risk-W'td Potential, M bbl	4
BOZ	300	0.1	30	
	200	0.8	160	
	100	0.1	10	
				200
GOA	450	0.2	90	
	300	0.4	120	
	150	0.4	60	
				270
BON	150	0.2	30	
	100	0.6	60	
	50	0.2	10	
				100
	Total			570

M̲ is millions

Column 4 shows the sum of the risk-weighted values for each area. For BOZ and BON these totals are the same as for the base case. Why? The reason is that the delay and acceleration probabilities are assigned the same value—are equal and less than the base case. Now check area GOA. Here the risk-weighted value is less than the base shown in line two of Table 13.1. Again, why? The reason is that delay is assigned a greater probability than acceleration; therefore, in a three-point probability system we say that the base value of 300 probably won't be achieved—but a more probable number would be less—on the average.

Once again a risk-weighted number deviates from the real world. The value of 270 million bbl is not the same as any of the potential outcomes: 450, 300, and 150 million bbl. The 270 is an average; furthermore, it is a risk-weighted average reflecting the probabilities assigned to the various outcomes. Note, however, that the risking here is for sale timing, not for variations in oil and gas potential per se.

In Chapter 9 we showed that three variables with three parameters generate 27 separate possible outcomes. Therefore, the three basins, each of which has three different possibilities, have 27 different possible combinations. As we shall see later, the 570 value for the risk-weighted sum of the nine cases is the real mean, even when we have considered the other 18 cases.

On Table 13.3 we have a rearrangement of the data to show how to generate the 27 cases. On the left are the various outcomes that can occur for each basin. Please note the column designation of a, b, and c and the row designation of 1, 2, and 3. We will be using these designations in Table 13.4 to show how the cases are derived. We have, in a

TABLE 13.3   Building 27 cases, two-year period

		Reserve Sizes, Millions of Barrels			Probabilities of Occurrence		
		Early a	Base b	Delay c	Early a	Base b	Delay c
	Col. → Row ↓						
BOZ	1	300	200	100	0.1	0.8	0.1
GOA	2	450	300	150	0.2	0.4	0.4
BON	3	150	100	50	0.2	0.6	0.2
Totals		900	600	300			

TABLE 13.4   The possible events

	Individual Possibilities			Potential* Available	Individual Probability
1	a_1	a_2	a_3	900	0.004
2	a_1	a_2	b_3	850	0.012
3	a_1	a_2	c_3	800	0.004
4	a_1	b_2	a_3	750	0.008
5	a_1	b_2	b_3	700	0.024
6	a_1	b_2	c_3	650	0.008
7	a_1	c_2	a_3	600	0.008
8	a_1	c_2	b_3	550	0.024
9	a_1	c_2	c_3	500	0.008
10	b_1	a_2	a_3	800	0.032
11	b_1	a_2	b_3	750	0.096
12	b_1	a_2	c_3	700	0.032
13	b_1	b_2	a_3	650	0.064
14	b_1	b_2	b_3	600	0.192
15	b_1	b_2	c_3	550	0.064
16	b_1	c_2	a_3	500	0.064
17	b_1	c_2	b_3	450	0.192
18	b_1	c_2	c_3	400	0.064
19	c_1	a_2	a_3	700	0.004
20	c_1	a_2	b_3	650	0.012
21	c_1	a_2	c_3	600	0.004
22	c_1	b_2	a_3	550	0.008
23	c_1	b_2	b_3	500	0.024
24	c_1	b_2	c_3	450	0.008
25	c_1	c_2	a_3	400	0.008
26	c_1	c_2	b_3	350	0.024
27	c_1	c_2	c_3	300	0.008
Total					1.000

*Millions of bbl

sense, a matrix to determine all combinations of possible outcomes. First, however, note the sums of each column. The sum of column a is 900; we know this is our upper limit. No outcome can exceed 900 million bbl, as this is the maximum for each basin. Column c shows a sum of 300 million. This is our lower limit. No single case can be less than 300 million bbl, as this is the least amount that will be offered in each basin under the delay case of one sale per area. These two numbers represent the extremes, and all other outcomes will be somewhere between them.

On the right side of Table 13.3 are probabilities assigned to the sale schedule for each basin. The probabilities for BOZ sum to 1.0 and relate to column a, row 1, column b, row 1, and column c, row 1, (a_1,

b_1, and c_1). The a_1, b_1, c_1 notation will show each specific outcome for a basin. The letters refer to columns, the numbers to rows.

BUILDING THE 27 CASES

Now that the basic ingredients are established, we can proceed to build the 27 possible outcomes. Each of the 27 possibilities contains one outcome for each of the three basins. The sum of the three basins represents one possible condition of the base case, delay, or acceleration. For example, one case is the sum of a_1, a_2, and a_3, or 900. This is our maximum case. This case has a low individual probability, however ($0.1 \times 0.2 \times 0.2 = 0.004$). It would occur *on the average* only once in 250 events.

Another possible case from Table 13.3 would be ($c_1 + c_2 + a_3$) or 400 million bbl. It has a higher individual probability ($0.1 \times 0.4 \times 0.2 = 0.008$). It would occur only once in 125 times, on the average. Note that we use the term *individual probability*. In a moment, we shall see that more than one possible outcome produces an answer of 400 million bbl.

All 27 possibilities are listed in Table 13.4. The method for their calculation can be followed from the letter and number code under the column headed "Individual Possibilities." Line 1 represents the first possibility, which we illustrated before—a_1, a_2, a_3. The next shown, line 2, is a_1, a_2, b_3. Follow these letter-number designations and you can sum the three basins to produce all 27 possibilities.

The reserve sums are shown under the column headed "Potential Available." Note carefully that several combinations produce identical values, just as several combinations of two dice can produce a seven.

The last column shows the individual probabilities for each of the 27 possibilities. Again, note that the sum of all probabilities is 1.000.

What do we do about the possibilities that give identical values? We make a distribution.

MAKING A DISTRIBUTION

On Table 13.5 we build a distribution. Following rules laid down in Chapter 1, class intervals are established and for cumulative purposes, later, the individual cases are arranged in order, the largest first. The rearrangement of the data shows interesting facts.

1. The two highest and two lowest values are represented only *once*
2. All others occur two or three times but never more than three

We could make a distribution from the first column; *if* we considered each possibility equally likely, it would fairly represent our expected frequency. Remember, however, that we do *not* consider each outcome equally likely. We are definitely interested also in the probabilities of each possible outcome.

The second column on Table 13.5 lists the individual probabilities for each outcome. The third column groups the individual probabilities for the identical outcomes. For example, three possible combinations can produce 600 million bbl. The sum of their probabilities (0.008 + 0.192 + 0.004 = 0.204) represents the probability of the occurrence of 600 million bbl. This value, 0.204, represents the highest probability for any value but is only slightly higher than the value of 450 million bbl. In like manner the individual probabilities are summed to give the combined probability for identical values.

Column 4 shows cumulative probability for the values, to be used in constructing a frequency diagram.

Fig. 13.1 has two parts. On the left is a *greater-than* cumulative probability distribution, which was constructed from the frequency distribution on the right.

Let's begin with the frequency distribution. It hardly represents any of the ideal distributions reviewed previously. It is essentially bimodal with the two peaks at 600 million and 450 million bbl. A glance at the frequency distribution seems to indicate that delay (smaller values than 600) is more likely than acceleration (values higher than a base of 600). The mean of our distribution is 570 million bbl, indicating that delay does have a slight edge. Remember we introduced this delay in GOA by saying that delay had a greater probability than acceleration. In the other two basins the base was the most probable outcome.

The cumulative frequency distribution on Fig. 13.1 is the culmination of the exercise. We have converted opinions about an uncertain set of conditions into a cumulative frequency distribution. This distribution can now be entered with other uncertainties in the form of distributions to bring to bear on the desired answer, all of the influences affecting the possible outcomes. We have quantified our opinion—and in usable form.

TABLE 13.5   Ranking of possible outcomes

No.	Possible Outcomes	Probability Individual	Grouped	Cumulative Grouped
1	900	0.004	0.004	0.004
2	850	0.012	0.012	0.016
3	800	0.004	0.36	0.052
4	800	0.032		
5	750	0.096	0.104	0.156
6	750	0.008		
7	700	0.024	0.060	0.216
8	700	0.032		
9	700	0.004		
10	650	0.008	0.084	0.300
11	650	0.064		
12	650	0.012		
13	600	0.008	0.204	0.504
14	600	0.192		
15	600	0.004		
16	550	0.024	0.096	0.600
17	550	0.064		
18	550	0.008		
19	500	0.008	0.096	0.696
20	500	0.064		
21	500	0.024		
22	450	0.192	0.200	0.896
23	450	0.008		
24	400	0.064	0.072	0.968
25	400	0.008		
26	350	0.024	0.024	0.992
27	300	0.008	0.008	1.000

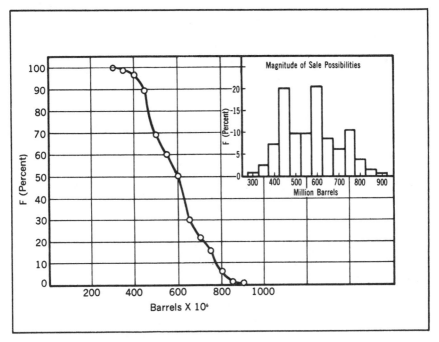

FIG. 13.1 Sale potential, cumulative frequency distribution

REVIEW

Opinions can be quantified into usable forms to shed light on factors affecting possible outcomes. Most often the desired final form is a distribution. Not all distributions will be normal, lognormal, or even smoothly continuous. They will, however, reflect opinion. We state opinions about each parameter and sum toward the final answer. As we shall see later, this step is one of the fundamentals of risk analysis.

CHAPTER 14

Basin assessment

If it happens, you must admit it was possible!

T he assessment of oil and gas potential is one of the integral parts of an exploratory program. An intuitive and subjective art in recent years, basin assessment today receives much more attention and concern than in previous years. The reason is simple: Our nation has become totally dependent on foreign supplies for over 40% of its daily usage of oil. The federal government in particular has recognized the importance of knowing how much oil and gas remain in unexplored areas of the Outer Continental Shelf and the inland areas of the United States. At present and for the next decade, we have no immediately available alternate to oil and gas. It becomes extremely vital, therefore, to know what our remaining storehouse holds in the way of undiscovered oil and gas fields. However, we do not know what is in this storehouse. We can only estimate what exists with great uncertainty. In fact, so much uncertainty is involved that we express our answers as a probability distribution, showing the full range of answers that might occur.

Thus, basin assessment is an exercise in risk analysis. In this chapter we shall review briefly the answers of published assessments and several methods for making basin assessments.

CURRENT ASSESSMENTS

Numerous authors have been interested in the remaining potential for oil and gas fields in the United States. Table 14.1 shows recent estimates of various individuals or organizations on remaining potential. These estimates range all the way from Hubbert[1,2] on the low side to high-side estimates by Exxon, line 5. The Potential Gas Com-

152

mittee[3] has an even higher estimate than Exxon, but it is not shown and is less up to date. In between are various estimates by companies and individuals. Methods used are not similar, and a few estimates (North,[4] not shown on Table 14.1) represent judgments about other existing assessments. The low estimate by Exxon, line 1, Table 14.1, is the amount technologically and economically attainable from the larger number, line 5, called a resource base.

TABLE 14.1   Mean estimates of total undiscovered liquids and natural gas—U.S.A.

			Amount	
Line	Source	Date	BB*	Tcf*
1	Exxon[(a)]	1976	63	287
2	Hubbert	1974	72	480
3	Mobil[(b)]	1974	88	443
4	USGS	1975	98	484
5	Exxon[(b)]	1976	118	582
6	Shell	1975	110	400
7	Shell	1978	60[(c)]	315
8	Nat'l Acad. Sc.	1975	113	530
9	USGS	1981	83	594

*Billions of barrels of crude oil (plus condensate and natural gas liquids) or trillions of cubic feet.
[(a)]Attainable portion of resource base, line 5.
[(b)]To 6,000-ft water depth; other estimates to about 600 feet.
[(c)]Excludes natural gas liquids.

Each individual company or organization, however, faces the same perplexing problem—thinking about the unknowable. Gradually, those outside the petroleum industry are beginning to understand that in thinking about the unknowable, there is much room for both difference of opinion and error. Remember the knowledge curve (Fig. 9.1).

The subject of basin assessment will be the object of many methodological attempts in the years to come. It will receive increasing attention of both government and academia. The truth is, however, that basin assessment has been around a long time. It has been only in the past few years that the methodology used by knowledgeable groups has been published.

In the area of basin assessment we can expect rapid evolution of published ideas because of the vital importance of this subject to our nation. The fundamentals will remain the same, however, and it is the fundamentals we will discuss.

AN ASSESSMENT CURVE

Before illustrating an assessment method used in Canada, let's first review an assessment curve. In Fig. 14.1 curve *a* represents a typical assessment curve. Numerous such curves are in the United States Geological Survey's (USGS) latest estimate of undiscovered recoverable resources.[5]

Curve *a* represents a basin with established production and thus has a 100% chance of containing at least 1 billion bbl. Note there is almost no chance of the basin containing more than 7 billion bbl. The mean of this distribution is 3.75 billion bbl at a 45% chance of the assessment being equal to or greater than this amount. (See Appendix B for a simple method of calculating the mean of any distribution.)

Curve *a'* represents an untested basin with a 50% chance that it contains no hydrocarbons at all. One can state this fact another way:

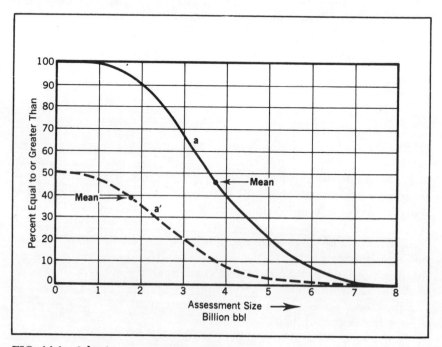

FIG. 14.1   A basin assessment

There is only a 50% chance of finding anything. The mean of curve a' is only about 1.7 billion bbl because of the large chance of finding nothing.

Finally, if each value on a' were one-half that of a, then a' would represent Curve a risked at 50%. In such a case the mean of a' would be one-half the mean of Curve a.

An assessment curve shows valuable information about a basin:

1. It shows the full spectrum of expected results, a minimum and a maximum concept
2. It can express the chance of a basin being totally dry—the chance of finding anything

With this reminder of the use of a cumulative frequency distribution, we are ready to illustrate an assessment concept.

THE DELPHI APPROACH

One of the earliest methods used in risk analysis has an unusual name: the Delphi technique. The name Delphi is an interesting choice for this technique. Any student of Greek mythology would recognize Delphi as the ancient city of Greece that was the site of the celebrated oracle of Apollo. Anything delphic is, therefore, oracular, ambiguous, and obscure in meaning. It would be well to remember this description. Although the Delphi technique will be illustrated, primarily because it is still used in some instances as an overall technique, it is not recommended as the best method. Its flaws will be obvious to you as we review the Delphi method.

The Method

The following method closely follows one outlined in detail in "An Energy Policy for Canada," Chapter Two, pages 31–40.[6] This reference will be reviewed subsequently.

Delphi techniques can begin at various stages of an assessment. They can also be used as a means of arriving at values for key variables. In its earliest usage Delphi was similar to a brainstorming session in that an overall answer was desired and estimated from the technique with essentially no intermediary steps.

Suppose we wish an assessment of the South Sea basin. It is unexplored; no wells have been drilled; our seismic data are sketchy, limited and of questionable value. We need a quick estimate of oil and gas potential. So we gather several knowledgeable explorationists in a room and pose questions. We are really applying our skill to extract opinions from the experts as described in Chapter 9. Everyone in the room recognizes the limit of real knowledge about the South Sea basin.

After reviewing the knowledge available from geology, geophysics, etc., we pose the following questions to our panel of experts:

1. What is the probability of something being discovered?
2. What is the largest quantity of oil and gas you can conceive as being discovered from this basin?

If we stopped with these two questions, we would have the end points of a cumulative probability distribution. Question one defines the 100% point of a greater-than curve, and question two defines the zero percent point of the distribution.

The Canadian paper recognized the possibility of asking for intermediate points. We could better define our curves with a request for five points. These questions could be asked in the form of a brief table:

Probability of Reserves Being Greater than Stated	Basin Potential (Billion Barrels)
0	—
0.25	—
0.50	—
0.75	—
1.00	—

Let's examine each point on our curve.

1. The zero point represents the maximum possible estimate. It is question two in the preceding illustration. You are saying there is no chance of the basin being larger than this amount.
2. The 0.25 probability means you feel there is only a 25% chance of ultimate reserves being greater than this number.
3. The 0.50 point is an approximate most-likely estimate. It is a median. One-half of your estimates are above this amount and one-half are below.
4. The 0.75 probability indicates you think there is at least a 75% chance that the basin contains reserves exceeding this amount.

5. The 1.00 probability is your low estimate. It would reflect question one of the previous illustration. It could also be a number less than 100% if you think there is some chance of the basin being completely dry. On the other hand, for a basin with a few productive fields, the 100% point represents the absolute certainty of what has already been found.

A poll of the experts yields the following results: The five points (0, 25, 50, 75, and 100) from each expert are plotted on Fig. 14.2. The individual curves have the participant number near the bottom end. Here we see the marked individuality of the estimates:

1. Participant four is the most conservative. He sees no chance of the basin exceeding 10 billion bbl
2. Participant five is the most optimistic. He estimates the basin's upper limit at 60 billion bbl
3. Note the shape of the individual curves. Participants two and five see some probability of very small potential. They also see better probabilities of a high potential than the other participants

You may see other bits of information from the individual curves. The next step is the calculation of an average or composite curve. Such an average is often compiled by a computer. In this particular application, where all curves describe the same quantity (barrels), we can manually calculate, with accuracy, an average curve.

TABLE 14.2 Probability reserve estimates South Sea basin—billion barrels

Probability	Expert				
	1	**2**	**3**	**4**	**5**
0	20	40	30	10	60
0.25	15	20	20	6	35
0.50	10	7	15	4	17
0.75	5	2	10	2	10
1.00	2	0	5	0	0

A COMPOSITE CURVE

The manner in which a composite curve is calculated is illustrated in Table 14.3. In the left column are even increments of billions of bbl.

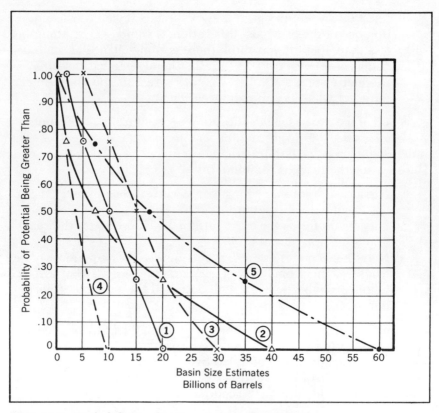

FIG. 14.2   Probability vs basin potential: five opinions

To the right are values of probability (percent, in this case) for each participant for this barrel number. We thus *average* the probabilities.

Why not average the reserve estimates at a given probability, i.e., reading horizontally, the five reserve estimates for each five billion barrel interval? The reason is simple: This method would not produce the right average, particularly on the high side. If you average the zero probability points of 10, 20, 30, 40, and 60 billion bbl, you get 32 billion bbl as the maximum for the South Sea basin. Such an answer is illogical since two of the participants, two and five, have estimated the maximum considerably higher than this. By averaging the percentage estimates you show a probability, though small, of high-side estimates up to 60 billion bbl.

TABLE 14.3 Probabilities (percent)—South Sea basin

Billions of Barrels	Participants					Arithmetic Mean
	1	2	3	4	5	
5	75	58	100	35	85	71
10	50	42	75	0	67	47
15	25	32	50		55	32
20	0	25	25		45	19
25		18	12		37	13
30		12	0		31	9
35		6			25	6
40		0			20	4
45					18	3
50					8	2
55					4	1
60					0	0

The arithmetic mean of the percentage estimates from Table 14.3 are plotted on Fig. 14.3. The composite shows several points:

1. Only a 70% chance that the South Sea basin has oil reserves greater than 5 billion bbl
2. A 50% chance of as much as 9.5 billion bbl
3. A 10% chance is indicated for 28 billion and a 5% chance for 37.5 billion bbl

Our composite curve is skewed sharply to the right with small chance of a high-side potential severalfold the median value of almost 10 billion bbl. The mean of our distribution is about 13 billion bbl, reflecting the skewness of our curve. There is only a 38% chance of the basin achieving the mean value or more.

WHAT NOW?

Fig. 14.3 represents our view of the potential for hydrocarbons in the South Sea basin. It is the composite of five opinions, showing in average the complete spectrum of possibilities. We could end the exercise here and go on to the next project.

However, one or two additional steps may be desired. Suppose you feel the distribution is skewed too far to the left or perhaps you think the low-side estimates (95% probability) discount the basin too heav-

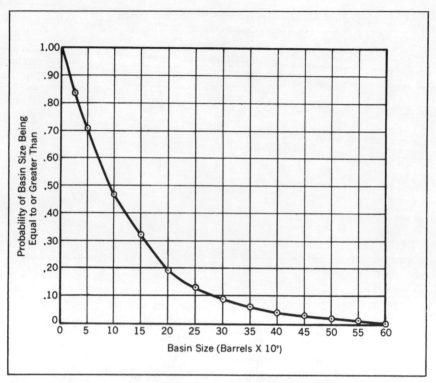

FIG. 14.3 Assessment of South Seas basin, composite of five estimates (cumulative probability distribution)

ily. You can reconvene the group and discuss each input point—but only if you feel there are sufficient data to warrant an additional session.

THE FLAWS OF DELPHI

The Delphi technique of brainstorming can often produce answers surprisingly close to reality, but it may also produce one not even in the ball park. For explorationists the basic flaw of Delphi is its emphasis on the answer rather than the pieces that make up the answer.

Consider our example of the estimates of field size (Chapter 9). We can survey the experts to get a total prospect size, but a better way is to use questions about ranges of pay thickness, areal extent, and recovery per acre. Triangular distributions are recommended here with their three values of minimum, maximum, and most likely.

These can then be combined to produce a complete spectrum of answers, based on the reality of measurable and understandable quantities.

So a better use of the Delphi technique is to gather opinions about the ingredients that make up the final estimate. Place your probabilities or distributions on the basic factors and a more realistic answer should result.

A fundamental of risk analysis is to Delphi the parts and sum to the whole.

A second major problem of Delphi is that for any basin it can ignore important facts. Geologic considerations of source, trap, environment, and structure might be individually risked, as shown in Chapter 9, to determine the likelihood of any production whatsoever.

Other equally important factors involve the number of known structures from seismic data and the expected field-size distribution. The USGS estimates of undiscovered oil and gas resources recognize the significance of lognormality and proper field-size distributions. These are important considerations in good basin assessments. The Canadian report also discusses field-size distributions briefly.

OTHER METHODS

In a critique of the USGS pre-1975 estimates, the National Academy of Sciences lists several methods of constructing basin assessments.[7] Various methods are also listed in the USGS Circular 725 and Circular 860. Nanz also lists methods for assessing basins.[8] Haun briefly described methods presented at a research conference sponsored by the American Association of Petroleum Geologists (AAPG), presented at Stanford University in August, 1974.[9]

In general these methods can be grouped as follows.

Volumetric Methods. A volumetric estimate begins with the physical volume of sedimentary rock in a basin or play. In a well-explored basin with many wells drilled, volumes can be estimated with reasonable accuracy. In a frontier basin volumes have less accuracy but can be estimated from geological and geophysical data—the latter largely seismic data.

Next a recovery per cubic mile of sediment is related to basin volume to estimate total recovery

$$\text{volume of sediments} \times \text{bbl per unit of sediments} = \text{bbl of oil}$$

This two-step approach is simplicity at its finest. However, it is loaded with flaws.

1. The most obvious flaw involves the choice of the right recovery per unit volume. The possible answers here are numerous. One can

    a. use the worldwide average from productive basins.
    b. choose a similar basin and apply its recovery.
    c. estimate a recovery based on judgments from *a* and *b*.

2. If *1a* is chosen, it may have little relevance to the real situation. In the absence of any better logic, you may wish to use it, but you should do so with your eyes open. The worldwide mean recovery is an average from many possible answers.

3. If *1b* is applied, you are saying you can pick a similar basin. Jones argues that each basin is unique and that there is a lack of correlation between geologic factors and recovery per unit volume.[10] He suggests an estimation method based on four factors:

    • source,
    • trap,
    • reservoir, and
    • migration

Each factor is important in the total estimate.

Today, few knowledgeable assessors advocate the volumetric method. It is a method of last resort that ignores too many critical geological, geophysical, and economic parameters.

Mathematical Methods. Various estimators have used mathematical models to estimate future undiscovered resources. Hubbert's studies are the most famous. In the late 1950s and early 1960s he was using a roughly bell-shaped curve to illustrate the production of a finite resource. The validity of Hubbert's methods for a continuously developing area is not questioned. Their application to areas not yet developed or having sporadic development leaves considerable doubt. Some production must occur before the shape of Hubbert's curve is known. Thus, the validity of Hubbert's method to the unknown, untested basins in the Outer Continental Shelf is questionable.

White et al. have used extrapolation of existing trends in mature basins to predict future discoveries.[11] Extrapolations of historic data

(Marsh[12]) establish the growth of existing discoveries. Existing discoveries in turn are extrapolated to an economic limit to establish estimates of future discoveries. The extrapolated units involve some measure of discovered reserves. If drilling levels and average depth per well were constant, the average discovery size could be extrapolated. Neither situation exists in the real world, so most users of this technique use barrels found per foot of exploratory drilling plotted vs cumulative barrels found. The value of cumulative barrels as one factor is its reduction of the element of time as an overpowering factor. Time is not completely eliminated because the barrels found per foot drilled are an annual factor.

Extrapolations also have their problems, but these are by degree much less serious than the volumetric base:

1. On the positive side, you are relating to history as you see it; negatively, you are assuming that history provides a sure key to the future
2. Changing economic conditions can affect your economic limit by influencing the amount of drilling to be done or the recovery from the reservoirs in new oil and gas fields found
3. Several forms of extrapolation exist—linear, logarithmic, etc. You must choose one you deem appropriate
4. Extrapolations must have a stable broad base of historic data. Lacking this strong statistical base they are valueless. Thus, extrapolations are of no value in frontier areas. There is no history to extrapolate

White et al. recommend a method of extrapolation developed by Baker. It produces multiple answers that can be converted into a cumulative probability distribution. Such output offers the advantage of allowing its combination with other distributions.

Geological Methods. Geological methods comprise the last general group of assessment techniques. These methods are the most popular for frontier areas if the data base is adequate. An inadequate data base pushes many estimators toward the volumetric methods.

Geologic methods take advantage of all geologic data, all geophysical data, and environmental and depositional conditions. They can include an estimate of the number of traps for oil and gas that exist in the frontier (Nanz). To be sure, judgments are involved. However, geologic methods allow the best consideration of the most significant unknown in frontier exploration, namely, "Do oil and gas fields exist in this basin?"

Frontier areas, basins, or plays usually involve either completely untested areas or untested sections of sedimentary rocks. In the latter case the deeper rocks usually remain untested. A deep unexplored section of sedimentary formation can have just as many unknowns and just as many risks as a new basin in which no well has ever been drilled.

In Chapter 9, on risking prospects, we touched on the problems associated with answering the question, "Is it there?" The same set of questions are involved in basin assessment. We might consider only the three factors of structure, reservoirs, and environment. Estimating the value of these factors for basin assessment necessitates judgments. Here the factors assume a broader scope, however. For example, it is not a question of whether structures do exist. The factors of reservoir and environment are equally broad. Was the oil and gas generated in economic quantities? Did it migrate to potential traps after the traps were formed? If so, has the oil or gas remained at the site of the trap?

In basin assessment as in risking prospects, risk factors are assigned to each key variable. Uncertainty is thus expressed in numerical form and, applied to barrel estimates, can produce a risk-weighted estimate of hydrocarbons for an untested frontier basin.

As with a payoff table showing expected value, in basin assessment a risk-weighted basin assessment is not a real-world number. It is only one of many possible answers and takes into account your estimates of the chances of this and other similar basins being dry. For this reason, basin assessment is most frequently expressed finally as a cumulative frequency distribution. Only from the composite of many such risked distributions can one estimate reasonably well the range in quantities of oil and gas to be found.

In summary, geologic basin assessment places value judgments on key parameters that are largely unknown. Through volumetric estimates, field-size distributions, or counts of known prospects, these judgments are applied to arrive at barrel estimates. The final product is most often a cumulative frequency distribution.

Combinations. Combinations of the three methods just described have been used. White et al. used both extrapolation and a volumetric method for an estimate of oil and gas potential for southern Louisiana. Geologic and volumetric methods are sometimes combined for untested basins.

What determines the method used? It depends partly on the estimator and his experience, but it is more directly related to the type and quantity of data available. Most estimators would agree with

Nanz that methods based on geology are the most reasonable and reliable, particularly for basins with some seismic information available. In a basin where no wells have been drilled and no seismic data are available, any method has limits. From the knowledge curve (Chapter 9) we learned that the less that is factual, the greater the range of possible opinion; and whether we like it or not, assessments under conditions of limited data are largely opinion. It should be expert opinion, but it remains opinion.

REALITY CHECKS

One practice every good assessor adopts quickly when data are sparse is the reality check. The easiest way to accomplish a reality check is to make two estimates of basin potential using two different methods. The answers should at least be similar; if not, check your input to each method and recalculate your answers. Relate your estimate to a similar basin for a reality check. Such a check assumes you believe a similar basin exists. Check your reasons for assuming similarity. They should involve the geologic setting, framework, and field sizes.

Increase your objectivity by assessing several basins at one time. The experienced estimator has the benefit of past assessments as a guide. One learns to assess by doing, as with most techniques, and making more than one assessment will increase you objectivity and the accuracy of your results.

Finally, remember that you are dealing with many factors that are unknown at the moment of your assessment. Your hope is that you make the best possible estimate from available data. But recognize that, especially when the facts are few, another might take the same data and arrive at a different conclusion.

ATTAINABLE POTENTIAL

An estimate of total resource potential must often be corrected for reserves that remain unattainable. Marsh describes attainable potential as "the amount of recoverable hydrocarbons in reservoirs and accumulations whose productivity and size make their development economically feasible in the foreseeable future."[13] Reserves to be attainable must be producible within the scope of present or imminent technology. Thus, the reasons some potential is not attainable are:

1. Field sizes too small to be economic
2. Ultradeep water, which raises costs, stretches technology, and rules out small accumulations of oil and gas
3. Hostile environments (massive icebergs, for example)
4. OCS fields too far from shore can result in poor economics, especially for gas fields
5. Political and economic factors (laws, wildlife refuges, etc.) can eliminate some otherwise attainable potential

A necessary step, then, in basin assessment is to adjust downward your total potential to that which is attainable. Such reductions can be judgmental as well as geological and economic. Yet the adjustment is necessary. You never bid on potential that cannot be obtained economically with existing or soon-to-be-developed technology.

SMALL FIELDS AND ATTAINABLE TECHNOLOGY

In any trend there exists a lower limit to the size of fields that can be developed economically. Even at shallow depths there is some field size that is so small, profits will not result. This field size represents the economic cutoff for any field-size distribution. Fields smaller than the cutoff size are noncommercial, and their discovery wells are classed as dry holes.

Granted, we produce a few small fields that never pay out just to get part of our money back, but you would not deliberately look for a field below your economic cutoff size.

Therefore, in using a field-size distribution for play assessment, the economic cutoff size is an important parameter.

FIELD-SIZE DISTRIBUTIONS (FSDs) AND SUCCESS RATE

We have dealt at length in several chapters on the meaning of success rate. As an average, it represents the chance of finding anything—or the chance of finding the smallest-size field or larger.

The economic cutoff size (ECS) is the smallest size that will support your play, and the average success rate relates to this field size or larger. The ECS is illustrated by line aa' on Fig. 14.4. Any field smaller than this size is considered uneconomic.

Let's assume in the trend under examination that the average success rate for fields larger than the ECS is 20%. What happens to the success rate if we change our mind about the economic cutoff size? Suppose a crude price increase permits the search for smaller fields.

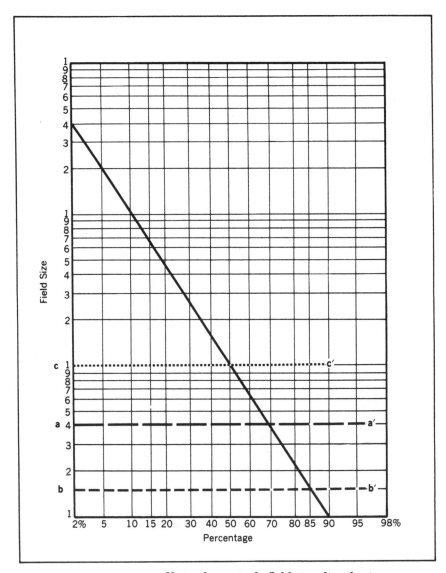

FIG. 14.4 Economic cutoff size for a single field-size distribution

If so, the total number of potential fields has increased because we have lowered our ECS. Correspondingly, we have raised our chances of success: Since there are more fields to find, we have expanded the possibilities for success. We may not have added many barrels, but we have increased the number of potential finds. Suppose the ECS is lowered to *bb'* as shown on Fig. 14.4. The new success rate can be calculated using the percentages (at ECS) for the two lines *aa'* and *bb'*

$$\frac{\text{new ECS cutoff \%}}{\text{old ECS cutoff \%}} \times \text{success rate (old ECS)}$$

$$= \text{new ECS success rate}$$

For *bb'* then the new success rate is

$$\frac{85.5}{69.0} \times 20 = 24.8, \text{ or almost } 25\%$$

A crude price cut would eliminate some fields by making them uneconomic. The decrease in the number of potential fields raises our ECS and lowers our chance of success. Line *cc'* on Fig. 14.4 illustrates a higher ECS, fewer fields, and reflects a lower success rate for the reduced number of fields, calculated as

$$\frac{50.0}{69.0} \times 20 = 14.5\%$$

Our original discussions of an FSD demonstrated the rareness of the largest fields in any trend or play. The chances of finding the large fields are less, simply because they are in the minority in your distribution. Raising the ECS, then, lowers your chance of success in a trend or play. In other words, your chances of failure increase as you raise the ECS. If you are succcessful, however, your discoveries will be among the largest; *your success rate will be affected more than total barrels found.*

FSDs, SUCCESS RATE, AND THE REAL WORLD

The foregoing abstract discussion of the relationship between ECS and success rate must be qualified to some extent. Under ideal circumstances a company has been able, occasionally, to lease an entire basin. A foreign concession could represent such a circumstance. Under these conditions your prospects could be listed by size and the largest drilled first. You could conceivably find the largest one first.

The concept and use of an FSD for assessment purposes does not rule out this favorable circumstance. The important point to remember is this: Large fields are the minority in every trend. Therefore, your chances of finding the more numerous small ones is larger. Even if you drill them in a predrill sequence of expected size, you can use the concept of an FSD

1. To estimate your ECS
2. To gain an understanding of expected size
3. To relate to the trend average success rate to illustrate the chances of finding a specific field size

---

REVIEW

Basin assessment is attempting to define quantitatively the unknown and possibly the unknowable. Yet it must be done; it is done by all companies planning investments in untested and semitested basins as well as by agencies in the federal government. The techniques are slowly being exposed to the printed page but with an increasing rate. The answers will always, however, be approximate for an untested basin. Only the drill can fully answer the greatest unknown—"Is it there?"

Basin assessment involves:

1. Gathering all facts available
2. Choosing a method or combination of methods to make the best assessment
3. Applying the method
4. Making reality checks

References

1. Hubbert, M.K. "Degree of Advancement of Petroleum Exploration in the U.S." AAPG Bulletin, Vol. 51, 1967, pp. 2207–2227.
2. Hubbert, M.K. "U.S. Energy Resources: A Review as of 1972, Part 1, 1974." Interior Committee Documents, Senate Office Bldg., Washington, D.C.
3. Potential Gas Committee. "Potential Supply of Natural Gas to the U.S." Potential Gas Agency. Golden, Colorado: Colorado School of Mines, 1973.
4. North, F.A. "A Sane Look at U.S. Gas Resources." National Gas Survey, Vol. 5, F.P.C., 1973, p. 113.
5. Dolton, G.L., et al. "Estimates of Undiscovered Recoverable Conventional Resources of Oil and Gas in the U.S." USGS Circular 860, 1981.
6. "Energy Reserves and Potential Resources of Oil & Gas." *An Energy Policy for Canada.* Phase I, Volume II, Chapter 2, p. 31ff.
7. Gillette, Robert. "Oil and Gas Resources: Did the U.S.G.S. Gush Too High." *Science,* Vol. 185, July 12, 1974, p. 127.
8. Nanz, R.H. "The Offshore Imperative—The Need for and Potential of Offshore Exploration." Presented at Colloquium on Conventional Energy Sources and the Environment, University of Delaware, April 30, 1975.

9. Haun, J.D. "Methods of Estimating the Volume of Undiscovered Oil and Gas." *AAPG Studies in Geology* No. 1, 1975, p. 1.

10. Jones, R.W. "A Quantitative Geologic Approach to Prediction of Petroleum Resources." *from* "Methods of Estimating the Volume of Undiscovered Oil & Gas." *AAPG Studies in Geology* No. 1, 1975, p. 186.

11. White, D.A., et al. "Assessing Regional Oil and Gas Potential." *from* "Methods of Estimating the Volume of Undiscovered Oil and Gas." *AAPG Studies in Geology* No. 1, 1975, p. 143.

12. Marsh, G. Rogge. "How Much Oil Are We Really Finding." *Oil & Gas Journal*, April 5, 1971, pp. 100–104.

13. Marsh, G. Rogge. "Forecasting Supply and the Timing of Production in Offshore Frontiers." *in* J.C. Davis, J.H. Doveton, and J.W. Harbaugh, convenors. *Probability Methods in Oil Exploration*—Amer. Assoc. of Petroleum Geologists, Research Symposium, August 20–22, Stanford University Preliminary Report, 1975.

CHAPTER 15

Competitive bidding

A

ll of the elements of risk analysis come together in a competitive bid for oil or gas leases on the Outer Continental Shelf (OCS). Five basic questions must be answered to arrive at a bid:

1. Are oil and gas present? (Is it there?)
2. How large is the deposit? (How big is it?)
3. What profits are possible? (Will it make money?)
4. What are reasonable bids? (How much can I afford to pay for it?)
5. What competition is possible? (What are the other guys going to bid?)

Competitive bidding exists in many industries, not just the oil industry. Many government contracts require competitive bidding. Furthermore, published literature on this subject is quite extensive. For example, Stark has published a list of over 100 papers and books dealing with competitive bidding.[1]

In this chapter our concern will be with competitive bidding as it applies to the oil and gas industry. We shall do this by first reviewing significant papers published on the subject and conclude by summarizing what these works "say" in composite.

BIDDING PATTERNS

A good place to start is with Paul Crawford's paper on Texas offshore bidding patterns.[2] In reviewing his work you will understand why we performed some of the exercises in Part I, Chapter Four. Particular reference will be made to the multiplication of the face values from rolls of the four dice to achieve a lognormal distribution.

Crawford begins with the logical premise that a final bid results from the multiplication of several factors, each of which exhibits uncertainty. Their product is a single answer. But the uncertainty in each factor (pay thickness, area, porosity, risk factor, etc.) is akin to one set of faces on the four dice. Another roll produces four different faces. Another competitor produces four different values for the same factors.

Thus, a study of competitive bidding begins with the important fact that single bids by different competitors should arrange themselves into a reasonable facsimile of a lognormal distribution.

Crawford includes plots of bids on six tracts, five of which show an approximately lognormal distribution.

Another key point comes from this paper. It stems from the number of factors considered. The greater the number of factors used to arrive at the product (bid), the greater will be the variance. The spread can be large between bidders if:

1. The variance is 20% to 30% above or below the average
2. The number of factors multiplied to arrive at the bid is three or more

An example of the very large range possible is Tract 230 in the Texas offshore sale of 1968. The ratio of the high bid to the low bid was 100:1.

In summary, we begin with two important facts. Bids on a single tract will be lognormal, and the range of bids can be very large.

NEXT—A BIDDING MODEL

We can now proceed to a bidding model. Our concern will center on what the model reveals, not its construction. Anyone interested in the latter can review thoroughly the reference article. It is the work by Capen et al.[3] on competitive bidding in high-risk situations using a simulation model. The model simulates the bidding game.

First let's trace briefly what is involved in any bidding process. It all begins with an estimate of field size, which is then translated to values of reserves per tract. From reserves ensues a schedule of production that converts easily to revenue; with the addition of exploration and development investment plus operating costs, we get cash flow and net profit. From risk and return concepts we translate profit into what we are willing to bid.

This process is in one sense nothing more than a typical economic evaluation of the type illustrated in *Exploration Economics*.[4] However, a major new factor enters the evaluation in the form of competition. You must address all of the factors normally included in an economic evaluation *plus* the consideration of what the other bidders might be doing.

Competitive bidding for oil and gas leases almost always involves great uncertainty and greater opportunity for loss than competitive bidding in other business activities. Granted there are uncertainties in a bid for constructing a building, laying a pipeline, or obtaining a fuel contract; the difference is one of degree. You can more easily lose your entire investment bidding on an oil and gas lease. Such a loss is much less common in other types of competitive bidding.

From prior chapters we have seen the variance possible in an estimate of field size. Reserve size and the estimation of risk are the most critical factors in competitive bidding. From the considerations on reserve size comes the first key point from the simulation model used by Capen, Clapp, and Campbell. There is much uncertainty in the factors resulting in estimates of field size and large variations possible in risk estimates. Therefore, the bidder who wins will most often be the one who overestimates the reserves on the tract. This key result occurs because of the nature of competitive bidding. You tend to lose the tracts you correctly estimate and win those you overestimate. The result is that your winnings—the high-side reserve estimates—tend to produce only modest profits, not what you hoped to average at a given sale. Capen et al. point out that your bids on the average may indeed produce desired profit goals but you don't win bids based on your average—only on the highest reserve or value estimates.

To effect a better strategy, Capen et al. recommend lower bids when:

1. You have poorer information than competitors
2. You are less certain than usual about your own size or value estimate
3. You expect more than three bidders

The last recommendation stems from the frequent occurrence of many bidders on the good tracts. The larger the number of bidders, the higher the winning bid, in general, and the better the chance of only modest profits, if any. Capen's model would steer the bidder away from the most popular tracts—in effect—by purposely submitting a lower than normal bid.

You might consider this rationale very defensive. Capen et al. defend this concept by showing the broad range that often exists between the highest (winning) bid and the second highest. That range, they say, leaves room for lower bids and still a reasonable chance to acquire properties. They do not deny that such a strategy will result in fewer tracts acquired, but they want to optimize profits, not just acreage acquisition.

THE WINNER'S CURSE

We might leave this excellent paper at this point, but it has much more to offer. The authors present an example illustrating why more bidders push you toward lower returns—by dropping out your lower underestimated tracts. This tendency they nicknamed *the winner's curse.*

From these discussions two more key factors emerge.

1. The chance of winning is more related to the estimate of reserve size than upon a particular bid level. Putting this in different words, modest increases in minimum rate of return do not drastically reduce your chance of winning acreage.
2. Because of the significance of the estimate of reserves, the greatest possibility for errors in reserve size exists in frontier areas.

Capen et al. conclude their article with comments about entering their model with factors reflecting a competitor's prior bidding patterns. Overall their paper has been one of the most important about the subject of competitive bidding to be published in recent years. It is recommended reading for all who want to learn more about the fascinating game of bidding and winning without losing your shirt.

Their principal point is of prime significance. Every bidder, on the average, evaluates his properties adequately; he will win, however, not on the average but when he overestimates value the most. This unique characteristic of competitive bidding pushes individual companies' returns below their expectations. The tendency to low returns is not the fault of the evaluators—the explorationists—but is a function of the competitive bidding system itself.

BIDDING AND PRODUCING RELATIONSHIPS

Lohrenz and Oden[5] analyzed the relationships between bidding levels and the subsequent amounts of production from leases acquired. Their analysis showed conclusions similar to those expected from the simulation model of Capen et al. and subsequent models—to be reviewed in this chapter. They analyzed leases sold up to and including the March 1962 sales.

Their principal conclusions were the following.

1. As the number of bids increased per tract the bonus increased as did the average bid. Better tracts got more bids and more money.
2. A small percentage of the leases produced most of the production—an evidence once again of lognormality of reserve size.
3. More bids and larger amounts of bonus were associated with the highly productive leases. This correlation shows that, in general, industry was able to select the best leases—as evidenced by more bids and more money per tract.
4. Since the ratio of production to bonus declined for leases with large bonus and a higher number of bidders, they infer that winning may not be the sole key to profits. The model of Capen et al. shows why this occurs, since the winner is the one who most probably overestimated the reserve size.
5. More drilling occurred on the high bonus leases, and it started earlier—thus the tendency was for these leases to be productive sooner.

OTHER MODELS

Models on competitive bidding have been around for decades. One early reference is by Friedman[6] published in 1956. Its effectiveness was based on previous bidding patterns of competitors. It was designed for single or multiple bidding situations involving contracts.

Of particular interest is a model proposed and tested by Hanssmann.[7] In his book, *Operations Research Techniques for Capital Investment,* he writes of an experimental model tested in a sale of mineral leases. He credits Friedman and Rivett (1959) with similar methodology.

Hanssmann's model employed the following steps.

1. Each prospect is assigned a point score supposedly reflecting value. This assignment was done in consultation with geologists and management.
2. Merging prospects from two prior sales with the upcoming sale all were grouped into four classes—A, B, C, and D— in order of decreasing value.
3. Industrywide bids from the prior sales established the relative monetary rank of the four groups as 16, 4, 2, and 1. (Hanssmann's ranking was based on several ratios; of particular interest was the ratio of the company's bid in coalitions—they were

higher. This situation happens in oil and gas lease bidding and in all competitive bidding. Joint bids are larger than single bids. Why—the risks for the individual companies are lowered. Speitzler found the same relationship.[8] He stated that "group consensus tends to be more risk-taking than the average of individual members of a group.")

4. A probability distribution was compiled for the highest competing bid from prior sales for each value group. Lognormal distributions resulted.
5. Final limits were set by management on an objective bidding level of $2.875 million and a spending level of $1.3 million. Furthermore, no bids were to be placed on A prospects.
6. Hanssmann then combines an estimate of expected value with the distribution made from the highest competitive bid described in 4 above. He is looking for the bid that produces the maximum expected value.
7. From this combination he develops the marginal gain in expected value and searches for the bid, for a prospect, that produces the highest marginal gain for an increment of bid.
8. Final bids are selected for prospects that optimize the expected value at the appropriate bid, using the marginal gain concept.

Hanssmann had a chance to compare his bids with the actual bids at the sale. The company prepared a set of "conventional" bids and used them for the sale. His bids from the study group were not submitted. Thus, a post-sale comparison could be made.

When the results were in, several interesting observations could be made:

1. The company decided to bid in coalition with several other companies
2. It did bid on an A prospect
3. More money was spent than the original instructions to Hanssmann's study group

HANSSMANN'S CONCLUSIONS

Despite these drastic changes in ground rules, Hanssmann makes a comparison of the two systems and concludes:

1. His "scientific" system acquired more acreage at less money than the conventional system. Thus, if the original goals had

remained the same, more tracts would have been acquired by his system.

2. His value system acquired more of the value points assigned by the geologists than did the conventional system. This was true even though the A prospect was assigned a high value.
3. The scientific system would have acquired acreage at one-half that paid by the conventional system bidding in coalition.

Hanssmann's model allowed the opportunity of a comparison of the two systems; but in addition, as with all models, it allows the ability to predict the consequences of alternate courses of action. Because his system produced better results, Hanssmann warns against last-minute, unexpected changes in objectives and strategy. These, he feels, carry the possibility for grave consequences.

THE IMPORTANCE OF COMPETITION

Dougherty and Nozaki[9] investigated the significance of competition using a model similar to that of Capen et al. They found that the optimum bid was a function of three factors:

1. The number of competitors
2. The aggressiveness of the bidding
3. The quality of your own estimate compared to competition

They conclude further that you should be conservative in bidding when the uncertainty of your own estimate of value increases; i.e., when the risks are greater, the bids should reflect that risk. Dougherty and Nozaki ranked knowing your competitors as of equal value to knowing how well your own estimate stacks up.

FIVE IMPORTANT FACTORS

Hubbell and Deroven[10] used a commercial economic model to test the sensitivity of several factors to rate of return. Their model's acronym was GUESS and is a product of Scientific Software Corp. The acronym stands for General Uncertainty Economic Simulation Systems. The five factors related to rate of return (ROR) were

- royalty
- depletion allowance
- crude oil price
- bonus
- reserves

Their work adequately tests a successful prospect for sensitivity to the five factors; however, the element of risk—the chance of complete failure—is not included in their work. As such, their ROR calculations are high and would be sharply reduced by true risk considerations. In addition, their bonus value, $125,000, is unrealistically low for a typical lease in the Outer Continental Shelf of the United States. The current minimum bid is several times this amount. Nevertheless, the paper does outline methods of testing sensitivity of various parameters.

The computer program they used, GUESS, also has capabilities for entering variables as distributions to be summed to a final composite distribution by Monte Carlo simulation. The answers produced by such programs are no better than their input, but the programs do allow a view of the complete spectrum of answers possible from your input—and that is important.

REVIEW

From published data about the competition for oil and gas leases in sealed bid sales, we can learn most of the essentials for better competitive bidding. The pertinent points from the literature are:

1. In a sale with many bidders your expectations could possibly be achieved by your average bid; but you will not win on your average bid. You will win when your reserve estimate is overstated relative to the next bidder
2. Frequently, the winning bid is disproportionately higher than the next highest bid, a reflection of lognormality
3. Because of point 2, there is some room for variations in minimum rate return that still make a winning bid
4. Estimates of reserve size and risk are still the most critical factors in the bid evaluation
5. However, the roll of competition assumes almost equal importance when the number of bidders is high

References

1. Stark, Robert M. "Competitive Bidding: A Comprehensive Bibliography." *Operations Research*, March–April 1971, pp. 484–490.
2. Crawford, Paul B. "Texas Offshore Bidding Patterns." *Journal of Petroleum Technology*, March 1970, pp. 283–289.
3. Capen, E.C., et al. "Competitive Bidding in High Risk Situations." *Journal of Petroleum Technology*, June 1971, pp. 641–653.

4. Megill, Robert E. *An Introduction to Exploration Economics.* 2nd ed. Tulsa: Penn-Well Publishing Co., 1979.
5. Lohrenz, John, and Hillary A. Oden. "Bidding and Production Relationships for Federal OCS Leases . . . ." paper given before the 48th annual SPE meeting, Las Vegas, September–October 1973.
6. Friedman, Lawrence. "A Competitive Bidding Strategy." *Operations Research* 4, 1956, pp. 104–112.
7. Hanssmann, Fred. *Operations Research Techniques for Capital Investment.* New York: John Wiley & Sons Inc., 1968, pp. 107–126.
8. Speitzler, Carl S. "The Development of a Corporate Risk Policy for Capital Investment Decisions." IEEE Transactions on Systems Science and Cybernetics, Vol. SSC-4, No. 3, September 1968.
9. Dougherty, E.L., and M. Nozaki. "Determining Optimum Bid Fraction." *Journal of Petroleum Technology,* March 1975, pp. 349–356.
10. Hubbell, Robert O., and Gordan A. Deroven. "How Five Major Bid Factors Affect Potential Lease Profit." *World Oil,* July 1975, pp. 67–69.

CHAPTER 16

The mechanics of prospect risking

I n the previous chapter we covered competitive bidding as a whole. This chapter becomes much more specific in dealing with bidding and outlines a method of handling the risks associated with tracts of varying value.

The economic evaluation of prospects by any analyst should involve a specific methodology. Such a methodology should consider both the chance of finding hydrocarbons and the numerous possible sizes of prospects on which a bid is to be submitted. Furthermore, the methodology must allow full expression of the explorer's model of his prospect. It must convert his geological-geophysical concepts into investment concepts.

The primary use of the methodology outlined in this chapter occurs in the sealed or oral bid sales for prospective leases. Such sales occur in the continental 48 states, but the predominant use has been among analysts facing the difficult problems associated with bidding for tracts in the Outer Continental Shelf.

The ultimate goal of all prospect risking (for a sale in the OCS by sealed bid) is tract value. However, tract value emerges only after appropriate and proper analysis and prospect risking. The key decisions and assumptions are made *about the prospect*.

The steps to achieve proper prospect risking combine the techniques of geological risk analysis[1] with size concepts related to modeling three sizes from a full spectrum of possible sizes.[2]

SIZING THE PROSPECT

In considering prospect size several volume parameters must be addressed. These volume factors and their relationship to the geologic controls governing the existence of hydrocarbons are:

Reserve, Volume	Geological Control
closure area	existence of fold, fault, facies
reservoir thickness	facies change, truncation, etc.
porosity	cementation, absence of solution
trap fill	source (maturation, migration); seal and timing; preservation
recovery	permeability, viscosity, drive

The sizing step involves consideration of these volume factors. Values are derived from which the range of possible sizes for the prospect can be viewed.

The uncertainties associated with volume factors are expressed in Table 16.1. Five volume factors are listed, and each is assigned three values. A most-likely value is assigned, and then a small and large value are assigned. The small size represents the smallest value of that particular parameter that is *expected* to be economically attractive. Granted, we may not know at this point what is expected to be economically attractive, but a reasonable and logical limit must be placed on the small values to avoid including absurd values. For example, for sand thickness, thin stringer sands—which would provide small shows but no real possibility for production—should not be included. The smallest sand thickness should have some reasonable chance of sustaining production for a commercial field. As will be explained later, that size is the closest to the success rate chosen. The high-side size results from the largest reasonable parameters expected to be productive. A more exact definition of "reasonable" will be reviewed later.

TABLE 16.1 Uncertainties associated with volumes

	Small	Most Likely	Large
Closure area, sq mi	10	15	20
Reservoir thickness, ft	10	50	90
Effective porosity	0.12	0.16	0.20
Hydrocarbon fill of trap volume	0.2	0.6	1.0
Recovery	0.35	0.40	0.45
Absolute product, million bbl	4	140	800
Monte Carlo product, million bbl	20	140	420

After Gehman et al.[3]

Let's examine the data from Table 16.1. The area of closure indicates a large field with modest uncertainty regarding areal extent. There is considerable uncertainty about the possible reservoir thickness. The values range from 10 feet for the small case to 90 feet for the large size. Effective porosity also has considerable variance—from 12% to 20%. Also, the uncertainty about hydrocarbon fill of the trap volume varies considerably, but the recovery estimates range from 35% to 45%.

Note on the last two lines on Table 16.1, the projected sizes for small and large cases. The first line shows the absolute product obtained from multiplying all of the small values. In millions of barrels, this totals four. In the final column the absolute product of all of the parameters for the large size totals 800 million bbl. Entering these small and large values into our computer program as triangular distributions, we in effect say they would never occur, i.e., their frequency of occurrence is zero. The Monte Carlo product, taken from the output of a computer program, is shown as 20 million bbl for the small size and 400 million bbl for the large size. Note that both numbers pull toward the most-likely value, which is unchanged. As will be explained later, we shall be using the 10th and 90th percentiles in our suite of prospect sizes and would "pull in" to those percentages for our small and large sizes.

The purpose of Table 16.1 is to show a way of expressing the uncertainties about prospect size. There is no mention of the word "probability," yet the explorer is allowed freedom to express what he feels about his prospect.

Having expressed our uncertainty about prospect size by means of the values shown in Table 16.1, we can obtain a computer-generated curve, using Monte Carlo techniques, that will depict all possible sizes. Some possible shortcuts to this method will be explained later. For now we shall assume we can access a Monte Carlo program that can stimulate all possible prospect sizes based entirely on the individual parameters of the explorer whose prospect is being examined.

You do not have to use all of the parameters shown, nor do you have to use triangular distributions, although they provide a very simple means of getting the data. Some programs allow several kinds of input, including mapped data relating to yield, area, and sand thickness. Sizing can also be produced from triangular distributions for only net pay thickness, recovery, and area. In most instances such input does enter a simulation model using Monte Carlo techniques so that all possible sizes are represented. The challenge is to use the best, most logical data for the input.

Fig. 16.1 is a representative example of three triangular distributions involving only pay, recovery, and area. No units are given, and no attempt is made to give the triangles any specific shape, although some parameters, e.g., recovery, exhibit lognormality. This type of input is the simplest that can be used for a Monte Carlo simulator. Again, it does not represent the only type of input; it is used here for illustration purposes. Be sure the explorer who is providing data understands the limitations of the triangular distribution. The small and large values are entered as having a frequency of zero. A common mistake in using triangular distributions is the lack of understanding of the use, by the program, of the minimum and maximum values. (Remember the discussion in Chapter 10?)

DISTRIBUTION OF SIZES

Fig. 16.2 demonstrates the cumulative probability distribution that results from triangular distributions. It is plotted on a linear scale with the 90th, 50th, and 10th percentiles marked with an X. These

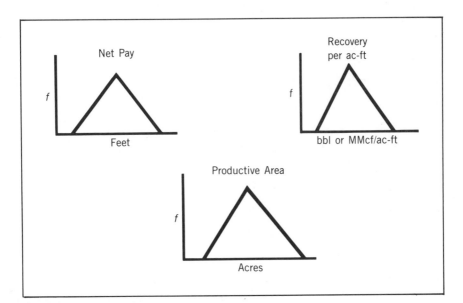

FIG. 16.1   Simulation input

percentiles form our low-side, most-likely, and high-side values for subsequent use in prospect risking.

For reasons to be explained in subsequent paragraphs, these specific percentiles are always used. The discrete sizes are necessary for several reasons:

1. A full spectrum of possible sizes presents an impossible evaluation problem. A few specific sizes must be isolated for evaluation
2. The specific sizes represent three segments (roughly thirds) of the spectrum. In evaluating the three sizes, each segment's economic potential can be reviewed
3. It so happens that in utilizing these particular percentiles and their resultant sizes, the mean of the distribution can be determined (for a lognormal distribution that is not highly skewed)

STANDARD PROBABILITIES

Just how and why these three percentiles are used is explained in the following paragraphs. This method is not universally used since each evaluation unit usually develops its own techniques. It is shown

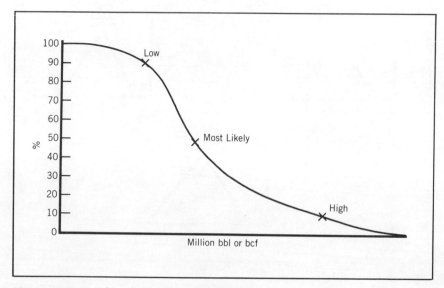

FIG. 16.2   Simulation output, prospect sizes

here to illustrate one method of achieving several desirable goals involving prospect risking. The use of three sizes is well known in the literature. One of the early uses was by Arps.[4] The USGS uses the 5th and 95th percentiles and a modal value (their most likely) to obtain the mean of distributions used in their assessments involving resource potential.

The practical value of three sizes is to reduce the economic calculations to a reasonable number. You need to know what a small-sized prospect will yield as well as a high-side size. But you also need to know about the mean because it is the only single number (size) that represents the entire distribution.

Fig. 16.3 shows another cumulative frequency distribution of prospect sizes. These data are plotted on log probability paper, which

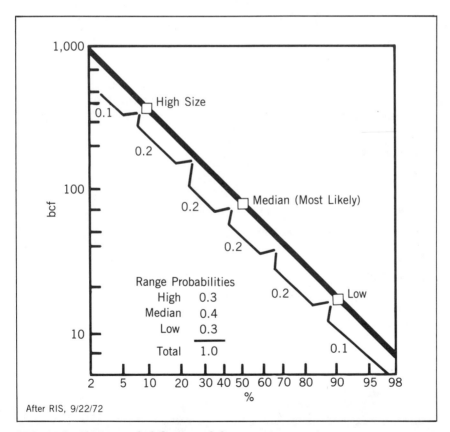

FIG. 16.3   Range probabilities and discrete sizes

results in a straight line for a lognormal distribution, as explained in
Chapter 4. The slope in this particular instance indicates a prospect
that can have a very broad range of sizes, which expresses much
uncertainty as to the prospect size. At the key percentiles the values
are

Percentile	Size, bcf	Case
90	16	Low
50	76	Most-likely
10	360	High

Fig. 16.3 was constructed to show the logic or methodology behind
the specific and standard probabilities suggested in this method of
risking prospects. The curve is split into rough thirds in the following
manner. The segment including the high-side size is assigned a 0.3
probability of occurrence. This probability is derived by splitting the
difference, on the percentage scale, between the high-side value and
the median size, or 0.2 to each. Adding the upper segment (above the
10th percentile) of 0.1 probability to the 0.2 makes a total of 0.3. This
value is assigned to the high-side case as representative of the upper
third of the distribution. Indeed, our distribution says that, if successful, about one-third of the possible prospect sizes would fall in this
segment of the curve.

Splitting the differences between the low-side and median value
yields 0.2 probability for each. Adding the bracketed segments together, we get (0.2 + 0.2) for the median case and (0.2 + 0.1) for the
low-side case. Note that these three probabilities are symbolic of the
segment but are *not* assumed to be absolutely applicable to the specific size for evaluation purposes. As we have noted previously, specific sizes can only be expressed (probabilistically) as that size or
greater relative to a specific percentage of occurrence. The result,
then, is as follows:

Size	Probability
High	0.3
Most-likely	0.4
Low	0.3
	1.0

The segment representing the most-likely value (the 50th percentile) is given the highest probability of occurrence, which is what you desire because most of the expected sizes will occur in this portion of the distribution.

You may have noticed that we have called the 50th percentile the most-likely value. We do this symbolically, knowing that the 50th percentile is the *median* and that the term "most-likely" stands, mathematically, for the *mode*. The reasons for our misuse of the term most-likely will be apparent as we proceed in this chapter. Just remember that the three percentiles represent segments of the curve as much as the actual percentiles themselves.

Why Standard Probabilities?

The use of the precise percentiles and standard probabilities for each discrete size has another very practical value. For a modestly skewed distribution it can produce the mean of that distribution. Swanson discovered empirically that a good approximation of the mean of a modestly skewed distribution can be derived by the following formula:

Case	Size × Probability	Value
Low	20 × 0.3	6.0
Median (most-likely)	37 × 0.4	14.8
High	70 × 0.3	21.0
	Mean	41.8

Using the probabilities shown above for the size of 20, 37, and 70 at the precise percentiles of 90, 50, and 10, the mean of the distribution is calculated at 41.8.

Why are we so interested in deriving the mean? Because the mean is the one single value best representing a complete distribution. Furthermore, the only additive value from one distribution to another is the mean. The low-side and high-side values from several distributions cannot be added together to get a composite, but the means *can* be added.

Since the distribution illustrated is lognormal, i.e., skewed to the right, the mean of 41.8 is larger than the median value of 37. In a greater-than plot, the steeper the slope, the larger the skewness and the greater the difference between the median and the mean—and the mean will always be larger.

We now have the complete philosophy behind the use of sizes from exact percentiles and standard probabilities for these sizes. As outlined in Appendix B, Swanson's rule must be used with caution for a highly skewed distribution. In general, if the ratio of value at the 10th percentile to that at the 50th percentile exceeds 5.0, you may wish to use the formula described in Appendix B to determine the mean. A practical example shows the variance from Swanson's rule:

Case	Size × Probability	Value
Low	16 × 0.3	4.8
Median	76 × 0.4	30.4
High	360 × 0.3	108.0
	Mean	143.2

Using Swanson's rule to derive the mean for the distribution expressed above by the values of 16, 76, and 360, we calculate a mean of 143. However, using the formula shown in Appendix B, the true mean is 159. Thus, in a highly skewed distribution Swanson's rule yields a biased answer—biased toward the smaller sizes in the distribution. In the particular case shown here, the value of the mean derived by Swanson's rule is 10% below the true mean.

Highly skewed distributions for prospects reflect much uncertainty about size. So philosophically you may wish for some "protection" from the maximum value where much uncertainty is expressed. If so, Swanson's rule gives such protection with its bias toward a smaller value than the mean. Furthermore, the greater the maximum value (the greater the skewness and thus uncertainty), the greater is the bias from Swanson's rule.

MODELS FOR THE PROSPECT

The next step relates geologic models to the prospect's distribution of potential sizes. A reasonable geologic model must be constructed to represent each of the three sizes: low side, median, and high side. Up to this point we have assumed that a Monte Carlo simulation has been run from prospect parameters and that the 10th, 50th, and 90th percentiles have produced three sizes to model. In actual practice, when modeling by Monte Carlo is first introduced, it is often difficult to get explorationists to see the value of simulation to get all potential sizes. Some encouragement may be necessary. A little help from top management goes a long way here. Many geologists and geophysicists see their prospects as a single value, a most-likely size. Such a concept may be all they considered; however, the economic principles involved require a distribution of sizes. Thus, additional data must be secured for a simulation.

On the other hand, top management may be the problem. It is unfortunate that some managements have an overwhelming desire to see a single value for a reserve size. There is much evidence to show that what is mapped is *not* the only structural configuration (or isopach) that can be drawn from existing data. Those who have experimented with giving different geologists identical data to prepare prospect maps know that different maps can come from the same data, and the range of values can be surprising. In any event the use of three sizes is a useful exercise even for managers who wish to see only the final choice. The exercise expands the explorationist's thinking to the other possibilities that can occur.

The geologist or geophysicist may have a most-likely and a high-side case already pictured, usually with the most-likely value mapped. If so, a low-side case can be estimated. Preferably, the low-side case should be expressed with geological values of key parameters. However, a low-side case can be estimated by plotting the most-likely and high-side values at the 10th and 50th percentiles (on log probability paper, of course) and then extrapolating the line to the intersection of the 90th percentile. Using this technique will give you a lognormal distribution of prospect sizes, a desirable goal. Nevertheless, a simulation based on reasonable variance in key reservoir factors is still the most desirable and, in the long run, the more consistent.

We must keep in mind, however, that simulations of all possible prospect sizes should not be accepted with the first run of the Monte Carlo model. All simulations must be held up to the light of reality, and corrections must be made if any of the key three values appear unreasonable. One of the most common mistakes in prospect risking is assuming that the simulation has produced the desired answer without checking its results against your concepts of reality. Many times several trials are needed to produce a reasonable answer. That means, of course, that some of your input values don't hold up to reality either.

What is a reality check? Well, suppose your simulation shows a high-side value at the 10th percentile that is larger than any field discovered to date. That's cause for checking, if not alarm. That is a reality check. Or suppose that the field sizes look reasonable, but when you put the logistics of development to the prospect, you find the reserve size of the average development well exceeds that of all prior wells to date. That is another reality check. The greater the uncertainty, the more important the need for reality checks.

A SHORTCUT TO BYPASS MONTE CARLO

Perhaps you just got a glimpse of a technique to bypass the Monte Carlo simulation. If you have a method of using three sizes to achieve the mean (and several are described in Appendix B), you can simply plot three sizes at the appropriate percentiles on log probability paper and check for approximate lognormality.

Let's illustrate this concept using Swanson's rule. We begin with what you have mapped. Assume it is a median value and put it on log probability paper at the 50th percentile. Now construct a high-side case based on your concepts of what a larger size could be, keeping in mind that it must be a reasonable size, not a max-max case. For example, in the method described here you must feel that you have at least a 1 in 10 chance of achieving the high-side value for it to be valid. You might say, "How can I tell what size has a 1 in 10 chance?" The answer is that you probably can do that as well as or better than picking a maximum case at the extremes of your distribution and then trying to estimate whether it is a 1 in 500 or a 1 in 1,000 chance. It is not prudent to run economics on a case that has only 1 chance in 500. Stick with a 1 in 10 shot! Next you must deal with a small-side case to be plotted at the 90th percentile. Here you are thinking of a value that, if productive, is almost a sure thing—a 9 out of 10 chance.

Now plot all three sizes on log probability paper at the appropriate percentiles—10, 50, and 90. (see Fig. 16.4). If they line up in an approximately straight line, you have a lognormal distribution and have bypassed the Monte Carlo simulation. You can always test the deviation from what is desired in the following manner. Draw a straight line representing a best fit of your three sizes on the log probability paper. Next calculate a mean using Swanson's rule based on the values from that line drawn. Then compare that value with the value calculated from the three plotted points (as opposed to those on the line). If the deviation is slight, you can feel safe in using your three values. We must always remember that we deal with much uncertainty in even our best mapped data, so a little deviation in our mean should not concern us too much.

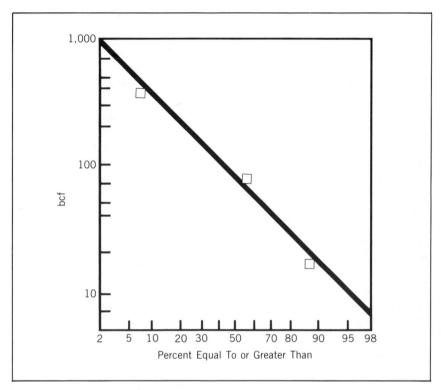

FIG. 16.4   Prospect sizes

The shortcut described is quick and simple and requires only the willingness to deal with values that you choose to derive your mean; in our example, these values are those at the 10th, 50th, and 90th percentiles.

Back to the Simulation

Whether using the shortcut or a Monte Carlo simulation, a low-side case must be derived. It must have a reasonable geologic concept backing it up. It may have less net pay, a smaller area, or a lower recovery (poorer porosity), but it should seem geologically possible—although less probable than the most-likely or mapped size.

The most-likely size should be close to the one considered most probable by the explorationist. Occasionally, a few explorers tend to think consistently on the high side of potential field sizes. Here again the Monte Carlo simulation is important. The cumulative probability distribution of sizes clearly shows if an estimate has a low probability of occurrence or if the input values are estimated unreasonably high, the result could be reserve sizes that are nonexistent in the trend to date. Monte Carlo simulation helps focus on reality. By itself, simulation does not produce any specific models as such. It does, however, accurately reflect the geologist's views of all potential reserve sizes.

The larger size from the 10th percentile should represent a high-side potential for the prospect. A combination of reasonable, geologically sound input should back up this case. The sizing of each parameter must reflect the knowledge that the assigned value is less probable than that for the most-likely case. Keep in mind that you can input triangular distributions for the key reservoir parameters and never mention the word probability. All you need is a low value, a high value, and a most-likely value. Finally, for the high-side case you should believe that you have at least a 1 out of 10 chance of finding a field that size. (This value changes if you are not using the 10th percentile to express your high-side case.)

Developing reasonable geologic models for the three cases may involve a little juggling to get the models to approximate the appropriate sizes. It is a required step, however, and it is a meaningful step. The explorationist should know the economic consequences of a small discovery. On the other hand there exists a small probability that a field size in the upper third could result. This possibility also should be reviewed and the economic consequences understood.

In the case of a single reservoir, the change from low-side to high-side values may result from slightly larger values for the three parameters of pay, area, and recovery. For cases involving more than one reservoir, both sizing and risking become much more complicated. Here the difference between low side and high side may involve a change from one productive reservoir (the low side) to several productive reservoirs, perhaps over a larger area (the high side). It's also possible that your discrete cases might result from a conclusion that two of four possible reservoirs appear to be the most-likely case. Then three cases might become variations of reservoir parameters, but always involving only two reservoirs. You can see that the number of possible combinations grows rapidly as one increases the number of potentially productive reservoirs. In any event the models you construct must represent the best geologic judgment related to the three key sizes.

For illustration purposes in this chapter, we will use the sizes shown on Fig. 16.4:

Case	Size, bcf	Percentile
Low	15	0.90
Most-likely	85	0.50
High	330	0.10

On log probability paper these sizes are approximately lognormal at the three key percentiles: 10, 50, and 90 (see Fig. 16.4). The precise sizes (shown on Fig. 16.3) were 16, 76, and 360. The modest variation from true lognormality will not seriously distort our economic calculations. Most of the basic data we shall deal with have more uncertainty than this slight variation. However, even though your models will not always fit the lognormal curve precisely, you should expect and work toward a rough lognormal correlation.

CALCULATING THE CHANCE OF SUCCESS

After the prospect has been carefully reviewed in terms of the uncertainty about size, we next consider the potential for the presence or absence of hydrocarbons or, more precisely, the probability of the presence of hydrocarbons. This factor is most often called the *success rate* or the *chance of success*. It may have such names as the *chance of adequacy* (in regard to a particular geological control) or it may be referred to as *existence risk*. In this chapter we shall use *success rate* and *existence risk*, knowing that they both mean the same thing.

Remember that we sized the prospect first. For sound reasons this step should take place before an attempt to determine the probability of the existence of hydrocarbons. Sizing first gives you valuable insights into factors affecting the control of hydrocarbons being present. As we have already mentioned, and we shall discuss this more, sizing also helps focus the proper attention on the factors affecting the minimum size.

Gehman et al. recommend consideration of five geological controls to estimate the probability of the existence of oil or gas (or both):

- trap closure
- reservoir
- porosity
- source (seal, timing, preservation)
- recovery

These five factors are assumed to control the geologic conditions that determine the presence or absence of hydrocarbons. They have varying probabilities of occurrence. The probabilities, when multiplied times each other, produce a composite estimate of success (existence risk), the chance of hydrocarbons being present. This estimate of the existence of oil or gas is used later to determine the risk-adjusted reserve for the prospect and for individual tracts.

An example taken from Gehman's paper is shown on Table 16.2. The geologic control is shown and the assigned probability is indicated in the right column. Gehman et al. have chosen great simplicity in that three controls are assigned values of 1.0 and two are assigned values of 0.5. You may like this kind of simplicity. It really says, we feel confident about trap closure, porosity, and recovery but are concerned about the reservoir and the source. In Gehman's example the product of the five probabilities amounts to 0.25, or a 25% chance of success.

There are many possible combinations of numbers for the five factors that would have produced a similar answer. Values of 0.9 could have been used instead of 1.0 for those factors in which you have the most confidence. Likewise, values of 0.4 or 0.6 might have been used for those controls in which you have less confidence. Gehman et al. chose not to be too fancy. The lesson here is clear: We cannot give precise answers for these probabilities. Gehman's illustration expresses with great simplicity the direction of feeling about the critical controls.

TABLE 16.2   Chance of success

Geologic Control	Chance of Adequacy (1.0 − Risk)
Trap closure	1.0
Reservoir	0.5
Porosity	1.0
Source (seal, timing, preservation)	0.5
Recovery	1.0
Overall chance of exceeding minimum potential = 1.0 × 0.5 × 1.0 × 0.5 × 1.0 = 0.25	

After Gehman et al.

What if you have no experience or backup data to determine the probability associated with a particular control? The best solution is to combine that control with the most logically related factor and use the combination as a single factor. You may have more data related to a larger field of controls. Existence risk has been estimated with as few as three or four geologic controls.[5]

This step—estimating the chance of success—presents the most problems and requires the greatest degree of subjective judgment, yet it must be done. It is not only important in its own right, but it affects the low-side case in particular and thus is crucial to evaluating the prospect properly.

WHAT ARE WE RISKING?

You may wonder about the meaning of the previous sentence for a moment. What is the relationship between the chance of success and the minimum size? It is more than a slender thread of relationship because the chance of success is in reality the chance of finding the minimum size *or more*. It is the chance of finding a prospect somewhere on the lognormal plot of all possible prospect sizes. But specifically it refers only to the minimum size or more. As we move up the prospect size curve, we know that our chance of finding a larger and larger field gets smaller. For example, if your lognormal plot of prospect sizes says that only half of the possible sizes are greater than 100 billion cubic feet (bcf) of gas, what is your chance of finding that size or larger if the chance of success is 20%? The answer is 10% because you only have a 20% chance of finding anything. But even if you find something, you expect only one-half of the sizes that may occur to be equal to or greater than 100 bcf.

We can look at this concept another way. The chance of success in an established, mature trend is definitely related to all of the producing fields. It includes a few marginal fields that were produced—not to make a profit, but not to lose all of the money already invested. Many one-well fields fall in this category. So your success rate is limited to producing fields, an obvious fact. Thus, your individual reservoir parameters must also be related to the reality of what produces. If in a given trend it takes 10 feet of sand to make a well, then your success rate should take this into consideration. In effect the existence risk is the chance of finding that minimum sand or more. Granted, you may not always know what a given parameter must be to be commercial, but we can take that into account later. For now, we must just recognize that it is important to see that there *is* a thread of relationship between the chance of success and the minimum (low-side) case.

Two examples may help clarify this point. First, we will make a comparison between onshore and offshore. A five-foot sand in a small field at a shallow depth might be economic on land but definitely not most places offshore. The fact that many small fields can be produced onshore means that the dry risk is lower. In other words, given the same geologic conditions and the same distribution of field sizes but different cost criteria, the dry risk is different—and offshore it is higher.

Second, suppose we have modeled several sizes on a prospect and have found the minimum size to be commercial if productive. Now we get a drastic cut in oil prices. Suddenly we find that not only the minimum size but even some of the larger sizes are no longer commercial. Our dry risk has increased sharply with price reduction, yet the distribution of field sizes is the same.

Thus, choosing the minimum values in volume considerations is inherently connected to dry risk. No matter how much we may wish to isolate them completely, we cannot sever this thin thread of relationship. The chance of success *is* related to the minimum size.

Your low-side case should be related to the experienced success rate and should be one you reasonably would expect to be commercial. You will find noncommercial fields; that is a fact. But they should not be reflected in your success rate to any great extent.

EXISTENCE RISK AND REALITY

The estimate of existence risk stems from multiplying several probabilities times each other. The answer must always be reasonable in the fact of reality. For example, the average of several prospects should be equal or close to the historic success rate for the trend. Obviously, a single prospect should vary from the average—some substantially. A single prospect may have more or less risk than the average for all prospects. However, the average success rate for a group of prospects with similar geologic objectives in the same trend should be at or near the historic success rate in a mature trend. Make a reality check whenever possible.

THE PROSPECT

Fig. 16.5 is a contoured view and cross section of a rather simple, uncomplicated prospect. Shown is a prospect that grows in pay thickness of the productive interval and in area as the size increases from the low-side case to the high-side case. The structural configu-

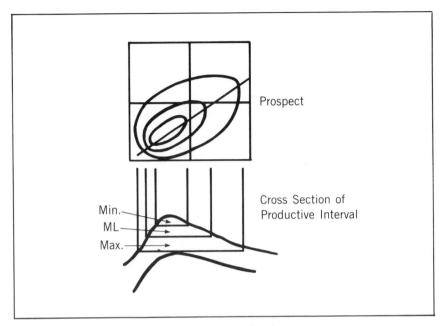

Prospect

Cross Section of
Productive Interval

Min.
ML
Max.

FIG. 16.5   One prospect and four tracts: the three cases

ration shows why the sizes have such a large range. In the example
each contour represents the limits of one case, i.e., low side, most
likely, and high side.

Fig. 16.6, a probability diagram, shows how we might look at this
prospect in terms of whether it is successful or dry. Note that we have
considered both the chance of success and the possible variations in
size. The probability tree branches to a dry case or a successful case. If
the successful case prevails, we have three possible sizes to review. Of
course, there are many more possible sizes, but we shall view these
three as representative of the distribution of prospect sizes. Probabilities can be assigned to each event. In the illustration we shall use,
specific probabilities will be used for the three branches, but you may
choose any values that best help you understand the risks and the size
implications of your distribution of sizes—provided you use another
means to establish the mean of the distribution.

Fig. 16.6 applies to any prospect that has only one reservoir as
potentially productive. It thus represents a tree diagram for all prospects in this simple case. We make this probability diagram individual to each prospect when we assign probabilities and reserves to the
three sizes: low-side, most-likely and high-side. So we begin with a

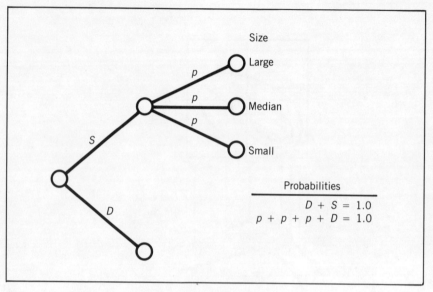

FIG. 16.6   Prospect outcomes, any prospect

diagram for any prospect and proceed to make it apply to each individual prospect. In our illustrations we shall use the probabilities of 0.3, 0.4, and 0.3. If you desire to place your prospect sizes at other than the 10th, 50th, and 90th percentiles, you must choose different probabilities.

As we have clearly demonstrated earlier, our sole purpose in using the 0.3, 0.4, and 0.3 probabilities is to get a value for the mean. However, there are many other practical reasons for using this relationship. For one thing, it relieves the geologist or geophysicist from the need to assign probabilities to his three sizes yet achieves the purpose of a systematic methodology for prospect risking. If you elect to risk-weigh the mean against the dry case, it can be used to estimate the acreage ownership for the mean case. Because your acreage ownership can vary with each of the three sizes, you need some means of calculating the ownership at the mean value. The three probabilities of 0.3, 0.4, and 0.3 can be used in the same manner as reserves to calculate the mean acreage ownership (see Appendix B).

Fig. 16.7 shows the prospect, a tree diagram for all prospects, and in the upper right-hand corner shows an example case that demonstrates relationships between the three sizes. This case assumes a 20% chance of success and an 80% chance of a dry case. Remember a dry case can mean more than one dry hole. It might even include some

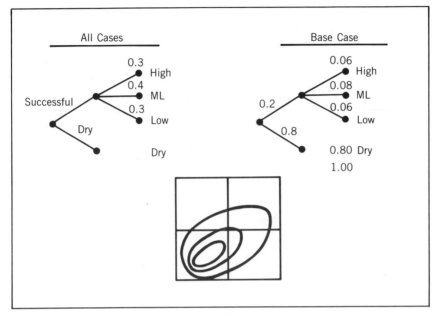

FIG. 16.7   Prospect outcomes

additional delineation seismic work before a second wildcat is drilled if the first one is dry or reveals unexpected information.

Because all probabilities must add to 1.0, note the probabilities assigned to the three successful cases (outcomes): 0.06, 0.08, and 0.06. They sum to 0.2, the chance of a successful case—the chance of finding a field on the prospect distribution of potential sizes.

The probabilities for the successful outcomes indicate several facts if viewed in a cumulative sense:

1. The chance of a successful outcome of any size is 20%
2. The chance of a prospect in the high segment is only 6%, the product of 0.2×0.3
3. The chance of a prospect in the most-likely or larger size is 14%, the sum of 8% and 6%. Thus, we have recognized that the most-likely case or larger has less chance of success than the small size
4. The 20% chance can *only* be associated with the low-side case. To say it another way, the high-side case has the lowest probability of occurrence, which is just what our geology indicates

TABLE 16.3   Prospect outcomes

Case	Size, bcf	Probabilities		
		Base	Alt. 1	Alt. 2
1 (High)	330	0.06	0.09	0.03
2 (ML)	85	0.08	0.12	0.04
3 (Low)	15	0.06	0.09	0.03
Dry	0	0.80	0.70	0.90
	Total	1.00	1.00	1.00

Table 16.3 tabulates the probabilities of a base case at 80% dry risk and two alternate cases as well as the reserve sizes of the high-side, most-likely, and low-side cases. The dry case, zero reserves, is shown just below the successful cases on the same line as the dry risks. Consider, for example, an alternate dry risk of 90%, shown as alternate 2. If any discovery has only a 10% chance of occurring under the method proposed herein, the probabilities for the successful cases become 0.03, 0.04, and 0.03.

THE ECONOMIC OUTPUT

Table 16.4 shows an abridged version of a typical economic output. We shall see other results later. In this table are listed the three successful cases, then the risk-weighted cases, and finally the dry case.

Risk-weighted reserves result from multiplying the mean reserve times the chance of success. Now you can see why we need the mean, the only single number that represents an entire distribution. The mean for our prospect is calculated using Swanson's rule as follows:

Size		Probability		Segment Weighted, bcf
330	×	0.3	=	99.0
85	×	0.4	=	34.0
15	×	0.3	=	4.5
		1.0		137.5

The risk-weighted reserve for the base case (80% dry risk) is 28 bcf (really 27.5). It represents the average of eight dry cases and two successful ones, or 0.2 times the mean reserve. If you assume the prospect

TABLE 16.4   Economic output

Chance of Success	Size, bcf	Millions of Dollars		DCFR, %
		AVP	PVP at HR	
100	330			
100	85			
100	15			
0	0			
10	14*			
20	28*			
30	41*			

*Risk-weighted size; includes dry case

is dry 8 times out of 10, then the consequence is finding an average of 28 bcf per prospect. A risk-weighted reserve is really an unreal number; it combines the estimate of failure with the probability of success into one number. However, if something is found, the dry risk no longer applies and we deal with real-world numbers, those associated with productive fields only. The probabilistic approach of including dryness and success in one number is used so we can see what we will do on the average. This view in turn helps us see the risk inherent in a single event.

The columns to the right of the reserve sizes on Table 16.4 [AVP, PVP at the minimum guideline discount rate (or HR for hurdle rate), and the discounted cash flow rate (DCFR)] symbolize a suite of yardsticks that are usually available from standard economic programs.

Any number of parameters can be tested for their sensitivity or to determine a minimum value, as shown in Fig. 16.8. Here, the desired DCFR is 15% and the present value of the risked cases is plotted against the dry risk. Such a plot enables you to ascertain the critical dry risk for a commercial venture. In the case shown a dry risk of slightly more than 60% can be tolerated and still have a present value of zero at 15%. This same plot can be used to test the minimum size, the maximum investment, the initial potential, or various levels of production. It is a most useful plot to isolate minimums, both financial and physical. For example, other possible variables could be net pay thickness, average wellhead price, and well cost.

An extremely useful plot is the one shown on Fig. 16.9. It aids in considering important parameters in tracts for sale in the OCS. The bonus that can be paid is shown as the ordinate, and the abscissa is the dry risk. A family of curves is shown, each representing a different

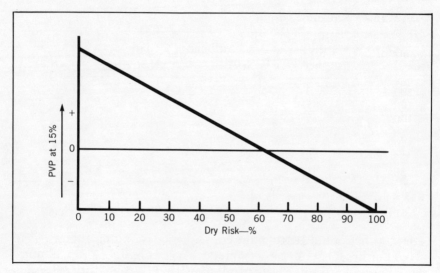

FIG. 16.8   Effect of risk on present value of mean prospect size

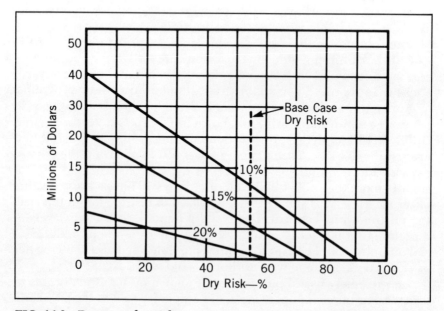

FIG. 16.9   Bonus vs dry risk

discount rate. Thus, three key parameters are shown—dry risk, bonus, and discount rate—and they are related to each other graphically. If a dry risk can be agreed upon, then the bonus that can be paid can be seen as a function of discount rate. If a specific discount rate is desired, then the maximum dry risk allowed can be shown as a function of a specific bonus. The figure is particularly useful on marginal leases in an area. It can be used to check the minimum bonus level on a tract to see if you are willing to enter a bid. The value of Fig. 16.9 is its ability to relate any combination of the three variables to arrive at a desired answer. Fig. 16.9 can be used for an entire prospect, but it is more commonly used for individual tracts if the prospect covers more than one tract.

Often a base-line dry risk is shown. It would appear as a vertical line intersecting all of the discount rate curves and would express the recommended estimate for dry risk of the evaluating or originating group. It can then be presented to management as the base case or recommended case. Yet by means of the figure, management can see the many related cases at or near the recommended one.

ESTABLISHING TRACT VALUE

We have finished our work on the prospect and now must proceed to the individual tracts because many prospects cover more than one tract. Fig. 16.10 depicts our prospect, with the letters a, b, c, and d assigned to each tract. Almost any valuation program can produce tract economics and the bonus bids for each tract, if given the appropriate input. To establish value, we must first decide how much of a prospect's reserve is on each tract. Fig. 16.10 shows such an assignment of reserve. We are not limited, at this juncture, to expressing value merely as a function of reserves. Value can be expressed as a percent of the prospect reserve, as a percent of the reservoir acre-feet; it can also be thought of as a percent of revenue or cash flow.

The left table in Fig. 16.10 shows the percent of reserves assigned to each tract for each of the three sizes: low side, most likely, and high side. The table to the right has the actual reserves assigned in billions of cubic feet. The low-side reserve is entirely on tract c, so all 15 bcf are assigned to tract c. The most-likely reserve size overlaps two tracts, c and d. The split is about 60/40 between the two tracts. The assigned reserves are 51 bcf to c and 34 bcf to tract d. The high-side case affects all tracts. For this case, based on the percentages indicated, the tract assignments are

Tract	bcf
a	33
b	66
c	132
d	99

Using these percentages, we have assigned reserve possibilities to all four tracts. We can see that tract c has the best possibility for production since it has reserves under all size conditions expected. It therefore has the least risk. Tract d is next in reserve size but is more risky since it will only be productive if the most-likely size or more is found. The most risky tracts are a and b. Neither is of value unless the maximum size is productive; of the two, b has the larger reserve. Just how we take our reserve assignments and combine them with risk is shown on Fig. 16.11.

The Prospect and the Dry Cases

Having assigned reserves to each tract, the dry case can be added. Remember, a dry case can always mean more than one dry hole. It can include several delineation wells and more seismic lines.

Case	Reservoir Size	Portion on Tract				bcf Per Tract			
		a	b	c	d	a	b	c	d
LOW	15	—	—	1.0	—	—	—	15	—
ML	85	—	—	0.6	0.4	—	—	51	34
HIGH	330	0.1	0.2	0.4	0.3	33	66	132	99

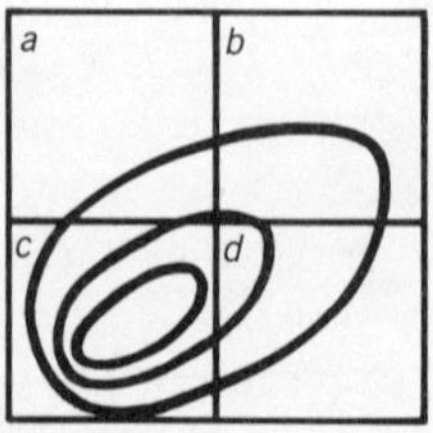

Prospect

FIG. 16.10   Tract reserves

Fig. 16.11 shows the possible outcomes for each tract, again by means of tree diagrams. The base case success rate has been estimated at 20%, so there is an 80% chance of a dry prospect. The probabilities for each diagram are the same, but they apply to different reserve sizes for each tract. As a consequence, the risk for each tract varies, based on its relationship to the prospect. *It is the prospect we risk, and what we think about each tract comes from our view of the prospect.*

For tract *a*, no most-likely or low-side reserves exist. Therefore, the probabilities relate only to the high-side case, which has the lowest probability of occurrence. There is only a 20% chance of finding any discovery at all and only a 30% chance of finding a reserve size in the high segment of the curve. So only a 6% chance exists for tract *a* to be productive (0.2 × 0.3 = 0.06). The chance of getting 33 bcf on tract *a* is 6%.

Tract *b* also contains reserves only if the high-side case is productive; however, it has 66 bcf—twice that of tract *a*. Its dry risk is the same as tract *a* (94%), but it has twice the reserve; so it is the next most valuable tract.

Tract *d* is only of value if the most-likely or high-side cases are productive; it has no reserves from the low-side case. Thus, the low-side case is, in effect, a dry case and the chance of success for tract *d* is

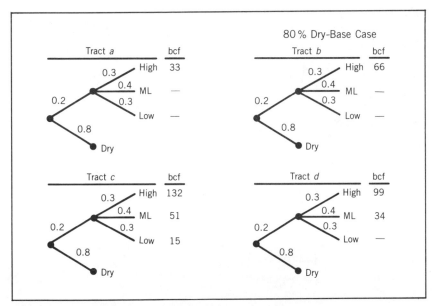

FIG. 16.11   Possible outcomes by tract, potential and risk

decreased by 6% from the 20% for the prospect and its dry risk is raised to 86%. With a 14% chance of success, tract *d* is less risky than *a* or *b* and also has more potential reserve. It is therefore the second most valuable tract of the four, ranking ahead of *a* and *b*. The success rate for tract *d* is derived as follows

$$(0.2 \times 0.3) + (0.2 \times 0.4) = 0.06 + 0.08 = 0.14$$

Tract *c* has potential reserves from all three sizes. It can then be assigned the greatest chance of being productive, 20%. In other words, it has the same chance of success as the prospect; after all, the prospect chance of success is the chance of finding the minimum size or more. So tract *c* is the most valuable. It has the largest reserve and the lowest risk.

The methodology just described provides a means of achieving the most desired goal in risking prospects to bid on tracts. It considers the prospect as a whole but recognizes that individual tracts have different reserve potentials as well as different risks. It is not a complicated method, nor does it presume an unreasonable accuracy because it deals more or less with segments of the curve of prospect sizes. Furthermore, we can use our segment relationship to compile the economic consequences of finding the mean for the prospect as well as each tract to weigh against the dry case to arrive at tract value.

VARYING THE DRY RISK

We showed in Fig. 16.9 that a suite of dry risks should be plotted against bonus at various discount rates to illustrate fully the interrelationship between these three key parameters. In Table 16.5 an alternative dry risk is shown for each tract. The alternative is 70% as opposed to the base case of 80%. The specific probabilities are shown for the three sizes along with a comparison between the two dry risks and their effect on the resultant success rates for the four tracts. As the dry risk decreases, the individual probabilities increase for the three segments of the prospect curve of sizes. For tract *a* at a 70% chance of a dry prospect, the success rate now becomes 9% compared with the 6% of the 80% dry case for the prospect. For tract *d* the success rate increases from 14% to 21% if the prospect as a whole has a 30% chance of success. Finally, tract *c*, the least risky tract, is assigned the success rate of the prospect: 30%.

TABLE 16.5 Tract evaluation input

	Tract *a*				Tract *b*		
	Size,	Probability			Size,	Probability	
Case	bcf	Base	Alt. 1	Case	bcf	Base	Alt. 1
1	33	0.06	0.09	1	66	0.06	0.09
2	—	0.08	0.12	2	—	0.08	0.12
3	—	0.06	0.09	3	—	0.06	0.09
Dry	—	0.80	0.70	Dry	—	0.80	0.70
		1.00	1.00			1.00	1.00

	Tract *c*				Tract *d*		
	Size,	Probability			Size,	Probability	
Case	bcf	Base	Alt. 1	Case	bcf	Base	Alt. 1
1	132	0.06	0.09	1	99	0.06	0.09
2	51	0.08	0.12	2	34	0.08	0.12
3	15	0.06	0.09	3	—	0.06	0.09
Dry	0	0.80	0.70	Dry	—	0.80	0.70
		1.00	1.00			1.00	1.00

THE STEPS IN PROSPECT RISKING

We have been through a series of steps to arrive at the proper size and risk to enable us to establish tract value:

1. Prepare a simulation run of potential prospect sizes
2. If you wish to bypass the simulation, construct three sizes for your prospect: a low-side, a most-likely, and a high-side case. Plot on log probability paper at the 10th, 50th, and 90th percentiles. If not approximately lognormal, you may wish to reconsider your sizes
3. Assign reserves to tracts
4. Evaluate discrete sizes for each tract plus a dry case
5. Select, by formation, key geologic parameters
6. Assign probabilities to these parameters
7. Calculate success rate
8. Combine mean size with dry case at desired success rate
9. Prepare alternative combinations at different dry risks
10. Make an economic run for tract value

We have covered all of the mechanics of risking in this chapter except the actual economic calculations of tract value. That subject is beyond the scope of this textbook, as we are dealing solely with the analysis of risk.

For convenience' sake, two typical forms are shown, Tables 16.6 and 16.7. Table 16.6 contains data about the three sizes and the calculation of the success rate. Table 16.7 lists other data that would be helpful when preparing for the economic evaluation.

REVIEW

This chapter showed in considerable detail a method of risking prospects. Its goal is to enable the explorationist to use his geologic input but to provide for the proper sizing of tracts systematically so they will not tend to be oversized and underrisked.

You may not care to use Swanson's rule; its advantage is that it dissolves the need for the geologist/geophysicist to guesstimate probabilities about size. On the other hand, it puts much dependence on the *mean* because it represents the entire spectrum of possible sizes in one number. If you use this method, you are saying that you feel confident about your distribution of prospect sizes. So check that distribution! Make sure it fits your gut-level feelings about the ranges of prospect sizes that are possible.

The method described is easy and simple, but it is only as good as your distribution of prospect sizes. Remember, however, that the distribution originates from your own mapped data—your geologic input.

Finally, we must remind you that the phrase "most likely" means *mode* to a mathematician. We have knowingly but conveniently applied the term to the median because we recognize that its use is only to derive the mean of our distribution.

Whatever method you use, at least you can see the need for consistency and perhaps you have gained an idea or two about your own risking concepts from the words in this chapter. Happy risking!

TABLE 16.6 Prospect Parameters

Date _____

Prospect Name: _____   Area: _____

Most-Likely Size (0.5) _____bcf   _____ millions of bbl

Depth: _____

Geologic Objective: _____
  Prospective Area
  Net Pay
  Recovery Factor
    Discuss or list critical
    parameters for each zone of
    assigned reserves.

Minimum Size (0.9) _____bcf   _____ millions of bbl
Geologic Objective: _____   Depth: _____
  Prospective Area
  Net Pay
  Recovery Factor

Maximum Size (0.1) _____bcf   _____ millions of bbl
Geologic Objective: _____   Depth: _____
  Prospective Area
  Net Pay
  Recovery Factor

Geological Control Factors—Chance of Sufficiency
  A. Trap/Seal   _____%
  B. Reservoir   _____%
  C. Source   _____%
  D. Timing   _____%
  E. Other (specify)   _____%
Geologic Chance of Success   _____%

TABLE 16.7   Prospect Evaluation Data

Prospect _____ County _____ State _____

Prospect Block—Acres _____ Bonus Paid M$ _____

Additional Geophysical Cost M$ _____

Other Exploration Costs (Rentals, etc.) _____

Your Working Interest _____

Drilling Data—100% Wells

Depth _____   Spacing _____

Succ. WC, M$ _____   Succ. Dev. Well, M$ _____

Dry WC, M$ _____   Dry Dev. Well, M$ _____

Reserves, Oil, Gas, & Condensate

	Low	*M-L*	*High*	*Mean*
Net Feet	_____	_____	_____	
Prod. Acres	_____	_____	_____	
Rec./ac-ft	_____	_____	_____	
Rec./Well	_____	_____	_____	
EUR-Field	_____	_____	_____	_____
W.I. Oil	_____	_____	_____	_____
W.I. Gas	_____	_____	_____	_____

Timing—Calendar Year

Lease Purchase _____   Drill Wildcat _____

Development Drilling	*Year*		*No. W.I. Wells*	
			Prod	*Dry*
	_____		_____	_____
	_____		_____	_____
	_____		_____	_____
	_____		_____	_____

First Oil or Gas Prod.
  (Mo/Yr) _____

Other Data

Risk Factors (Prob.) _____   Royalty _____

Gas—Intra/Interstate _____   Initial Oil Price _____

Initial Flow Rates _____   Initial Gas Price _____

GOR if Oil Production _____

References

1. Gehman, H.M., J.R. Kyle, and D.A. White. "Prospect Risk Analysis." from *Probability Methods in Oil Exploration*, AAPG Research Symposium, Stanford University, Preliminary Report, 1975, pp. 16–20.
2. Swanson, R.I. "Applying G-Risk Reserves Analysis to Prospect Economics." Unpublished memorandum, September 1972.
3. Gehman, H.M., R.A. Baker, and D.A. White. "Assessment Methodology—An Industry Viewpoint." from *Assessment of Undiscovered Oil and Gas*, Proceedings of the Seminar at Kuala Lumpur, Malaysia, March 3–8, 1980, p. 113.
4. Arps, J.J. "A Strategy for Sealed Bidding." *Journal of Petroleum Technology*, September 1965, p. 1033.
5. Megill, R.E. *An Introduction to Exploration Economics.* 2nd ed. Tulsa: PennWell Books, 1979, p. 114.

CHAPTER 17

More on prospect risking

W e have now reviewed the general basis for risking prospects, a process that dealt primarily with a prospect having a single prospective pay. We did not take into account other aspects of prospect risking.

Let's begin by discussing the allocation of the dry case. Structural conditions may exist which make it unlikely that an edge tract should be burdened with the entire cost of the dry case. After all, only one well may test the prospect and, if dry, condemn all of the other tracts as having no value. So we see that the dry case is easy when applied to the entire prospect. It becomes another subjective or judgmental decision when many tracts are involved.

One method is to consider whether you would drill a well on an edge tract if you had only that tract on the prospect. Assume that we leased tract *a* from our prospect in Chapter 16. It had only 33 bcf of reserve and had a 94% chance of being dry. If we got only tract *a*, we probably would not drill a well at all. We would probably wait to see if the winner of tract *c* would drill his well. He had the most desirable tract and most probably would drill soon to test it. We would then drill tract *a* only if tract *c* was a success and if the test showed that the gas-water contact was low enough to make the high-side case most probable. Using this approach we would not assign much if any of the dry case to the tract. We still would recognize that we only had 33 bcf on the tract and only a 6% chance of getting that reserve. So we would not bid much for this tract, even with no dry case assigned.

Now suppose we got all four tracts. We plan to drill one well on tract *c* and, if dry, we assume that it will condemn the entire prospect. Does tract *c* carry some of the burden of the dry case? If we assume tract *c* carries all of the dry risk, then we might end up with unusually favorable bids on tracts *a* and *b* because they have no dry cost assigned; this would be especially true if the reserve size is marginal. This method hardly seems fair. What should we do?

One method is to allocate the dry cost to tracts based on their proportion of the reserve. We would be dealing with the mean reserve of each tract as a percent of the prospect mean reserve. The amount of the dry case to be assigned to each tract would be its percentage of the mean reserve of the prospect. At least in this case, the bid is burdened with some share of the dry case, even though the well will be drilled on tract *c*.

This concept of assigning the cost associated with the dry case is not easy to fix absolutely. Each case is somewhat independent of all others, as each prospect is usually different. Again, as so often is the case in our business, sound judgment is called for with the objective of bidding on a reasonable but profitable basis on all tracts. You must decide, and where there are many tracts on a single prospect, it is not an easy decision to make. Consistency should be used and a careful record kept of the decision made for future reference.

THE PROBLEM OF MULTIPLE RESERVOIRS

In an established basin the large quantity of historic data helps the explorationist zero in on an appropriate success rate for the minimum size or more. Data are also available by formation for all of the producing pays. However, the problem of establishing the average success rate for a prospect becomes more complicated as the number of potentially productive reservoirs increases. If one assumes that the chance for each reservoir to become productive is *independent* from that of the other reservoirs, then binomial probability can help us understand the chances of success associated with the various combinations of productive reservoirs. Remember, however, that we are assuming the success rate for each reservoir is independent of all other reservoirs. There are ways to handle *dependent* success rates, but they will be discussed later. For now we shall show some vital points about risking prospect with multiple reservoirs, assuming independent variables for the geologic controls governing our estimate of the chance of success.

Incidentally, the thought processes for prospects with multiple reservoirs apply to development wells with multiple pays. The major difference is the lower dry risk associated with development wells.

THE TWO-RESERVOIR PROSPECT

The risks associated with a two-reservoir prospect are shown in Table 17.1. The potential pays are the Devonian and the Ellenburger. In the area the Devonian has been productive about one time in five, a success rate of 20%. On the other hand, the Ellenburger in the same area has not been as successful. Its success rate averages only 15%.

As shown on Table 17.1, four events are possible from the two reservoirs. They can be described by the binomial $(D + S)^2$, where D = dry and S = successful. The binomial shows us the four events. When listed individually, they are DD, DS, SD, and SS. Because two reservoirs are involved and also because each reservoir has a different success rate, the probability of each event differs. The probability of both zones being dry is 0.8×0.85, or 0.68—68%. At the other end of the spectrum, the probability of both pays being productive is only 0.03, a very small chance of 3 in 100. Therefore, the most probable

TABLE 17.1   Risking of a two-reservoir prospect

Potential Pays	Historic Probability of Success (*S*)	Dry (*D*)
Devonian	0.20	0.80
Ellenburger	0.15	0.85

Possible Events $(D,S)^2$†

	By Pay			
No.	**DV**	**EL**		**Probability of Occurrence***
1	*D*	*D*		$0.80 \times 0.85 = 0.68$
2	*D*	*S*		$0.80 \times 0.15 = 0.12$
3	*S*	*D*		$0.20 \times 0.85 = 0.17$
4	*S*	*S*		$0.20 \times 0.15 = \underline{0.03}$
			Total	1.00

Summary	No. of Events	Probability
All dry	1	0.68
1 successful, 1 dry	2	0.29
All successful	$\underline{1}$	$\underline{0.03}$
	4	1.00

Using the summary

Event	Probability
One or more discoveries (0.29 + 0.03)§	0.32

*Assumes *independent* variables
†$(D,S)^2 = (2)^2 = 4$
§Probability of finding anything

occurrence if the prospect becomes a discovery is only one productive reservoir. Remember, this entire exercise is contingent on our faith in the success rates assigned to the two reservoirs.

THE THREE-RESERVOIR PROSPECT

If we now expand to three possible reservoirs, we introduce additional cases. We have exactly the same number of possibilities as we did in our three-well wildcat program, shown on Table 7.2. The cases expand exponentially because we are dealing with the binomial $(D + S)^n$ where n is the number of possible pays and D and S the two possible outcomes for each pay. In the three-pay prospect the total possible events are $(2)^3 = 8$. There are eight possible events for the three formations as shown in Table 17.2.

In this example, a third reservoir is considered as possibly productive, the Fusselman. Three events produce only one successful pay and two dry. Three events result in two successful and one dry, but these events have a *much* lower probability (0.06) than one successful and two dry (0.33). The most-probable event, if a prospect is drilled and completed as a discovery, is one successful pay and two dry.

Note the small probability of three successes: only three chances in 1,000 that all three will be productive. The probability of three productive pays is a direct function of the success rates tied to each. The point illustrated by the three-formation example, with low individual success rates, is that the probability for all to be successful is very small. Even if each pay had a 30% chance of success, the probability of all being successful would be only 0.027, or about 3 chances in 100. Although small, the tenfold increase shows the high sensitivity of this event to modest changes in individual success rates.

In general, as the number of pays increases, the probability that all will be successful decreases rapidly. On the other hand, as the number of potential pays increases, the chance that all will be dry decreases, but slowly.

THE FOUR-RESERVOIR PROSPECT

The two points just expressed are even more aptly illustrated with a four-reservoir prospect. On Table 17.3 a fourth potentially productive pay is added: the Montoya. Its historic success rate is low, 10%, the same as the Fusselman.

Now the chance of all dry has gone down to 55%, meaning that there is a 45% chance of finding something, i.e., the chance of one or

TABLE 17.2   Risking of a three-reservoir prospect

Potential Pays	Historic Probability of Success (S)	Dry (D)
Devonian	0.20	0.80
Fusselman	0.10	0.90
Ellenburger	0.15	0.85

Possible Events $(D,S)^3$

No.	By Pay DV	FS	EL	Probability of Occurrence*
1	D	D	D	$0.80 + 0.90 \times 0.85 = 0.612$
2	D	D	S	$0.80 \times 0.90 \times 0.15 = 0.108$
3	D	S	D	$0.80 \times 0.10 \times 0.85 = 0.068$
4	S	D	D	$0.20 \times 0.90 \times 0.85 = 0.153$
5	D	S	S	$0.80 \times 0.10 \times 0.15 = 0.012$
6	S	S	D	$0.20 \times 0.10 \times 0.85 = 0.017$
7	S	D	S	$0.20 \times 0.90 \times 0.15 = 0.027$
8	S	S	S	$0.20 \times 0.10 \times 0.15 = \underline{0.003}$
				1.000

Event	Number of Events	Probability
All dry	1	0.61
Only 1 successful	3	0.33
Only 2 successful	3	0.06
All successful	$\underline{1}$	$\underline{\quad}$
	8	1.00

Using the summary

Event	Probability
One or more discoveries (0.33 + 0.06)	0.39
Two or more discoveries (0.06 + 0.00)	0.06

*Assumes *independent* variables

more successful pays. Note that the number of possible events has increased to 16. Our binomial here is $(D + S)^4$. The number of events is $(2)^4 = 16$. The probability of all four zones being productive is so low it is less than one chance in 1,000. Furthermore, the chance of three successful and one dry is 0.01 (1%), or 1 chance in 100. Again, the most-probable event is one productive formation and three dry (0.36).

Table 17.4 illustrates these two extremes if we assume uniform success rates for each reservoir. The only variable becomes the number of formations.

From this illustration we can see the rapid decrease in all reservoirs being successful as the number of pays increases. The more gentle decline in the probability of all dry is also clearly demonstrated.

The lesson from the illustrations involving multiple reservoirs for a prospect is simple: It takes a very high success rate for individual reservoirs to have a high-side case that considers all of them successful. This statement is not to infer that we do not have many producing fields that have more than one reservoir. If this is true in a given play, then the success rates for the individual pays should reflect this fact. But given low success rates for individual reservoirs, the probability that more than one will be productive is slight for the most-likely case, as has been demonstrated. Care should be exercised in determining a legitimate high-side case. You should feel there is at least a 1 in 10 chance of the case occurring, a 1 in 10 chance of having that size or more.

MULTIPLE RESERVOIRS WITH COMMON RISKS

Next, let's look at prospects whose reservoirs have common risks. Now we do not have independent variables for our geologic controls on hydrocarbon existence.

What happens when some factors affect the productivity of all of the potential pays, thus the risks are *not* independent? If a risk is common to all reservoirs on an individual prospect, then the calculation becomes a two-step process.[1] You first calculate the risks for individual reservoirs, then apply the common risk to all reservoirs in the group. The result is, as you would think, a larger dry risk—the probability of all being dry. There is a partial compensation in prospect potential in that if one formation is productive, the probability of the others being so is enhanced and the upper ranges of prospect sizes are increased. We shall dwell mostly on the concepts involving the chance of success and the dry risk.

For illustration purposes, the following conditions are assumed.

Given
   1. A prospect, Greenbriar, South, has three possible pays:
      • Devonian
      • Fusselman
      • Ellenburger

TABLE 17.3   Risking of a four-reservoir prospect

Potential Pays	Historic Probability of Success (S)	Dry (D)
Devonian	0.20	0.80
Fusselman	0.10	0.90
Montoya	0.10	0.90
Ellenburger	0.15	0.85

Possible Events $(D,S)^4$

No.	DV	FS	MT	EL		Probability of Occurrence*
1	D	D	D	D	$0.80 \times 0.90 \times 0.90 \times 0.85 =$	0.551
2	D	D	D	S	$0.80 \times 0.90 \times 0.90 \times 0.15 =$	0.097
3	D	D	S	D	$0.80 \times 0.90 \times 0.10 \times 0.85 =$	0.061
4	D	S	D	D	$0.80 \times 0.10 \times 0.90 \times 0.85 =$	0.061
5	S	D	D	D	$0.20 \times 0.90 \times 0.90 \times 0.85 =$	0.138
6	D	D	S	S	$0.80 \times 0.90 \times 0.10 \times 0.15 =$	0.011
7	D	S	D	S	$0.80 \times 0.10 \times 0.90 \times 0.15 =$	0.011
8	D	S	S	D	$0.80 \times 0.10 \times 0.10 \times 0.85 =$	0.007
9	S	S	D	D	$0.20 \times 0.10 \times 0.90 \times 0.85 =$	0.015
10	S	D	S	D	$0.20 \times 0.90 \times 0.10 \times 0.85 =$	0.015
11	S	D	D	S	$0.20 \times 0.90 \times 0.90 \times 0.15 =$	0.024
12	S	S	S	D	$0.20 \times 0.10 \times 0.10 \times 0.85 =$	0.002
13	S	S	D	S	$0.20 \times 0.10 \times 0.90 \times 0.15 =$	0.003
14	S	D	S	S	$0.20 \times 0.90 \times 0.10 \times 0.15 =$	0.003
15	D	S	S	S	$0.80 \times 0.10 \times 0.10 \times 0.15 =$	0.001
16	S	S	S	S	$0.20 \times 0.10 \times 0.10 \times 0.15 =$	0.000
						1.000

Summary	No. of Events	Probability
All dry	1	0.55
3 dry, 1 successful	4	0.36
2 dry, 2 successful	6	0.08
1 dry, 3 successful	4	0.01
All successful	1	—
	16	1.00

Using the summary

Event	Probability
One or more discoveries $(0.36 + 0.08 + 0.01)$	0.45
Two or more discoveries $(0.08 + 0.01)$	0.09
Three or more discoveries (0.01)	0.01

*Assumes *independent* variables

TABLE 17.4 Success and failure vary with increase in number of reservoirs

| No. of Reservoirs | Uniform Chance of Success, Each Reservoir | | | | | | | |
| | 10% | | 20% | | 30% | | 40% | |
	All S	All D	All S	All D	All S	All D	All S	All D
1	0.10	0.90	0.20	0.80	0.30	0.70	0.40	0.60
2	0.01	0.81	0.04	0.64	0.09	0.49	0.16	0.36
3	—	0.73	0.01	0.51	0.03	0.34	0.06	0.22
4	—	0.66	—	0.41	0.01	0.24	0.03	0.13
5	—	0.59	—	0.33	—	0.17	0.01	0.08
6	—	0.53	—	0.26	—	0.12	—	0.05

2. Two key geologic controls govern the existence of hydrocarbons: trap and source
3. The assumed independent success rate for each pay is:

Pay	Probability
DV	0.20
FS	0.10
EL	0.15

4. The chance of adequacy of the individual geologic controls and their relationship to the overall success rate is:

| | Probability for Controls | | | | Overall Probability |
	Trap		Source		
DV	0.50	×	0.40	=	0.20
FS	0.50	×	0.20	=	0.10
EL	0.40	×	0.375	=	0.15

Under these conditions the chance of at least one productive pay is one minus the probability that all reservoirs will be dry, or

$$1 - [(1 - 0.20) \times (1 - 0.10) \times (1 - 0.15)] =$$
$$1 - (0.8 \times 0.9 \times 0.85) = 1 - 0.612 = 0.388 \text{ or } 39\%$$

The chance of at least one productive pay is commonly referred to as the *success rate*.

Let's now assume that *source* risk is common to all reservoirs—that geologically if one pay has no source, the others do not either. Furthermore, we will assume, based on a survey of surrounding somewhat similar prospects, that our common source has only a 35% chance of being present on this structure.

Now our calculations of the chance of having at least one productive pay are much more related to a single risk and are calculated as follows

$$0.35\ [1 - (1 - 0.5) \times (1 - 0.5) \times (1 - 0.4)] =$$
$$0.35\ [1 - (0.5 \times 0.5 \times 0.6)] = 0.35\ (1 - 0.15) = 0.298$$

In this instance a common geologic control *lowers* the chance of at least one productive reservoir. Furthermore, the chance of success will always be less than the chance of adequacy of the common risk, i.e., 0.298 is less than 0.35.

One can prove this fact by examining several different levels of chance of adequacy for several reservoirs. To keep the illustration simple, we will deal again with only two geologic controls—trap and source—and we shall keep the chances of adequacy the same for each of the three pays. In one instance we shall consider the trap and source independent; in the other, source risk will be common to all reservoirs:

	Geologic Controls Chance of Adequacy (1 − Risk)		Chance of At Least One of Three Pays Productive	
Case	Trap	Source	Source Independent	Source Common
1	0.5	0.5	0.58	0.44
2	0.6	0.6	0.74	0.56
3	0.7	0.7	0.87	0.68

Three Possible Productive Pays

Sample calculations for case 3 are

$$0.7\ [1 - (1 - 0.7)^3] = 0.68 = \text{common source}$$
$$1 - (1 - 0.49)^3 = 0.87 = \text{independent source}$$

Note again the strong relationships for the three cases shown between the value of the common risk applied to each reservoir and the final success rate (chance of at least one productive). In the case of a common source, the success rate cannot exceed the chance of adequacy of the source. Also, a risk common to all reservoirs consistently lowers the chance of at least one productive well below the value for independent risks for reservoirs. *A general or commonly related risk reduces success rates.*

Table 17.5 shows another illustration of the mathematics involved in dealing with four reservoirs where the risks are either independent or common relative to individual geologic controls. If the chances of adequacy for all controls are independent, then the chance of at least one productive formation is 0.75. However, if the source is a group risk (common to all reservoirs), its probability is entered in the equation first, as shown, and the probability of at least one productive pay is lowered to 0.56.

TABLE 17.5   Risk analysis of multiple reservoirs

| Geologic Control | Chance of Adequacy | | | |
	DV	FS	MT	EL
Reservoir	0.80	0.70	0.80	0.80
Trap	0.60	0.50	0.60	0.70
Source	0.70	0.50	0.50	0.70
Overall chance (S)	0.34	0.18	0.24	0.39
Chance of dry (D)	0.66	0.82	0.76	0.61
	1.00	1.00	1.00	1.00

Chance of at least one productive = one minus the chance of all dry

Chance of at least one productive = $1 - (0.66 \times 0.82 \times 0.76 \times 0.61)$
  (one or more) $= 1 - 0.25 = 0.75$

If source is a group risk (common to all reservoirs) and is estimated at chance of adequacy (S) of 0.6, then the chance of at least one productive is:

$$
\begin{aligned}
&\quad\quad\quad \text{DV} \quad\quad\; \text{FS} \quad\quad\; \text{MT} \quad\quad\; \text{EL} \\
&= 0.6 \times [1 - (1 - 0.48)\,(1 - 0.35)\,(1 - 0.48)\,(1 - 0.56)] \\
&= 0.6 \times [1 - (0.52 \times 0.65 \times 0.52 \times 0.44)] \\
&= 0.6 \times [1 - (0.07)] \\
&= 0.6 \times 0.93 \\
&= 0.56
\end{aligned}
$$

TREE DIAGRAMS WITH MORE THAN ONE RESERVOIR

Obviously, the tree diagrams to illustrate prospect sizes and risks become more complicated with additional potential pays. Fig. 17.1 illustrates a prospect with several potential pays; the exact number need not be specified since it is our final decision as to the most probable occurrences that must be depicted. In the illustration several reservoirs have been considered, their individual success rates documented. It is estimated that there is a probability of 0.67 of one pay if the prospect is productive and a 0.33 probability that two pays may be productive. Each of these is then projected to a high-side, a most-likely, and a low-side case to show the two different conditions. The individual probabilities would be the multiples along the tree limbs, e.g., the probability for the high-side case with two zones is the product of $0.45 \times 0.33 \times 0.3 = 0.045$ or 4.5%. This illustration is only one means of handling more than one reservoir.

Another method might be to consider the high-side case as two reservoirs and the most-likely and low-side cases as variations on a one-reservoir case. In this instance you would have a tree diagram

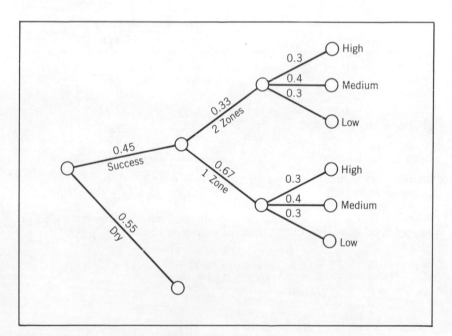

FIG. 17.1   Prospect tree diagram, six cases

similar to a single reservoir example with only one branch from the success limb of the tree diagram instead of two as shown in Fig. 17.1.

Each prospect is unique and so are the considerations for size, risk, and potentially productive pays. There are numerous ways multiple-pay situations can be handled. Consistency is again urged with a well-documented presale list of assumptions so that postsale results can be compared. We grow by learning from such comparisons.

REVIEW

This chapter has extended our look at risking prospects by examining the problem of multiple reservoirs, the difficulties associated with assigning the costs of the dry case to tracts and tree diagram concepts involving more than one reservoir. Because of the individuality of each prospect, a cookbook approach cannot be recommended that will answer all needs. Nevertheless, it is hoped that enough of the salient points have been reviewed to give the reader some pathways that will lead to proper risking and adequate consideration of all critical factors.

References

1. Gehman, H.M., R.A. Baker, and D.A. White. "Prospect Risk Analysis." *Probability in Oil Exploration*. AAPG Research Symposium, Stanford University, Preliminary Report, 1975, pp. 16–20.

CHAPTER 18

The ever-present overbid

S ince 1954 the federal government has held auctions for leases on the Outer Continental Shelf. The auctions are conducted by submitting sealed bids. The high bidder, if his bid is accepted, obtains the right to explore for oil and gas; if successful, he can develop and produce the field found. Although bidding methods vary, most involve a variable cash bonus plus a fixed or sliding-scale royalty from any production discovered.

We reviewed much of the available literature on competitive bidding in Chapter 15, including the classic paper by Capen et al.[1] An article by G. Rogge Marsh discusses the various bidding methods and compares them at a given set of conditions (field size, discount rate, etc.)[2] His article is of value to anyone wishing to compare the various bidding systems because it considers both the seller's and the buyer's positions.

One of the most frequently mentioned topics in any discussion of a sealed bid sale in the OCS is the amount of money "left on the table." This sum is most often called the *overbid*. In this chapter the characteristics of the overbid will be reviewed and its intrinsic nature to the sealed bid auction will be documented. The ultimate success of the bidder will not be reviewed. Final economic success depends on the discovery of new fields whose development will yield acceptable profits. We shall deal *only* with the explorer's first hurdle: winning tracts.

A DEFINITION OF OVERBID

The overbid has a fairly standard definition within the petroleum industry, partly the result of its use by the principal publication concerning each sale put out by the Offshore Oil Scouts Association. However, there have been other definitions or calculations of the

224

overbid in the media and in some reports about the industry. An overbid is "the amount of money the first bid exceeds the second bid."
When expressed as a percentage, this difference is always related to
the *winning* bid. Now, suppose there is no second bid? What then is
the overbid? Prior to 1983 the report sponsored by the Offshore Oil
Scouts Association (issued by Bonner & Moore) considered a single
bid an overbid of 100%. Most of the statistics shown in this chapter
are based on this concept. However, from 1983 onward the rules were
changed so that the minimum bid (required by the federal government) was considered the second bid and the overbid was then the
difference between the winning bid and the minimum bid. Keep this
in mind if you use the Bonner & Moore reports for years after 1983.
The change was really occasioned by a sharp increase in the minimum bid required by the federal government—from $25 to $150 per
acre. For this reason there are no historic data relative to the change
made in 1983.

Since the federal government evaluates many of the tracts put up
for lease, it is always a "silent" bidder. Thus, when tracts are rejected
by the government, and a few usually are, the overbid becomes mean-
ingless. Regardless of the change in definition, with the proper data
base you can correct the historic data and calculate an overbid dealing only with those tracts that have a second bid. Many feel this practice is the most realistic.

THE HISTORIC FACTS

Since the beginning of federal offshore sales in the OCS and Alaska
in 1954, overbids have averaged 51% of the winning bids. This percentage includes single bids as overbids. If we deal only with those
tracts that had a second bid, the overbid percentage drops to 45%.
The percent overbid varies slightly from area to area as shown by the
two segments of Table 18.1.

For all sales through 1982, the U.S. Treasury has received a total of
$21.5 billion in overbids. There is a modest difference between the
overbid percentage in a frontier and that in an established basin. As
will be shown later, part of this difference can probably be attributed
to the level of competition. This large average percentage over such a
long period of time should make us wonder if the overbid is not an
integral part of the bidding game in which bids are sealed and one
does not know another's bid.

Notice that the overbid was always related to the winning bid in
Table 18.1. It is not always calculated this way in various accounts of

TABLE 18.1   Federal sales (1954–1982)

			All Bids		
Area	No. of Sales	High Bid, $B	Overbid $B	%	Total Single Bids, $B*
GOM	56	31.8	15.8	50	3.3
ATL	7	2.9	1.7	57	0.2
PAC	9	4.1	2.2	54	0.3
AK	9	3.7	1.8	50	0.3
Totals	81	42.5	21.5	51	4.1
		Tracts with Two or More Bids			
GOM		28.5	12.5	44	
ATL		2.7	1.5	54	
PAC		3.8	1.9	51	
AK		3.4	1.5	45	
Totals		38.4	17.4	45	

*B = Billion

OCS lease sales in the media and in the financial houses reporting on sale results of participating companies. The different calculation is confusing to the uninformed reader because he is hearing two different percentages about the same event. Both are correct *if* adequately defined. An example of the preferred and usual calculation is as follows:

Winning Bid	Second Bid	Overbid
$10 million	$6 million	$(10 - 6)/10 = 0.4 \times 100 = 40\%$

Again, the overbid was stated as a function of the winning bid, not the second bid. In some reports regarding overbidding, we find the calculation as follows:

Winning Bid	Second Bid	Overbid
$10 million	$6 million	$(10 - 6)/6 = 0.67 \times 100 = 67\%$

It makes quite a difference which way the calculation is made, and you can easily see the confusion if both numbers are used by different writers to describe the same event. The distinction is drawn here so the normal practice will be noted and the obvious confusion demonstrated.

WHY OVERBIDDING EXISTS

It is the bane of the explorationist that he must always deal with a management that would like successful bids with essentially no overbid. However, as we shall see, this goal is impossible. The very manner in which bids are constructed plus the fact that little is known about competitive bids prohibits no overbids. A simple mathematical calculation shows why overbids are intrinsic to sealed bid sales because of the manner in which prospect potential is calculated. Note the following example:

Case	Pay, ft	Rec./Ac., bbl/ac-ft	Area, Acres	Reserve Size, bbl × 10^6
Base	100	100	1,000	10.0
+10%	110	110	1,100	13.3
−10%	90	90	900	7.3

In this example a base case calculation of reserves is made for an oil field with an estimated size of 10 million bbl. Two other examples are shown. One is 10% higher in each parameter; the other is lower by 10%. In effect, the spread between each parameter, i.e., the high and the low, is 20%. However, the difference between the high and low reserve estimate is not 20% (2.0 million bbl) but 6.0 million bbl. If the difference is related to the low estimate, the total difference becomes 83%.

The simple process of multiplication produces a much larger spread in the final answer than the change in any of the individual parameters. The spread is a consequence of an exponential relationship that explains the large difference between the first and second bid. This example is not meant to infer that each high bidder used the highest value for each parameter or that the lowest bidder used only the lowest values. One would expect mixtures of high and low values; however, the example does show that small variations in individual parameters produce much larger variations in the final product.

Not only is the difference a function of the difference between parameters, but it is also a function of the number of parameters involved:

	One Parameter	Three Parameters	Five Parameters
Calculation	$\dfrac{1.1x}{0.9x}$	$(1.22)^3 = 1.83$	$(1.22)^5 = 2.73$
Difference in Product	22%	83%	173%

The symbol x represents the various parameters, and in the calculation they cancel out. In the three cases shown, we are left with a ratio expressing the difference from the low estimate (in the one-parameter case, 22%). The exponent represents the number of parameters multiplied. As the number of parameters increases, the ratio between the low and high products of multiplication increases.

Product variations increase exponentially as parameters increase. This characteristic of prospect evaluation is the primary cause for the range of bonuses offered in multiple bids for a single tract. It produces, therefore, the ever-present, ubiquitous overbid.

MULTIPLE BIDS AND LOGNORMALITY

The bonus offered for a tract in any sealed bid sale is the result of multiplying a number of different factors. Since individual explorers can view each factor somewhat differently, it is not surprising that there is a wide variation in the bids submitted on individual tracts in a sealed bid sale. Fig. 18.1 represents an idealized example of five bids on a single tract. In a perfect lognormal distribution, bid values would be evenly spaced (in percentages) along a straight line on log probability paper. For purposes of analysis, Fig. 18.1 assumes such is the case.

In this idealized lognormal distribution the five bids and their characteristics are as follows:

Bid Rank	Bid, $\overline{M}$	Difference From Next-Higher Bid, $\overline{M}$
1	30.0	—
2	13.5	16.5
3	7.7	5.8
4	4.4	3.3
5	2.0	2.4

$\overline{M}$ = million dollars

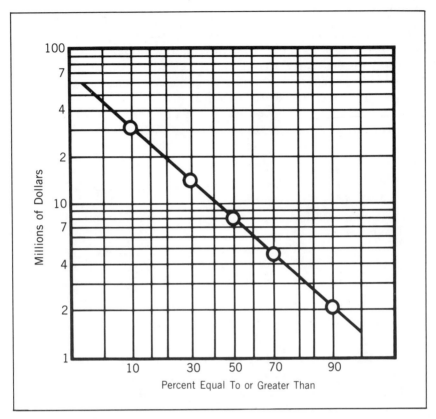

FIG. 18.1   Bids distributed lognormally

There is much empirical evidence to support lognormality for the distribution of bid values. An example is Paul Crawford's paper on Texas offshore bidding patterns described in Chapter 15.[3]

The five bids on Fig. 18.1 exhibit a sharply skewed distribution with more small values than large ones. Because the scale of bonus values is logarithmic, there is a large difference between the first and second bids: $16.5 million, a 55% overbid.

In the real world, bids do not line up this uniformly, but the illustration serves a purpose. It discloses the large percentage difference between the first and second bids when they are part of a lognormal distribution. Any multiplication process produces a suite of products (in this case bids) that will approximate a straight line when plotted on log-probability paper. Remember our experiment in Chapter 9 where we had several geologists multiply three geological controls? Because each used slightly different values, their estimated success rates produced a lognormal distribution. Again, we have evidence of the intrinsic nature of the overbid in the process of submitting sealed bids for tracts of land of unknown potential value.

Many uncertainties accompany the calculation of expected value in the assessment of oil and gas prospects. These uncertainties produce a lognormally distributed range of bid values when the trap and its potential petroleum and profit alike are evident to a large group of prospect buyers. However, other factors can modify lognormality in bid distributions on highly visible prospects:

1. Most bidders are risk adverse, i.e., the potential reward has decreasing incremental value to the risk taker as the expected value of the prospect increases to the high levels commonly seen in OCS bidding. Some refer to this aversion to risk as the *choke point*
2. In the Gulf of Mexico where 7 out of 10 OCS sales have taken place, the geologic limitations imposed by reasonably predictable structure and stratigraphy constrain the high side of trap potential

A departure from lognormality is sometimes observed in the smallest bids also. It is caused by at least three factors

1. The economic threshold for offshore fields, which concentrates competition on the larger opportunities perceived
2. The Department of the Interior's (DOI) minimum bid per acre
3. The threat of bid rejection

These factors eliminate some small bids that would be expected if the distribution were entirely lognormal. The result on portions of the curve showing high-side bids and small bids is sometimes an exponential distribution as the best fit for bids on some tracts.

TWO REAL-WORLD EXAMPLES

We mentioned that real-world examples of lognormal distributions do not line up as straight as the five points shown in Fig. 18.1. Two examples follow that show actual cases. The first is taken from the Gulf of Mexico. On Fig. 18.2 the nine bids on a tract in sale 69 are shown. The tract is West Cameron Block 202, and the sale was held in November 1982. Even though three bidders had similar evaluations for the tract at from $8–10 million, the nine bids ranged from almost $20 million to a low of about $120,000, a considerable range. You can see the approximate lognormality indicated by the solid line drawn through the points. It is not a perfect correlation, but it is adequate to show the rough lognormality of several bids on the same tract.

A second example is taken from an onshore sale involving sealed bids. It is deliberately chosen to illustrate that lognormality is not confined to an area but to the process called *sealed bidding*. The example shown is the lease sale involving the Dix Ranch in south Texas (see Fig. 18.3). Note the roughly lognormal trend of the 12 sealed bids. Also note the large difference between the first and second bids. Bid values are shown in dollars per acre rather than the total bonus. Getty submitted the winning bid; Exxon placed the second bid at roughly one-half Getty's bid.

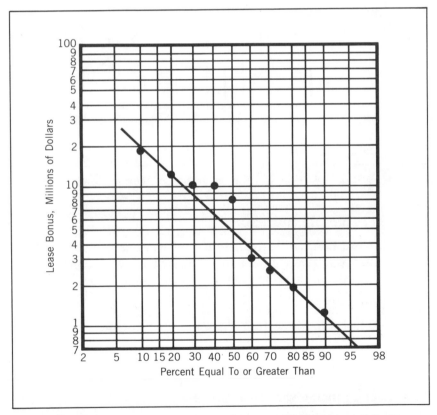

FIG. 18.2   Bids on West Cameron Block 202, Gulf of Mexico, Sale 69, November 1982

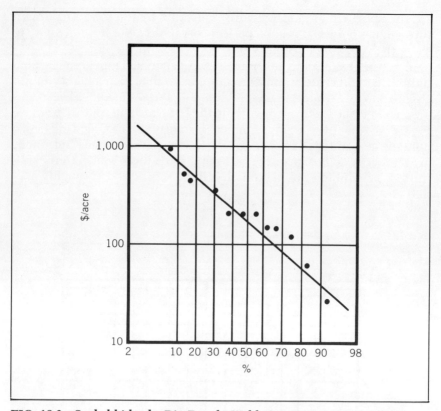

FIG. 18.3   Sealed-bid sale, Dix Ranch, Webb Co., Texas, March 2, 1981

SUCCESS IS ON THE HIGH SIDE

We can use another illustration to show what happens in a sealed-bid sale that produces winning bids with a high-side bias. One of the natural consequences of the sealed-bid sale is an average bid higher than the average of all bids submitted. We have said that only the bidder who is the most optimistic wins.

The 10 tracts in Table 18.2 illustrate this principle.

Given:
1. Ten tracts are for sale
2. Three companies bid on each tract
3. Each company wins some of the tracts

Now let's look at the bids submitted. On line one, we see in the last column that your bids averaged $26.5 million, i.e., $265 million was exposed by your 10 bids. Company A's average bid was $26 million. Company B's average bid of $21.5 million was the lowest of the group.

You win tracts 1, 3, and 7 because your bids are the most optimistic. Company A wins tracts 2, 6, 8, and 9 for the same reason. Company B's winning tracts were 4, 5, and 10.

Now see the end results. Your winning bids averaged $53.3 million per tract, Company A's average was $30 million, and Company B's winning bids averaged $33.3 million per tract. In each case the winning average was significantly higher than the average of the 10 tracts.

TABLE 18.2　A sealed-bid sale of 10 tracts, U.S.A., OCS

	Tracts										Average Value
	1	2	3	4	5	6	7	8	9	10	
Your bids	50	10	40	30	5	15	70	10	30	5	26.5
Company A's bids	40	30	20	10	15	30	40	20	40	15	26.0
Company B's bids	10	20	10	40	20	10	60	5	10	30	21.5
Your winning bids	50		40				70				53.3
Company A's winning bids		30				30		20	40		30.0
Company B's winning bids				40	20					40	33.3

You only win when you are the highest bidder. Because bid value is directly related to your estimate of prospect potential and risk, it is possible that the winner overestimated the reserve size of the tract he won; and he may have underestimated the prospect size of tracts lost. Because only the largest estimate wins, the winner loses any benefit he might have had from averaging the 10 tracts.

Finally, although your bids on the two tracts with the highest prices were larger than those of Companies A and B, your bids exceeded the second bid in each case by only $10 million.

Table 18.2 illustrates a natural phenomenon produced by a sale involving sealed bids. The consequence is that the winner gets only those tracts on which he has the largest estimate of prospect potential or the lowest dry risk. We should not be surprised, therefore, to find that presale, most-likely estimates (on a productive basis) are larger, on the average, than the actual reserves found. It is a consequence of the bidding process.

THE ROLE OF COMPETITION

We discussed the role of competition briefly in Chapter 15. Competition is by far the most important unknown factor in the bid equation. Potential bidders or combines of bidders may be known prior to a sale or assumed from past practices. But each sale is unique: in time, in geologic setting, in its economic environment for the companies as well as the nation, and in the manner in which it may be viewed by a specific company. The factor of competition causes the greatest pondering by top management. Value, right or wrong, can be assessed and risked, but what competition will do can only be implied with extremely limited accuracy. No company is completely consistent in its bidding strategy. The record is sprinkled with individual companies that completely misread the competition for a specific sale, and the misreading can go both ways—an overestimation or an underestimation of competition.

There is, however, another factor. In producing trends competition is primarily on a tract by tract basis. Differences in perceived value produce different bids on the same tract. Oil and gas accumulations tend to be present in groups of related fields or plays. The normal OCS leasing unit is either 5,760 acres or 2,304 hectares (about 5,693 acres). The tracts are smaller than most geologic plays, so there is a strong positive dependency between play risk and tract risk in frontier basins. Two bidders may develop similar volumetric assessments on a tract basis but bid very differently. In frontier basins a company must evaluate a total potential for a basin or play. Here the associated geologic and economic risks control participation in a sale and, consequently, the order of magnitude of bids on tracts. An optimistic appraisal by one company or bidding group can cause that group or company to sweep the sale with high overbids, with most of the competition unexpectedly shut out.

Table 18.3 lists 15 sales where a single company spent 26% or more of the total bonus, and it shows the top bidder in each sale. It is safe to assume that in almost all instances the company with the large percentage of the bonus spent did not believe, prior to the sale, that its success would be so high. The variety of companies involved shows clearly that no single company is immune to misjudging competition. The data on Table 18.3 emphasize, again, the possibilities that exist to misread the competition completely for a specific sale.

Note also the overbids. The highly successful bidders had, in all but 4 of the 15 instances, a significantly higher overbid than the average for all successful companies, shown as the industry. The spread

TABLE 18.3   Highest participation sales and leading bidder, company net basis (1967–1981) (Sales in which a single company spent more than 25% of the total bonus)

	Percent of Total Bonus	Date	Area	Company	Bonus $M*	Co.	Industry
		Sale				Overbid, %	
1	86	10/80	GOA	Arco	94	58	59
2	49	10/77	C.I.	Phillips	196	80	65
3	49	12/81	M. Atl.	Shell	157	80	79
4	40	5/68	Texas	Texaco	235	48	47
5	36	2/68	Calif.	Exxon	218	66	47
6	33	12/79	Bf. Sea	Exxon	347	54	49
7	33	3/78	S. Atl.	Exxon	33	63	73
8	30	2/76	GOM	Gulf	53	13	44
9	30	8/76	M. Atl.	Exxon	343	54	36
10	29	12/79	N. Atl.	Mobil	241	79	67
11	28	5/81	Calif.	Chevron	621	63	54
12	28	5/81	Calif.	Phillips	620	63	54
13	27	2/75	GOM (TX)	Shell	75	87	71
14	27	6/77	GOM	Gulf	314	48	51
15	26	4/76	GOA	Shell	148	48	38
Total					3,695		

*$\overline{M}$ = Million
GOA = Gulf of Alaska; C.I. = Cook Inlet; Bf = Beaufort; GOM = Gulf of Mexico

varies from sale to sale and may be partly a function of the uniqueness of each sale as well as a misreading of competition.

Most OCS discoveries were probably evaluated accurately presale by *some* bidder. Unfortunately, the winner gave up much of the profit he might have obtained because his bid exceeded the next bidder by 40–50%.

Thus, we see again the "winner's curse" as described in Chapter 15. If a bidder could win all of the tracts on which he bids, he would win some of the low estimates as well as the high ones. If there were 10 bids, the property was recognized by 10 bidders as having a prospect with possible commercial value. However, there were nine other companies who thought less of the property than the winner, a sobering thought for management.

The greater the competition, the greater the number of companies who think less of a given tract than the winner; yet each wanted the tract, even though his value was not the winning one. A few companies deliberately bid more conservatively, or not at all, if they feel that competition on a tract will be intense. Capen et al. espouse such a strategy. Other companies bid value and let the chips fall where they may. There are probably as many different bidding strategies as there are bidders, but we must assume that all begin with some concept of value and diverge from there to a substrategy.

One might assume that overbids would vary from frontier (unproductive) basins to established basins. However, as shown in Table 18.1, there is only one percentage point difference between the Gulf of Mexico average overbid and that of the nine sales in Alaska. On the other hand, there is a 10-percentage-point spread between the Atlantic, a frontier, and the Gulf.

OVERBIDDING AS A FUNCTION OF BIDS PER TRACT

Dougherty and Lohrenz demonstrated that the overbid is a function of the number of bids per tract.[4] Obviously, the greater the number of bids per tract, the greater the competition for that tract. This competition tends to reduce the percent of overbid. This general tendency can be demonstrated by looking at the sales as a whole, with each sale plotted as a single point.

Fig. 18.4 is such a plot. It includes all federal sales from 1962 through 1981. Single bids are included as an overbid of 100% in this plot; but, as shown by Table 18.1, the monetary volume is not sufficient to distort seriously the general conclusions.

Two sales appear almost as extraneous points:

1. The December 1970 sale in the Gulf of Mexico where 1,043 bids were submitted on 117 tracts (8.9 bids per tract with a 41% overbid)
2. The third mid-Atlantic sale of December 1981 where 240 bids were submitted on 50 tracts (4.8 bids per tract with a 79% overbid)

These highly competitive sales, one a frontier and the other in a mature established basin, are omitted from the least-squares fit of the data points shown in Fig. 18.4. The correlation coefficient for the trend line plotted is 0.65. If the two sales listed above are included, the correlation coefficient is lowered to 0.51.

One can clearly see from Fig. 18.4 a general tendency for the percent overbid to decrease as the number of bids per tract increases. Increased competition decreases the percentage difference between the first and second bids.

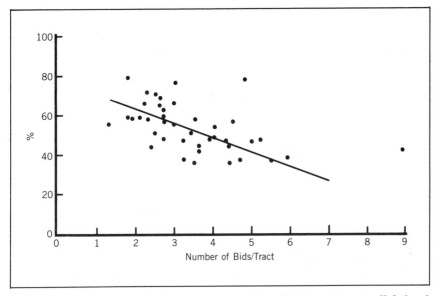

FIG. 18.4   Percent overbid vs average number of bids per tract, all federal sales for 1962–1981

THE HISTORIC PERSPECTIVE

Now let's look at a historic perspective of sales to track the changes in overbid percentage. Fig. 18.5 shows the history of federal lease sales in the Gulf of Mexico since 1954. The total amount of high bids per sale is plotted on a three-year average to smooth the cycles of bidding over 28 years. The scale for this curve is on the left. The percent overbid per sale is also plotted as a three-year moving average, with its scale on the right.

The first peaks of lease bonus investment occur in the period 1972–1974 and were the industry's response to price increases, the OPEC embargo, and the rapid, widespread adoption of seismic modeling techniques for identifying and quantifying gas accumulations. During this period of intense competition, overbids dropped to 40%. When exploration groups could find little of interest during many of the sales between 1975 and 1978, the average overbid percentage climbed to 60%. The higher percentage was the result of less competition because during this four-year period there was a slight but noticeable decrease in the average number of bids per tract.

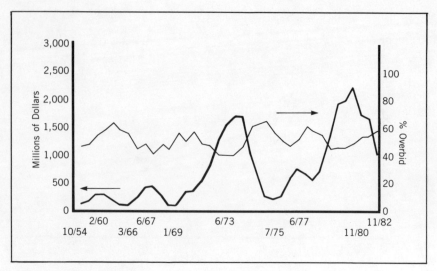

FIG. 18.5 Total high bids in 41 sales, Gulf of Mexico, 1954–1982 (3-sale average)

Rapidly increasing oil and gas prices in 1979 and 1980 brought more bidders with record bonuses to vie for new profit opportunities. Higher prices caused a drop in the threshold size of fields needed for economic development. The percent overbid dropped back to the mid-40s again as competition increased.

The last three points show a sharp reversal. This change is related to the oversupply of oil and gas that existed beginning about 1981. It is also related to much lower expectations by the industry for future price increases at the wellhead for crude oil and natural gas.

Thus, the percent of overbid does respond to competitive changes. However, a linear regression with time of the overbid percentages for the entire 28-year period produces a line that is virtually flat. In other words, the industry has not been able to lower its overbid percentage over a long period of time.

Over 500 oil and gas fields have been found on the acreage purchased in the 41 lease sales shown by Fig. 18.4. The average size of the fields in the Gulf of Mexico is about 55 million bbl of oil equivalent (boe). In the late 1970s sizes were smaller. Despite the drop in size, bidders made record bonus offers in quest of new hydrocarbon resources. Even with the explosion of exploratory data and the industry's ability to process these data during three decades of discovery in the Gulf of Mexico, the ubiquitous overbid is still alive and well at about 45% (50% if single bids are included as 100% overbids). The billions of dollars in overbids paid to the U.S. government by the oil industry for the right to explore in the public domain have maximized the revenues from lease bonuses.

Sales of OCS tracts involving sealed bids represent a paradoxical situation for the bidders. They recognize that the distribution of bids is roughly lognormal. The sale data for most of history also show the overbid varying, on the average, between 40% and 60%. So for each sale the bidder is faced with this long history in mind. But a key element that makes it difficult to lower the overbid is the inability to predict competition. We have demonstrated the significance of reserve size differences. We know that there are other key elements, some of which will be reviewed later. But competition is a key element that has defied solution, proved by both Table 18.1 and Fig. 18.5. If we look only at sales from 1976 to 1981, the average number of bids per tract was 4.3, corresponding to the 45% overbid. However, if the average bids per tract drop to three, the expected overbid would be 59%. These relationships can be confirmed by checking Fig. 18.4.

Remember, we have dealt only with results of the bidding strategy. Nothing has been said about which tracts are productive or about the ultimate economic consequences.

THE GEOMETRIC AVERAGE AND THE MMS

The Minerals Management Service (MMS) has used the geometric mean of the industry bids plus its own evaluation as a measure of tract value. This value is then used as a factor in determining the basis for rejecting certain bids. The geometric average is commonly 25% of the high bid and 50% of the second bid when there is a large number of bidders. If the geometric mean is a measure of *fair* market value, certainly the federal government must be pleased with the large multiple of this value received on high-interest tracts.

The U.S. government in various periods of the OCS history has received large sums of money from bonuses for tracts leased. Each bonus, of course, includes the overbid, itself a large number. In the Gulf of Mexico alone, from January 1975 to January 1983, the money received in *overbids* amounted to over $9 billion. This sum exceeds the total drilling cost of the roughly 2,500 exploratory and development wells drilled on those leases through January 1983. The overbid is part of the preinvestment in a lease and is a large part of the cost of operating in the OCS. It probably has reduced the rate of return of the petroleum industry on U.S. offshore operations by from three to five percentage points.

ORAL BIDDING

Oral bidding is sometimes suggested as the answer to overbidding. In this type of auction, the tract would be placed up for bid, and any interested participant would bid against competition until the price was so high he was no longer willing to bid. Oral bidding is used by some states and several of the Indian tribes in their sales of oil and gas leases. Although there is no proof that oral bidding raises less cash for the seller, it seems certain that it can reduce overbids. There has been a minimal amount of experimentation in this area. A series of experiments by Coppinger et al. confirms the intuitive view that the sealed bid auction is "preferred since it tends to provide the highest prices."[5] The reduction in overbids in itself could mean less cash for the seller, depending upon the bidding strategy of the second-highest bidder.

There is another intuitive reason to believe that oral bidding might reduce the price paid for tracts. In such bidding the eventual winner has much more information about his competition. It seems unreasonable to believe that the ultimate second bidder would consistently exceed his maximum value for a tract by 45% (the average overbid); so the winning bidder theoretically has this range in which to win.

With this preliminary discussion, let's examine some of the pros and cons of an auction using oral bidding. On the positive side:

1. It would produce essentially no overbidding because the winning bid would be slightly larger than the second bid
2. It would provide companies with broader bidding options. A losing bidder could quickly reallocate his bonus budget to remaining tracts
3. The money saved from no overbids would be reallocated to finding and developing other prospects
4. It would raise the return for the bidder, and in some instances properties would be developed that are now surrendered because the lease write-off exceeds the present value of the reserve to be developed
5. It would provide a *realistic fair market value* for leases receiving bids
6. More ideas by more operators would be tested with money saved by oral bidding. The results would produce more discov-

eries and greater economic benefit for both industry and government

On the negative side:

1. The government would probably receive less money in the near term. Some would be recovered in taxes on higher profits from leases that became productive
2. It would draw more criticism about receiving less than *maximum* market value

———————————————————————————————

REVIEW

With these facts behind us, what can we say about the sealed bid process and its relationship to overbidding?

1. Overbidding is an intrinsic part of sealed bidding
2. Overbidding probably appeals most to Congress as the answer to the cry for "fair" market value for the tracts leased
3. Prior studies by Capen et al. and Capen[6] have shown that the economic result of sealed bid sales is a tendency to depress a company's rate of return below what might have been obtained
4. Because of the depression of rates of return, the government is the chief beneficiary of the sealed bid system
5. The consumer has the satisfaction that his government has submitted its tracts in an open sale (although by sealed bid) with no limits on entrants
6. Sales by sealed bid are an optional investment. No company has to play this difficult game if it does not think it can win at the odds presented. And there are some specific sales where companies have stayed away in droves

As long as the auctions for leases in the OCS are by sealed bid, substantial overbids will occur. Overbids are an intrinsic part of the sealed-bid auction and 40 years of history show that the percent overbid varies but modestly over time.

Furthermore, no single company's successful bidding has been without overbids, nor has any single company consistently beaten the average overbid of the industry. Including only those tracts receiving a second bid, the average overbid has been 45% from the beginning of sealed bid sales in the OCS. Overbids are ubiquitous in sealed-bid sales.

References

1. Capen, E.C., R.V. Clapp, and W.M. Campbell. "Competitive Bidding in High Risk Situations." *Journal of Petroleum Technology*, June 1971, p. 641.
2. Marsh, G. Rogge. "An Analysis of Methods For Leasing the U.S. Outer Continental Shelf." *Journal of Petroleum Technology*, July 1980, p. 1262.
3. Crawford, Paul B. "Texas Offshore Bidding Patterns." *Journal of Petroleum Technology*, March 1970, pp. 283–289.
4. Dougherty, E.L., and J. Lohrenz. "Statistical Analyses of Bids For Federal Offshore Leases." *Journal of Petroleum Technology*, November 1976, p. 1377.
5. Coppinger, Vicki M., Vernon L. Smith, and Jon A. Titus. "Incentives and Behavior in English, Dutch and Sealed Bid Auctions." *Economic Inquiry*, Vol. 18, January 1980.
6. Capen, E.C. "The Difficulty of Assessing Uncertainty." *Journal of Petroleum Technology*, August 1976, p. 843.

Megill, R.E., and R.B. Wightman. "The Ubiquitous Overbid." *AAPG Bulletin*, April 1984. (This chapter draws heavily from this paper. Permission granted for such use by the American Association of Petroleum Geologists.)

CHAPTER 19

The fundamentals of risk analysis

T he final chapter summarizes the principles involved in the analysis of risk. We will be summing up the fundamentals, commenting on some problems inherent in all risk analysis, and reviewing the steps in setting up a solution to a problem requiring risk analysis.

First, a review of the fundamental concepts necessary for the best analysis of risk.

THE FUNDAMENTALS

In the search for new oil and gas fields, risk analysis takes the judgments of explorationists and engineers and translates them into the language of probability. Risk analysis thus helps a manager make reasonable decisions where the key parameters have considerable uncertainty.

The mathematical models used to synthesize risk analysis employ Monte Carlo simulation. Occasionally we find the mistaken conclusion that Monte Carlo simulation is risk analysis. The word *simulation* is the clue. The judgments we input as probability distributions can be summed to a final distribution. That distribution simulates our concept of the risks involved. It is only as good as our input. It takes into account only the variables submitted.

1. The first fundamental of risk analysis, then, is this: You must know enough about your proposed analysis to isolate the key variables. An obvious or inadvertent omission will result in poor output. It may be so poor, in fact, that you have not analyzed the real risk at all. Furthermore, we constantly face the

danger, when facts are few, that our concept of how a parameter may vary is extremely limited.

2. After isolating the key variables, you must find a means to quantify these variables. Unfortunately, quantification faces problems.

For example, Table 19.1 illustrates the varying amounts of data affecting drilling decisions. The table is based on the premise that for objective probability we have some real-world empirical experience upon which to base probabilities or quantification. Subjective probability stems from essentially no data.

On the first line of Table 19.1, development drilling, we have the most information. The statistical base here gives a reasonable view of the future and some assurance of real-world probabilities. Development drilling typifies objective probability.

Outpost drilling contains less data and therefore requires some subjective judgments. Wildcat drilling in a mature trend has a reasonable data base but more subjective judgments. In a frontier we may have extremely limited data. Some theorists would say that in wildcat drilling we have no data base from which to estimate probabilities. Others would say your opinions—technical judgments or gut feelings—are a form of subjective probability.

In prior chapters we used single-number estimates of probability (geologic success estimates) and triangular distributions to quantify key variables. The choice depends upon the mathematical model used and how your data are input. Sometimes data are so few that the geologist faces a real dilemma in trying to describe his uncertainty.

On Fig. 19.1 we see the situation faced by many explorationists. With few facts, many explorationists feel comfortable only

TABLE 19.1   Objective vs. subjective probability

Type of Drilling	Type of Probability	
	Objective	Subjective
Development	X	
Outpost	X	X
Wildcat—mature trend	X	X
Wildcat—frontier		X

with words, such as poor, fair, good, or excellent. The theorist says numerical expression allows the discipline of math to describe dissimilar opportunities with greater consistency and adequacy. But when the facts are few, our opinions range widely. We should expect it to be so. Even quantifying the words poor, fair, good, and excellent can be done in more than one way, as shown in Fig. 19.1.

Despite the fears associated with quantification the second fundamental is absolutely necessary. Use your best judgment and find a satisfactory method of quantifying your uncertainty.

3. Another fundamental consideration in risk analysis involves your basic view of uncertainty. Most parameters have up-side and down-side possibilities in addition to a most-probable value. Your view of a parameter should reflect both the up side as well as the down side. A triangular distribution does reflect these values, one reason for its popularity.

It is in time-related variables that the possibility exists for a limited view of the variable. Fig. 19.2 illustrates this problem. Here are two views of uncertainty; on the left is what some have called the cone of uncertainty. It reflects, in forecast form, both positive and negative views of the future. On the right is what an associate calls the horsetail view of uncertainty. Only negative tomorrows are viewed here. This view asks only what alternatives can produce bad results. White et al. have shown that even extrapolations related to time can be constructed to give the up-side and down-side extrapolations on a basis related to history.[1]

In quantifying any parameter, consider the good outcomes as well as the possibly bad outcomes.

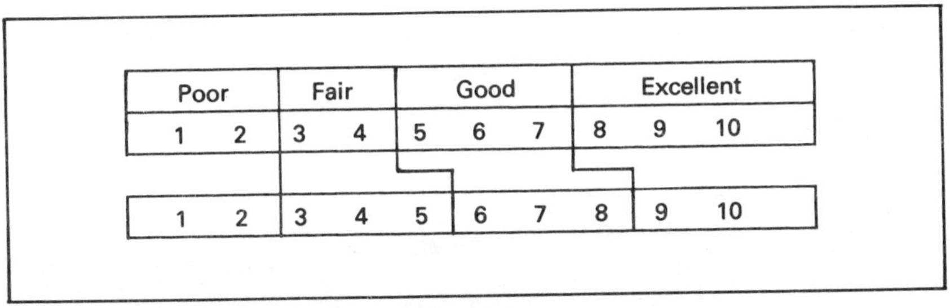

FIG. 19.1   Expressing uncertainty: ranking a variable

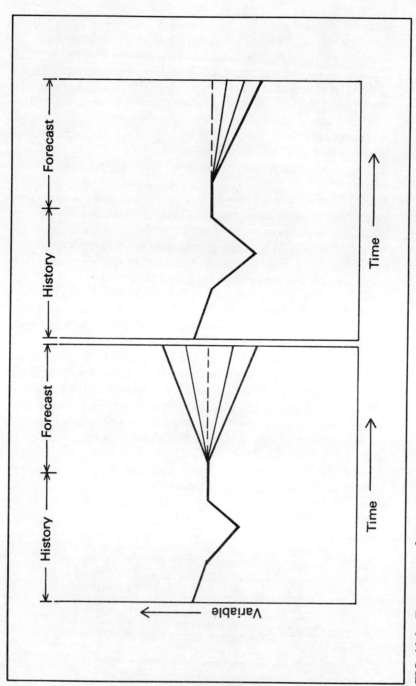

FIG. 19.2   Two views of uncertainty

4. A fourth fundamental of risk analysis involves understanding your model. Even if your model is a simple equation, you should comprehend its affect on your input. This admonition was stated in Chapters 10 and 11 regarding triangular distributions, but it applies equally to the model itself.

   If you don't have or can't understand a mathematical consultant, you can test your model independently. Substitute a range of cases and illustrations until you understand the effect on the output of the changing conditions of your input.

   One of the dangers of the computer age is that users assume the programs are all written properly. Often a program may have some flaw not detected by the user. A hand-calculated case, obviously simple as a matter of convenience, will often expose a false concept or equation in your model.

5. A most important fundamental of risk analysis was brought out in Chapter 14. In the discussion on the Delphi method, one fundamental was stressed: put your estimates of probability into your key variables *before* simulation in your model. Don't massage the final answer (except in the next case discussed) for probability adjustments; go back to the basic ingredients. There you have a better grasp of the limits, and your input should reflect your judgments at that point. An exception to this occurs in point six.

6. The scientist, analyst, or forecaster must constantly strive for credibility. He achieves what credibility is possible—and complete credibility is never possible for the unknown—by tying to reality.

   A fundamental of risk analysis, therefore, is to search for reality checks. These can be found by comparison to similar but known situations, by correlation, or by checks of limits set by reality. Search, then, for means to support credibility.

   If you hold your answers up to the light of reality and you don't like the result, what then? Go back to your input. *Answers in risk analysis are only as sound as their weakest assumption.* Reexamine your input and see what factor produced the questionable answer.

   Some examples of answers lacking credibility or at least rating a recheck of the input are:

   a. The mean field size estimated is larger than any field yet discovered in the trend

   b. Your composite geologic success factor for a number of prospects is greater than the trend average

    c. Your assessment of a basin produces recoveries higher than comparable basins in the world

    d. Your field sizes produce well sizes (bbl or bcf per well) larger than previously known in the trend

       Many other examples are possible. Each of these four examples shows cause for rechecking, even though the analysis may be showing you the right answer. You could have the best prospect in the trend; your basin could be better than similar basins around the world; your sand thickness could be above the average for the trend. Nevertheless, for credibility's sake you need a ready explanation for why you think so, and you may have to go back to your beginning assumptions to substantiate your case.

7. As a final fundamental, express the uncertainty of your solution in the form of a cumulative probability distribution. Such a distribution best expresses the range of uncertainty in a complex problem or projection. In addition:

    a. It demonstrates the fallacy of a single answer

    b. It illustrates all foreseeable answers based on your estimates of uncertainty

    c. It provides a mean value and shows the most frequently occurring values at its steepest slope

    d. It reminds us again that we do our managers a disservice when we show only a single answer to a problem, forecast, or projection that has great uncertainty

THE NEVER-ENDING PROBLEMS ASSOCIATED WITH RISK ANALYSIS

After you have done your very best in setting up an analysis of risk, have made reality checks, and have satisfied yourself that you have considered all of the right variables, you will still have problems. Many of them are never-ending.

Yearn for Certainty

One example is management's natural yearn for certainty. In a large corporation much time is spent trying to reduce risks as much as possible. Sometimes this yearn for certainty makes us victims of the search for a single answer. The worst thing an analyst can do for a manager is to obscure the line between what is known and what is unknown.

Cut It in Half

Another problem in risk analysis is associated with the "cut-it-in-half" manager. We've all met one. Maybe you've been one! The idea is that if it still looks good with half the reserves, it's safe. Let's face a fact, however: one misses some good deals with such a pessimistic view of the future. For every cut-it-in-half manager we may need a "two-times" manager. The future can be both positive and negative. If every analysis faces a 50% cut, a lot of time and money may be wasted on risk analysis. You don't really look at the risks when you cut it in half, and you are ignoring all prior risking. It is a true example of double-dipping your risking process.

The reason this problem will never completely go away is that in most corporations the penalty for errors of commission is several times greater than penalties for errors of omission.

Overoptimism

One problem in risk analysis particularly affects explorationists. Our profession, because of its high chances for failure, puts a premium on optimism and on selling geologic ideas. Sometimes this aspect gets out of hand. It results in oversell, and we inadvertently blind ourselves to the flaws in our analysis. Optimism *is* important, but so is realism.

Experience

Strangely, one problem is experience. Judgment and experience are important. They are just as important today as at any period in history. ("Judgment comes from experience and experience from bad judgment.") However, in a rapidly changing world, experience can be a handicap. Each of us needs to have the humility to remember the new ideas we rejected—ideas that later proved successful. It's no crime to be limited by our experiences. It's a shame, however, to have our experiences result in a closed mind.

The All-important Outcome

A big problem in risk analysis and decision-making under vast uncertainty is separating the right decision from the outcome. Uncertainty means the outcome can have wide variance. Often a good tactical decision is made, but the outcome is poor. Unfortunately, the world of reality tends to judge the quality of a decision only by the outcome. Often "Monday-morning quarterbacks" don't have all of the facts or choose to ignore a few.

Good outcomes can come from bad decisions and poor outcomes can result from good decisions. When a bad decision is obscured by serendipity or a fortuitous outcome, risk analysis takes a ribbing. However, in a long-term game of high risks, you will go broke without an intelligent, consistent way to handle risk.

ASSESSING UNCERTAINTY

No discussion of the fundamentals of risk analysis would be complete without a brief review of one of the key papers evaluating an important element in risking—that of our own inability to assess the degree of uncertainty. The classic paper on this subject is the one referred to earlier by E.C. Capen.[2]

In this important paper Capen addressed the degree to which all of us overestimate our ability to deal with the uncertain. In the absence of knowledge (or to put it more harshly, in our ignorance), we all tend to think we know more than the facts ultimately reveal. The result, as revealed by several examples by Capen, is that we tend to *underestimate* the degree of uncertainty when we have no precise quantitative background data upon which to rely.

In a number of experiments conducted before local sections of the Society of Petroleum Engineers, Capen asked several questions for which the answers were probably not known to the audience. He did not ask for specific answers but only a range that included the right answer (think of the 10th and 90th percentiles as a range of 80%). What Capen found was that, regardless of the range asked for, about two-thirds of the answers did not fall within the range specified. In other words, we all think we know more than we really do when faced with absolute uncertainty.

Capen's practical answer to this dilemma is to ask for a range, say, of 80% and then, given the range, assume that it is really only a 30% or 40% range. Using this approach the extremes become much greater for the estimator, and the chance of the range including the right answer increases remarkably. He also commented that persons using a Monte Carlo simulation to get their ranges uniformly had better ranges and that the true answer was included in their final range.

To expand your understanding of the uncertainties of risk analysis, the paper is recommended reading. It is one of the most important contributions to this subject in the past decade.

A REVIEW OF STEPS IN RISK ANALYSIS

Our previous section on the fundamentals of risk analysis is almost in itself a step-by-step approach to an analysis of risk. Nevertheless, a brief review will reiterate the significant steps in an analysis of risk.

1. Gather your data. A normal start in any analysis, this step is no less important for an analysis of risk. One of the initial things you want to discover is how much is not known.
2. Isolate the key variables. Past experience may have to be a key. On the other hand, you may not know what some of the key variables are until you have gone through the problem and run some sensitivity cases.
3. Quantify the key variables. Triangular distributions are recommended for uncertain variables with many possible answers. For other variables, consider the positive as well as the negative to avoid overrisking. For exploratory problems remember the important significance of lognormality.
4. Be sure that your concepts of uncertainty are put in at the variable level, not at the final answer level.
5. Enter your input into whatever model you use.
6. Check the answer for reality; protect your credibility.
7. Express the final answer in the form of a cumulative frequency distribution. This approach will not let you fall victim to the single-answer syndrome. In a very uncertain investment (one with many possible outcomes), the probability of a single value being the answer is near zero.

We need to remember one last concept. Every complex business decision has to be made in light of the relevant facts that are known— but also in recognition of what is unknown and possibly unknowable.

Risk analysis provides insights when the unknown is a major factor. It helps sort out reasonable approaches from many possible approaches.

Current concepts of risk analysis, although far from perfect, do provide better insights about investments with great uncertainty.

THE RISK OF THE UNIQUE EVENT

Exploration is a process that commits company funds to an unknown future. The unknowns involve not only geologic uncertainty but a number of critical economic factors such as price, cost, inflation, and possible changes in tax laws. Exploratory funds, therefore, are committed to a sum of unknowable expectations—not to facts.

It is this challenge that lends excitement to the search for oil and gas fields. It is this element that constantly reminds the explorationist that risk is the essence of his business—that risk taking represents the basic and constantly underlying principle of his work.

All business enterprises face risks and unknowns. The important difference for the explorationist is the number of times he is faced with a unique, unrepeatable investment opportunity for which there is no prior experience or statistical probability to guide his decision.

The explorationist understands that he can never eliminate risk from his work. But he also knows that the best results from his efforts will be that management will have taken the right risks.

References

1. White, D.A., et al. "Assessing Regional Oil & Gas Potential." from *Methods of Estimating the Volume of Undiscovered Oil and Gas Reserves.* AAPG Studies in Geology No. 1, 1975, p. 143.
2. Capen, E.C. "The Difficulty of Assessing Uncertainty." *Journal of Petroleum Technology*, August 1976, p. 843.

Epilogue

I f the goals set forth in the beginning of this book have been achieved, then your further reading in the arena of risk analysis will be easier. You will have mastered and gained new insights into some of the fundamentals of the analysis of risk. You are the judge.

There are other areas of study in the field much more complex yet deserving of study. Utility theory, Bayesian concepts, and more complex statistical applications would add to your knowledge. This introduction should make these additional readings easier to absorb and use.

The many ideas and theories relating to the analysis of risk are being challenged today and have always been challenged.[1,2] Until more professionals understand both the benefits and limitations of risk analysis, managers will go on making difficult decisions without the help of a better understanding of the dimensions of their decision. The real challenge of risk analysis is to the teacher who must find simple, semimathematical means of explaining difficult concepts. He must also, if given the opportunity, show that his methods can produce results not only better than other methods but at less cost. Once this is accomplished he will find a ready audience for his work.

Additional Reading

1. Hall, William K. "Why Risk Analysis Isn't Working." *Long Range Planning*, December 1975, p. 25.
2. Carter, E.S. "What Are the Risks of Risk Analysis." *Harvard Business Review*, 1972, pp. 72–82.

Appendix A • triangular distribution

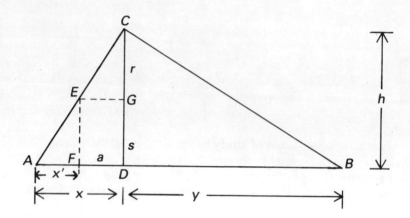

Given:

$$h = r + s$$
$$a = x - x'$$

The purpose of this appendix is to show that the area of any part of a triangle can be expressed as a percentage of the total triangle in terms of values of the base line.

Before proceeding further, however, please refer to the Reference Triangle, which is the last page of this appendix. Its purpose is to familiarize you with the basic segments of the triangle that will be used in the appendix. Below the triangle you will find definitions of the terms. After reviewing this page, you are ready to proceed.

PART I

Our aim in these relationships will be to find ways of defining area entirely as functions of x and y. To begin with, we will make use of the obvious fact that the area of $\triangle AFE$ is equal to the area of $\triangle ADC$ *minus* the area of the polygon $FDCE$.

Setting this thought up in the form of an equation (remember that the area of a $\triangle$ is one-half the base times the height) we have

254

$\frac{sx'}{2}$ (the area of $\triangle AFE$) $= \frac{xh}{2}$ (area of $\triangle ADC$) $- sa$ (area of

polygon $FDGE$) $- \frac{ra}{2}$ (area of $\triangle EGC$)

which without the words reduces to $\frac{sx'}{2} = \frac{xh}{2} - sa - \frac{ra}{2}$; multiplying both sides of the equation by 2 we have

$$sx' = xh - 2sa - ra = xh - sa - sa - ra$$
$$sx' = xh - ra - sa - sa = xh - (r + s)a - sa$$

We know that $(r + s) = h$, so we can substitute and have

$$sx' = hx - ha - sa$$

We now substitute for a which, as we said, equals $(x - x')$

$$sx' - hx - h(x - x') - s(x - x') = hx - hx + hx' - sx + sx'$$

The hx values cancel and we have

$$sx' = hx' - sx + sx'$$

which reduces to

$$hx' = sx$$

We have covered a lot of equation territory for a simple relationship. If you are interested, you can check our simple relationship by constructing a triangle on graph paper with rectangular coordinates and you will see that hx' does always equal sx. Our use of this simple equation will be to substitute for values of s, and from the equation we know that

$$s = \frac{hx'}{x}$$

PART II

Now we can go back to our main purpose—to show that a part of the total area can be expressed as a function of the total area in terms of the base line alone. As we will see later, we have to express this idea in two segments. One segment deals with the areas left of the most-likely value, the other segment with areas to the right. We shall deal first with the area to the left of the most-likely value.

This time, rather than using a we shall begin with $(x - x')$ as the value of a. Our ratio of any triangular area to the left of the most-likely value (ML) becomes:

$$\frac{\frac{xh}{2} - s(x - x') - \frac{r}{2}(x - x')}{\frac{h(x + y)}{2}} = \frac{\text{area of any } \triangle \text{ left of ML}}{\text{area total } \triangle}$$

Multiplying the top and bottom of the fraction by 2, we have

$$\frac{hx - 2sx + 2sx' - rx + rx'}{h(x + y)}$$

Rearranging to take advantage of the relationship $(r + s = h)$ we have

$$\frac{hx - (r + s)x + (r + s)x' - sx + sx'}{h(x + y)} = \frac{hx - hx + hx' - sx + sx'}{h(x + y)}$$

The hx values cancel out and we have

$$\frac{hx' - sx + sx'}{h(x + y)}$$

But $hx' = sx$ and, substituting for sx, the hx' values cancel out. Our equation becomes

$$\frac{sx'}{h(x + y)}$$

From the previous section we developed the relationship that $s = \frac{hx'}{x}$; substituting for the value of s we have

$$\frac{\frac{hx'\,x'}{x}}{h(x + y)} \quad \text{which equals} \quad \frac{\frac{(x')^2}{x}}{(x + y)} \quad \text{(the h's cancel)}$$

We can show our ratio now in an equation form

$$\underset{x'=0}{\overset{x'=x}{CF}} = \frac{\dfrac{(x')^2}{x}}{(x + y)}$$

which is read: The cumulative frequency for values of x' from 0 to x equals x' squared, divided by x, and this quantity then divided by the sum of $(x + y)$.

Newendorp[1] defines $x/(x + y)$ as "m" and x' as $x(x + y)$ or $x = x'/(x + y)$. His form for the equation is x^2/m, which in our nomenclature would be shown as: $\dfrac{\left(\dfrac{x'}{x + y}\right)^2}{\dfrac{x}{(x + y)}}$. It can be reduced to our equation of $\dfrac{\dfrac{(x')^2}{x}}{x + y}$. Going back to our equation, you can see that when $x' = x$, the ratio reduces to a simple $x/(x + y)$.

So, in triangular distributions at the most-likely value the cumulative frequency of values equal to or less than ($\leq$) x will be $x/(x + y)$.

PART III

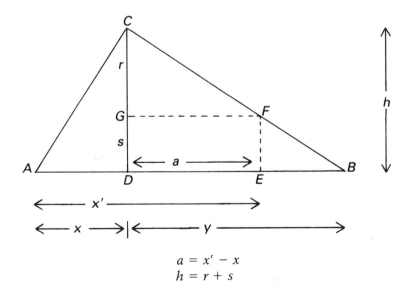

$$a = x' - x$$
$$h = r + s$$

We will use the same approach for the right side of the most-likely value as for the left. We can sum up the areas as follows

$$\text{Area } EBF = \text{Area } ABC - \text{Area } ADC - \text{Area } DEFG - \text{Area } GFC$$

$$\frac{s[(x + y) - x']}{2} = \frac{h(x + y)}{2} - \frac{xh}{2} - sa - \frac{ra}{2}$$

Multiplying both sides of the equation by 2 we have

$$sx + sy - sx' = hx + hy - hx - 2sa - ra$$

The hx's cancel and we substitute for a, which equals $(x' - x)$

$$sx + sy - sx' = hy - 2s(x' - x) - r(x' - x)$$
$$= hy - sx' - sx' + sx + sx - rx' + rx$$

Combining $sx + sx'$ values on the right side we have

$$sy = hy - rx' - sx' + rx + sx = hy - (r + s)x' + (r + s)x$$

But $(r + s) = h$ so, $sy = hy - hx' + hx$, and our beginning relationship becomes

$$sy = h(y - x' + x)$$

We will use this relationship to substitute later for s. You can prove this mathematical statement by drawing a triangle to some easy scale and inserting the proper numbers in the equation.

PART IV

We now return to our area ratios. For the right side of x, we will use the ratio of the little triangle EBF as related to the large triangle ABC. Our ratio is

$$\frac{\dfrac{s(x + y - x')}{2}}{\dfrac{h(x + y)}{2}} = \frac{\text{area of the small } \triangle}{\text{area of the whole } \triangle}$$

Multiplying both numerator and denominator by 2 we have

$$\frac{s(y - x' + x)}{h(x + y)}$$

Now we can substitute for the value of s derived above

$$\frac{\dfrac{h(y - x' + x)}{y}(y - x' + x)}{h(x + y)}$$

The h's cancel; multiplying top and bottom by y we have

$$\frac{(y - x' + x)(y - x' + x)}{y(x + y)}$$

or

$$\frac{y^2 - yx' + xy - yx' - x'^2 - xx' + xy - xx' + x^2}{y(x + y)}$$

Rearranging we have

$$\frac{x^2 + 2xy + y^2 - 2yx' - 2xx' + x'^2}{y(x + y)}$$

Factoring we have

$$\frac{(x + y)^2 - 2x'(x + y) + x'^2}{y(x + y)} = \frac{[(x + y) - x']^2}{y(x + y)}$$

Note for the special case of $x = x'$ this ratio reduces to $y/(x + y)$. We shall need this relationship later.

Returning to the form of our ratio as

$$\frac{(x + y)^2 - 2x'(x + y) + x'^2}{y(x + y)}$$

and dividing by $(x + y)^2$ we then have

$$\frac{1 - \dfrac{2x'}{x + y} - \dfrac{x'^2}{(x + y)^2}}{\dfrac{y}{(x + y)}}$$

However, by definition we know that

$$\frac{x}{x+y} + \frac{y}{x+y} = 1.0$$

Therefore

$$\frac{y}{(x+y)} = 1 - \frac{x}{(x+y)}$$

Our ratio now becomes

$$\frac{\left[1 - \dfrac{x'}{(x+y)}\right]^2}{1 - \dfrac{x}{x+y}}$$

This is the ratio of the very small triangle to the large triangle. To get the proper value for cumulative frequency, we must subtract this value from one. By doing this we get the ratio of the area up to x', which is what we want—not the area of the small triangle. So our final expression becomes

$$\underset{x'=x}{\overset{x'=(x+y)}{CF}} = 1 - \frac{\left[1 - \dfrac{x'}{(x+y)}\right]^2}{1 - \dfrac{x}{(x+y)}}$$

We can prove the logic of this last step several ways. Consider only the ratio (not the ratio subtracted from 1.0). What happens as x' approaches $(x + y)$ the maximum? The ratio goes to zero, as it should, because the area of the small triangle goes to zero.

Consider another way. What happens to the ratio when x' becomes x? Under this condition the ratio becomes $y/(x + y)$ and the small triangle has enlarged to become the exact complement of $x/(x + y)$. This latter value was the ratio for the small triangle starting from the left of x. This proof satisfies our definition $[x/(x + y)] + [y/(x + y)] = 1.0$ and says that the area to the left of the ML value plus the area to the right of the ML value equals one. This was our beginning assumption.

Newendorp[1] defines $x'/(x + y)$ as x and $x/(x + y)$ as m, so his ratio is shown as

$$1 - \frac{(1 - x)^2}{1 - m}$$

SUMMARY

Using triangular distributions the base-line values alone can be used to convert the distribution to cumulative frequency values. Referring to the reference triangle, we have these definitions:

x = the most-likely value minus the minimum
y = the maximum value minus the most-likely
x' = any and all values along the base line (minus the minimum value)

Our final equations:

1. For values of x' equal to or less than ($\leq$) x

$$\operatorname*{CF}_{\substack{x'=x \\ x'=0}} = \frac{\frac{(x')^2}{x}}{(x + y)}$$

2. For values of x' equal to or greater than ($\geq$) x

$$\operatorname*{CF}_{\substack{x'=(x+y) \\ x'=x}} = 1 - \frac{\left[1 - \frac{x'}{(x + y)}\right]^2}{1 - \frac{x}{(x + y)}}$$

REFERENCE TRIANGLE

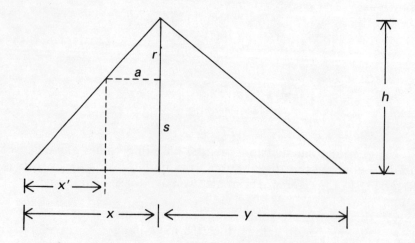

x = most likely minus the minimum
y = maximum value minus the most-likely
x' = any value of x from the minimum to the maximum
h = height of triangle
$r + s$ are segments of h such that $(r + s) = h$
a is a segment of $x + y$
    —to the left of x it is defined as $x - x'$
    —to the right of x it is defined as $x' - x$
$x + y$ = entire range of values of x' from the
       minimum to the maximum

Remember that the area of any triangle is equal to one-half the base times the height. Thus for the large triangle the area is

$$\frac{1}{2}(x + y)\, h$$

Reference

1. Newendorp, Paul D. *Decision Analysis for Petroleum Exploration.* Tulsa: PennWell Publishing Co., 1975, p. 274.

Appendix B • shortcuts to calculating the mean of a distribution

---

G iven a cumulative-frequency distribution, it is often desirable to know the mean of the distribution. Several methods of estimating the mean and standard deviation are available from the field of order statistics.[1]

The United States Geological Survey (USGS) approximates the mean by adding the values at the 5th and 95th percentiles to the modal value and then dividing by three. The USGS refers to this number as the *statistical mean*.[2] The difficulty with this mean is that you must know, calculate, or be given the modal value.

Another method is suggested by Levin and Kirkpatrick.[3] Their method uses the following formula

$$1 - \overline{X} = \frac{P + 4ML + O}{6}$$

where:

$\overline{X}$ = mean
ML = most-likely value
P = pessimistic value
O = optimistic value

As you can see, there is no precise definition for the pessimistic or the optimistic values, a possible limitation in using this formula. This lack of precision inhibits a comparison of this method to those that tie to a precise percentile in a cumulative-frequency distribution.

A much simpler method was discovered by R.I. Swanson.[4] In his method, referred to as Swanson's rule (Chapter 16), all data can be read from the cumulative-frequency distribution—either the linear plot or the plot on log probability paper. Three steps are involved:

1. Read the values of the parameters as plotted from the 10th, 50th, and 90th percentiles. These values are considered to represent the high, low, and middle *segments* of the distribution
2. Multiply these values by the probabilities of 0.3, 0.4, and 0.3, respectively
3. Sum the segment-weighted values for the mean

For modestly skewed distributions this method is close to the actual mean generated by 5,000 iterations from a Monte Carlo simulation. However, as we mentioned in Chapter 16, Swanson's rule begins to be biased toward the median value as the distribution becomes highly skewed.

A sample calculation of a mean using Swanson's rule is illustrated as follows

Percentile	Variable Value	Probability	Segment-Weighted Value
10	200	0.3	60
50	100	0.4	40
90	50	0.3	15
			Mean = 115

How accurate is Swanson's rule? Modifying the work of James, Fig. B.1 shows the relationship between Swanson's rule and the true mean of a lognormal distribution.[5] On the figure a plot of the ratio of Swanson's rule to the true mean is made vs the ratio of the values at the 10th percentile to the 50th percentile. For the V_{10}/V_{50} ratio the typical prospect range is shown, as well as the basin-play range for field-size distributions.

Even if the high-side value (V_{10}) is five times larger than the most-likely (V_{50}), Swanson's rule is only 10% lower than the true mean. For a prospect with this much uncertainty in potential sizes, you may not be disturbed by a 10% downward shift toward the median value. However, when the V_{10}/V_{50} ratio reaches 15, Swanson's rule underestimates the mean by 45%. Thus, Swanson's rule should not be applied to obtain the mean of play or basin assessments.

The formula for calculating the true mean of a lognormal distribution is

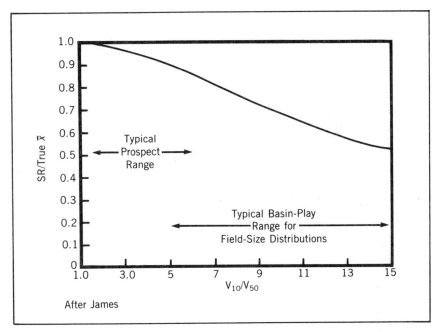

FIG. B.1 Comparison of Swanson's rule to true mean, lognormal distributions

$$\overline{X} = e^{(a + 1/2b)^2}$$

where:

$\overline{X}$ = mean
$a = \ell n\ V_{50}$
$b = \ell n\ V_{10}/V_{50}$
V = parameter value at the percentile indicated in the subscript

THE USES

The mean is the only value that can be added directly from one distribution to another for data that are lognormal. For this reason alone, it is a popular parameter for the lognormal distribution. If you must settle on only one value to represent a distribution, the mean best expresses that value. So the mean of reserve sizes, acreage ownership, profits, discounted profits, etc., can be added from one distribution to another. Also, given the values of these amounts at the 10th, 50th, and 90th percentiles, Swanson's rule can be used to get the mean value.

Here is a practical example. Assume that you have calculated the present value profit at 10% for the reserve sizes indicated at the 10th, 50th, and 90th percentiles. You can use the probabilities from Swanson's rule to calculate the PVP @ 10% for the mean:

Percent	PVP, 10%	Probability	Segment-Weighted PVP @ 10%
10	400	0.3	120
50	200	0.4	80
90	100	0.3	30
			Mean = 230

You will find this shortcut quite valuable in using distributions and relating them to other economic relationships.

One final reminder about the mean: Our example above was labeled segment weighting because we were dealing with unrisked productive sizes, i.e., zero dry risk. In risk weighting the mean (of the three productive cases), you are not saying that the mean size has that specific chance of success. You are risk weighting the entire distribution, which is represented by the mean. The chance of success for a specific size or more is related to its position on the distribution and, as we have shown, that chance diminishes as we move to larger and larger sizes in our distribution.

References

1. Eisenberger, Isidore, and Edward C. Posner. "Systematic Statistics Used for Data Compression in Space Telemetry." *Journal of the American Statistical Association*, Vol. 60, No. 309, March 1965, p. 97.
2. Miller, Betty M., et al. "Geological Estimates of Undiscovered Recoverable Oil and Gas Resources in the United States." Geological Survey Circular 725, 1975, p. 21.
3. Levin, R.I., and C.A. Kirkpatrick. "Quantitative Approaches to Management." New York: McGraw-Hill, 1975, pp. 488–522.
4. Swanson, R.I. Unpublished memorandum, September 1972.
5. James, W.R. "A Theoretical Foundation for Swanson's Rule." Unpublished memorandum, June 1983.

Appendix C • binomial probability tables

Individual Binomial Probability
$B(x, n, 0.30)$

Values of x

TABLE 1

n	0	1	2	3	4	5	6	7	8	9	10	11	12	13	14	15	16	17	18
2	.49	.42	—																
3	.34	.44	.19	—															
4	.24	.41	.26	.08	—														
5	.17	.36	.31	.13	.03	—													
6	.12	.30	.32	.19	.06	.01	—												
7	.08	.25	.32	.23	.10	.03	—												
8	.06	.20	.30	.25	.14	.05	.01	—											
9	.04	.16	.27	.27	.17	.07	.02	—											
10	.03	.12	.23	.27	.20	.11	.04	.01	—										
11	.02	.10	.20	.26	.22	.13	.06	.02	—										
12	.01	.07	.17	.24	.23	.16	.08	.03	.03	.01	—								
13	.01	.05	.14	.22	.23	.18	.10	.04	.01	—									
14	—	.04	.11	.19	.23	.20	.13	.06	.02	.01	—								
15	—	.03	.10	.17	.22	.21	.15	.08	.03	.01	—								
20	—	.01	.03	.07	.13	.18	.19	.16	.11	.07	.03	.01	—						
25	—	—	.01	.02	.06	.10	.15	.17	.17	.13	.09	.05	.03	.01	—				
30	—	—	—	.01	.02	.05	.08	.12	.15	.16	.14	.11	.07	.04	.02	.01	—		
35	—	—	—	—	.01	.02	.04	.07	.10	.13	.14	.14	.12	.09	.06	.04	.02	.01	—
40	—	—	—	—	—	.01	.02	.03	.06	.08	.11	.13	.14	.13	.10	.07	.05	.03	.02
45	—	—	—	—	—	—	.01	.01	.03	.05	.07	.10	.12	.13	.13	.11	.09	.07	.04

Cumulative Binomial Probability

$B(x$ or more, n, 0.10)

						Values of x													TABLE 2
n	0	1	2	3	4	5	6	7	8	9	10	11	12	13	14	15	16	17	18
2		.19	.01	—															
3		.27	.03	—															
4		.34	.05	—															
5		.41	.08	.01	—														
6		.47	.11	.02	—														
7		.52	.15	.03	—														
8		.57	.19	.04	.01	—													
9		.61	.23	.05	.01	—													
10		.65	.26	.07	.01	—													
11		.69	.30	.09	.02	—													
12		.72	.34	.11	.03	—													
13		.75	.38	.13	.03	.01	—												
14		.77	.42	.16	.04	.01	—												
15		.79	.45	.18	.06	.01	—												
20		.88	.61	.32	.13	.04	.01	—											
25		.93	.73	.46	.24	.10	.03	.01	—										
30		.96	.82	.59	.35	.18	.07	.03	.01	—									
35		.97	.88	.69	.47	.27	.13	.06	.02	.01	—								
40		.99	.92	.78	.58	.37	.21	.10	.04	.02	.01	—							
45		1−	.95	.84	.67	.47	.29	.16	.08	.03	.01	—							

Cumulative Binomial Probability

$B(x$ or more, n, 0.20)

Values of x TABLE 3

n	0	1	2	3	4	5	6	7	8	9	10	11	12	13	14	15	16	17	18
2		.36	.04	—															
3		.49	.10	—															
4		.59	.18	.03	—														
5		.65	.26	.06	—														
6		.74	.34	.10	.02	—													
7		.79	.42	.15	.03	—													
8		.83	.50	.20	.06	.01	—												
9		.87	.56	.26	.09	.02	—												
10		.89	.62	.32	.12	.03	.01	—											
11		.91	.68	.38	.16	.05	.01	—											
12		.93	.73	.44	.21	.07	.02	—											
13		.95	.77	.50	.25	.10	.03	.01	—										
14		.96	.80	.55	.30	.13	.04	.01	—										
15		.96	.83	.60	.35	.16	.06	.02	—										
20		.99	.93	.79	.59	.37	.20	.09	.01	—									
25		1–	.97	.90	.77	.58	.38	.22	.11	.05	.02	.01	—						
30		1	.99	.96	.88	.74	.57	.39	.24	.13	.06	.03	.01	—					
35		1	1	.98	.94	.86	.73	.57	.40	.25	.07	.03	.01	.01	—				
40		1	1	.99	.97	.92	.83	.71	.56	.41	.27	.16	.09	.04	.02	.01	—		
45		1	1	1	.99	.96	.91	.82	.70	.56	.41	.30	.17	.10	.05	.02	.01	—	

Cumulative Binomial Probability

$B(x$ or more, n, 0.30)

Values of x TABLE 4

n	0	1	2	3	4	5	6	7	8	9	10	11	12	13	14	15	16	17	18
2		.51	.09	—															
3		.66	.22	.03	—														
4		.76	.35	.08	.01	—													
5		.83	.47	.16	.03	—													
6		.88	.58	.26	.07	.01	—												
7		.92	.67	.35	.13	.03	—												
8		.94	.74	.45	.19	.06	.01	—											
9		.96	.80	.54	.27	.10	.03	—											
10		.97	.85	.62	.35	.15	.04	.01	—										
11		.98	.89	.69	.43	.21	.08	.02	—										
12		.99	.91	.75	.51	.28	.12	.04	.01	—									
13		.99	.94	.80	.58	.35	.17	.06	.02	—									
14		.99	.95	.84	.64	.42	.22	.09	.03	.01	—								
15		1	.96	.87	.70	.48	.28	.13	.05	.02	—								
20		1	.99	.96	.89	.76	.58	.39	.23	.11	.05	.02	.01	—					
25		1	1	.99	.97	.91	.81	.66	.49	.32	.19	.10	.04	.02	.01	—			
30		1	1	1	.99	.97	.92	.84	.72	.57	.41	.27	.16	.08	.04	.02	.01	—	
35		1	1	1	1	.99	.97	.94	.87	.77	.64	.49	.35	.23	.14	.07	.04	.02	.01
40		1	1	1	1	1	.99	.98	.94	.89	.80	.69	.56	.42	.30	.19	.12	.06	.03
45		1	1	1	1	1	1	.99	.98	.95	.91	.84	.74	.62	.49	.37	.25	.16	.10

TABLE 5   Probability of all dry holes

		$(x = 0)$	
n	$p = 0.1$	$p = 0.2$	$p = 0.3$
2	0.81	0.64	0.49
3	0.73	0.51	0.34
4	0.66	0.41	0.24
5	0.59	0.35	0.17
6	0.53	0.26	0.12
7	0.48	0.21	0.08
8	0.43	0.17	0.06
9	0.39	0.13	0.04
10	0.35	0.11	0.03
15	0.21	0.04	
20	0.12	0.01	
25	0.07		
30	0.04		
35	0.03		
40	0.01		

Index